Praise for Joe Robinson and *Work to Live*

"Joe Robinson is a Paul Revere for our times, warning Americans that we are under attack by the Overwork Ethic. Too many of us are putting jobs above all else in life—with dire consequences for our health, our loved ones, our happiness, and even the quality of our work. In this lively, compelling, and very important book he makes a call for a new American revolution in how we lead our lives. *Work to Live* inspired me to look at things differently in my world, and it can do the same for you."

—Jay Walljasper, editor, *Utne Reader*
and coauthor of *Visionaries: People and
Ideas to Change Your Life*

"*Work to Live* is a rousing manifesto for those martyrs among us working way too late, way too long, and way too hard while life—real life, the stuff of dreams and not data—stands jilted at the altar. But *Work to Live* is no mere lament; Robinson provides an annotated road map for escaping the stranglehold of careers, and offers hope for both the reader and the nation. Soulful yet pragmatic, *Work to Live* may change your life—or rather, help you get it back."

—Jonathan Miles, book editor of *Men's Journal*

"Chronic overtime is a major health hazard that has been ignored for too long. If you go to work at 7 A.M. and come home late at night, you are going to pay for it. Joe Robinson shows in a very entertaining way that stepping back and making time for your life isn't something to feel guilty about. It's medicine. It's vital to your health."

—Dr. Steven Lamm, New York University
Mt. Sinai Medical School, author of *Younger at Last:
The New World of Vitality Medicine,*
and commentator on ABC's *The View*

D1011738

Joe Robinson (signature)

Work to Live

...

The Guide to Getting a Life

JOE ROBINSON

A Perigee Book

A Perigee Book
Published by The Berkley Publishing Group
A division of Penguin Putnam Inc.
375 Hudson Street
New York, New York 10014

First edition: January 2003

Visit our website at www.penguinputnam.com

Library of Congress Cataloging-in-Publication Data

Robinson, Joe.
Work to live : the guide to getting a life / Joe Robinson.
p.   cm.
Includes bibliographical references and index.
ISBN 0-399-52850-4
1. Quality of work life.   2. Work and family.   3. Life skills.   I. Title.
HD6955 .R62 2003
650.1—dc21
2002030365

Printed in the United States of America

10 9 8 7 6 5 4 3

*To my parents, John and Helen Robinson, and to summer vacations
in windblown Falcons and station wagons.*

And to every overworked American, yearning to break free.

Contents

"Twenty years from now you will be more disappointed by the things you didn't do than by the ones you did do. So throw off the bowlines. Sail away from the safe harbor. Catch the trade winds in your sails. Explore. Dream. Discover."

—Mark Twain

"Unless one is able to live fully in the present, the future is a hoax. There is no point whatever in making plans for a future which you will never be able to enjoy. When your plans mature, you will still be living for some other future beyond. You will never, never be able to sit back with full contentment and say, 'Now, I've arrived.' Your entire education has deprived you of this capacity because it was preparing you for the future, instead of showing you how to be alive now."

—Alan Watts

Acknowledgments

...

First and foremost, I'd like to thank the thousands of working Americans who sent E-mails, signed petitions, and called in to talk shows around the country in support of the Work to Live vacation campaign. Their frontline tales of the overwork insanity and enthusiastic calls to do something about it inspired me to try to get the full story on this destructive siege out and to put to rest the superstitions that squeeze out our lives.

I'm particularly grateful to all of you who shared your work-life struggles in interviews for this book. Thanks for going on the record about your jobs, a gutsy thing to do in a land where work can do no wrong. Your willingness to shine the light on the dark recesses of the 24-7 workplace will give others the strength to do so and to break free of the self-destruction model held out as the matter of course. Thanks for getting involved.

I'd like to thank others who helped along the road. Intrepid photographer Gilles Mingasson provided the crucial tip that resulted in the article in *Time* that broke the vacation story to a national audience. Good one, Gilles. I'd like to pass along my special thanks to Steve Lopez, now at the *L.A. Times,* who wrote that piece with gusto. I also want to give a well-deserved hand to the gang at *Utne Reader.* Thanks to Jay Walljasper, Karen Olson, Dan Carroll, and Leif Utne for supporting the campaign and for their ongoing commitment to work-life issues.

You wouldn't be reading this if it weren't for the encouragement and dogged efforts of my agent, Faye Bender, of the Doris S. Michaels Literary Agency, whose unfailing belief in this project got it to the starting gate and me to that first blank page. Thanks for making me know I had to do this thing, against all rational judgment. I'm very grateful to Perigee's Jennifer Repo, who made this book happen. She saw the need for the message and the form to get it out there. Thanks for your efforts on my behalf and your skills with the book form. Your six-week vacation will be coming shortly. I'd like to thank Perigee publisher John Duff for his support and for the opportunity to state the case for a sane workplace; Michelle Howry, who hit the ground running with editorial reassurance and enthusiasm for this book; and Cristel Winkler, for her assistance on all the floating pieces of the puzzle.

I'd like to express my appreciation to all the economists, psychologists, doctors, researchers, professors, management and business experts, and authors who were kind enough to lend their expertise to this project. I would especially like to thank Penn State's Lonnie Golden for helping steer me through the arcane world of overwork policy, for the hand in formulating reforms to the Fair Labor Standards Act, and for pitching them with me in Washington. Boston College's Juliet Schor pioneered the overwork issue and has been a guiding light for me since we first talked about this subject eight years ago. Dr. Arie Shirom of Tel Aviv University gave me invaluable assistance, sharing his research on stress and burnout and his use of the Shirom-Melamed Burnout Questionnaire. I also received critical support from respite research pioneer Dov Eden, also of Tel Aviv University. Other noteworthy assists were provided by Cornell's Kate Bronfenbrener, Eileen Applebaum at the Economic Policy Institute, Ellen Ostrow of Lawyers Life Coach, Pam Ammondson of Clarity Quest, Rick Service of *Business and Health,* Tom Freston of MTV

Networks, and employee-rights attorneys Renee Barge and Matt Righetti. Many thanks to Charlie King for the use of "Bring Back the Eight-Hour Day."

I would like to give a special nod to Dan Sullivan and Joan Patch at the Strategic Coach, a company beating the overwork insanity at its craziest, one entrepreneur at a time. The Strategic Coach®, the Justification Model™, and the Achievement Model™ are trademarks of the Strategic Coach, Inc., and are used with permission.

On the European front, I'd like to thank Barcelona-based work-life professor Steven Poelmans, and, in Hamburg, Germany, Dr. Desiree Ladwig of Balance EWLA, for their insights on how the other half lives and for connecting me with work-life experts around the Continent. Thanks also to my man in Mannheim, Germany, Juergen Lattenkamp, for his contributions and travel tales, and to my brother, Tom Robinson, for reports from the front lines.

For his usual sterling work, I'd like to thank Michael Justice for the photo (and Mount Whitney launch). Other members of the band included Marty Herman (on hook turn), Jeff "World's Luckiest Man" Sievert (on the *wu-wei* trail in Kansai—thanks, guv), Kyoko "Brown" (on Osaka soul), Ran Klarin (on rhythm patrol), and Marisol Saens (on voice, guitar, and sushi).

I'd like to acknowledge the musical muses that powered this book: Joyce, Pat Metheny, Marisa Monte, Horace Silver, Pat Martino, David Sanchez, Jane Bunnett and The Spirits of Havana, McCoy Tyner, Michael Brecker, Djavan, Eliane Elias, Mike Stern, John Patitucci, Wayman Tisdale, and Steve Cole, among many others. And the top three CDs I could always count on to pry some words loose: Miles Davis' *Kind of Blue;* John Coltrane's *A Love Supreme;* and at number one on the *Work to Live* inspirational charts, the amazing *Joey Calderazzo.* There's no living without great music.

Finally, I want to thank my parents, who instilled in me a reverence for the vacation on our summer road trips. It never mattered where we were going, only that we were on the move to far-away mountains and states where there were exotic brands of milk and pop. They also taught me that it's not what you do but who you are that counts. Sorry, Jeff, looks like I'm the luckiest man.

And one more thing: Thank *you* very much for reading and spreading the word. I hope this book helps you steer a course out of coworker madness—to a richer personal and family life, to balance, and to some stunning tropical lagoon where you haven't seen a watch for at least a couple of weeks.

Work to Live

...

The Guide to Getting a Life

Introduction

...

"If you are going to let the fear of poverty govern your life . . .
your reward will be that you will eat, but you will not live."

—George Bernard Shaw

M aybe you've felt it on the morning commute as you braced yourself for the ten-hour siege ahead, or at your desk as you contem-
plated an ancient vacation photo and wondered if you were really ever
there. Or maybe it's staring back at you in the form of kids (yours) who
you haven't seen awake for a few days, or the Matterhorn of laundry you
haven't had time to get to for a month—that gnawing void within, the
creeping sense that something's missing. And it is: a little thing called
Life. Your gut is onto it before you are, and it poses the question you
can't bring yourself to ask: Is this all there is?

Gulp. That's not the kind of question we like. Why couldn't it be
something a little less cosmic, like, "What's the capital of Paraguay?"
Or "Should I get a hot fudge sundae?" But no. Enquiring guts want to
know what's up on the existential front, because they have a low threshold for emptiness and one-dimensionality. It's nothing to be alarmed
about. It's all part of our biochemical need to be more than worker ants.
As much as we're led to believe that work and success at it is all we
need, it's not. There has to be more to life. That's not a hope; that's a
fact.

Life satisfaction, all the research tells us, depends on the experience
of life, something squeezed out by the 24-7 workplace. We need to
have a social life, a personal life, time to explore and play, learn and

grow, and indulge in things that feed the soul, not just the resume. Balance. Harmony within, so that we have it without. The Chinese sages called it Tao: the course of nature, the alignment of all that you are with all that is at this moment. Or, as British philosopher John Stuart Mill put it: "Human nature is not a machine to be built after a model and set to do exactly the work prescribed for it, but a tree, which requires to grow and develop itself on all sides." The balance of nature, it turns out, includes you and your psyche, as you will find out from the experts ahead.

A lot of us have been going the machine route, pushed to believe that only one side of life counts: the job, and that all else is inconsequential. It's left us starved for the "living" we're supposedly making. How long has it been since you took a real vacation, one at least two weeks long, where you really got away from the grind and relaxed? When was the last time you learned a new hobby or had time for one you used to love? When did you last read a book with no career goal in mind? How long has it been since you walked barefoot in a park, smelled a flower planted in the ground, not a florist's display case, noticed shapes in the clouds?

If it's been a while, you're not alone. The standard of living we so exhaustively pursue has become a contradiction in terms. "Standard of non-living" is a little more like it. The harder and longer you go after it, the less real living there is. Not much of that around when you need carbon dating to estimate the last time you went to a concert, and the only friends you see regularly are Mylanta and Paxil. We may have the second-highest per-capita gross national product in the world, but is it any wonder that by another measurement, life expectancy, the U.S. is only twenty-fourth in the rankings?

The 24-7 workplace has pushed the 9-to-5 workday well into the night and, via assorted screeching devices, into your home and weekends. The lines between work and home have become so blurred that the only way you can tell them apart is that one has a bed. Almost 40 percent of us are now working more than fifty hours a week, according to *U.S News and World Report*. In fact, we are now working more hours a year than Americans have since the 1920s. And if you think it's bad now, projections call for us to be working sixty hours a week by 2010. Let's hear it for progress!

You might be able to regenerate your fried brain cells and lose that zombie gait if there was ever a break in the action. But as hours on the job have skyrocketed, time off has shrunk. The U.S. is dead-last among industrialized nations in time off, wheezing in the burnout basement. How pathetic has it gotten? An adventure travel company in Michigan, Journeys International, conducted a trip giveaway contest, with the winning couple receiving an all-expenses paid trip to Peru to visit the mystical Andean Inca site of Machu Picchu. But the winners never went. They couldn't get two whole weeks off from their job and wound up forfeiting the trip.

As we crash catatonically on the couch after another ten-hour day or complete another year of watching the world whiz by without us, we have to confront the painful truth: It ain't working. I'm not talking about the work ethic. Hard work is a given in the opportunity society. Sink or swim. We get that, we live that—to the bottom of the Tylenol bottle. It's the crazy, insane *overwork ethic* that needs a pink slip forthwith, the assumption that fifty- and sixty-hour weeks are normal and that there's no limit to an employer's right to your time.

Yes, there's a lot to get done out there, but as you'll find out in the pages ahead, there's no compelling reason to do it in the myopic way we have been—at the expense of our personal, family, social, civic, and spiritual lives. We're overdoing it, not because our jobs require it, but because we're in the grip of some very self-destructive illusions about work. Number one is the notion that the quantity of hours on the job and the degree of pain doing it is equivalent to the quality of performance, and, therefore, your self-worth—when, in fact, it's just the opposite. As you will learn, chronic overtime produces lousy work, flimsy esteem, and sick employees with no time to think about what they're doing or why. Secondly, we're held hostage to this workstyle by the illusion that it's this masochism that makes us more productive than any other country in the world. Yet a number of European countries are more productive than we are—with their citizens working up to *three months* less than we do in total hours every year. And finally, there's the illusion about free time, which we are deluded to believe is worthless. In fact, it's the engine of productivity, innovation, and something quite extraordinary: actual living.

These fantasies have helped to trap us in the idea that work is so much more important than every other part of life that we *can't* put any limits on it. It's an old adage in the management trade that work expands to fill the available time, which we've been conned into believing should be any time. All must make way for the sacrament of productive endeavor.

Work has become the most sacred of all cows, permitted to park its ubiquitous rear end in front of you just about anywhere you are. Blind faith in anything, even in an item as hardwired into our identities and self-worth as work, can lead to excess, and that's what we've got in today's overworked place: record levels of burnout, stress-related absences, and depression. Divorce in families who work long hours is rampant, sending a large number of the children of those families into poverty in single-parent households.

Then there's the personal toll. You drag through the day under a nagging cloud of gloom. You're afraid you can't make it, ashamed you can't take it. Barbara, a publicist for a record company in New York, tells a familiar tale these days of exhaustion and guilt. "I kept feeling like, what's wrong with me?" she says. "I've got a job people would kill for, but I'm exhausted. I'm thinking, why am I so ungrateful? But then I work 9:00 A.M. to 7:00 P.M., hardly ever leave the office for lunch, and there are always events several nights a week. When I get home, I don't want to talk on the phone, so I've lost contact with my friends. It's like a bad relationship. I'm so codependent on my job I've excluded everything else from my life."

We can't draw the line on the job, because of the taboo against any hint that there might be something wrong with the creed that runs us: Work is the only source of self-worth. We've gotten our identities so wrapped up in the job as the sole provider of esteem that any restraint of hours seems sinful, turning us into blaspheming slackers. But like the rest of the mythology that keeps us living to work and postponing our personal lives, there's nothing behind this accusation but fear and its henchmen—guilt, bravado, and stubbornness. It's all in our heads.

It was in mine for many years. Though I had always been an avid vacation fan, I approached work in the hell-bent style that is held out to be the model for American Dreamers. I was consumed with it as the fount of all esteem and importance. Like the overworked addicts I now debate, I embraced the idea that being able to take more of a pounding than the next guy was something to be admired, that the job was an exercise in who could endure the most pain, a triathlon in pants. I'm good at endurance, so good that I once worked at least a part of every day for one year, something I knew lesser mortals couldn't hack. But, luckily, my vacation side won over death wish. My passion for travel and adventure showed me the absurdity of total focus on objective and destination, when it was what happened along the way that made the whole trip. I became the journey guy I already was, like we all are, but are too bamboozled by the shiny prizes to see. I came to see the contest of working to absorb punishment as the religious rite it has become. Indian ascetics may stand on one leg or keep an arm raised for years as exercises in atonement. We demonstrate our worthiness by the penance of overwork. (If they knew how truly superior our life denial talents are, India's extreme penitents would trade their contortions for a salary gig immediately.)

And all the extra work doesn't ensure esteem. As you will see ahead, it can't. And it doesn't even guarantee a job in a volatile marketplace. "We all think if we work harder, we'll be more appreciated or successful, but that's not necessarily true," notes Paula Ann Hughes, a consultant and management professor at Texas Women's University and former president of the University of Dallas. "Often you're not going to get the recognition that you're hungry for. It just won't come. I think we need to realize that."

We've been locked in the pattern of overdoing it for the same reason hand-washers keep heading for the sink—a compulsive fixation born out of irrational fear. We fear the germ of nonproductivity: living. This book is for all of you who don't want to sacrifice your brief stint on this planet to that fear anymore. It's for everyone who feels that a standard of living is meant to be lived, touched, felt, and tasted, not treated as a statistical bludgeoning device.

Standards of output don't tell the whole story. They can't measure quality of life, which requires input, the actual experience of life. *Work to Live* is a call for a new standard, one that lets you judge success by your own measuring stick, not by others' conceptions of requisite job titles, toys, and wealth. Its gauge is immersion in living—input—instead of accumulation. We seem to have plenty of stuff, based on the staggering proliferation of public storage facilities going up on every other block these days. They commemorate the emphasis on *having* over *being* that has consumed our better judgment.

Keeping score of the symbols of output is keeping us stuck. They're the wrong indicators of what we want them to measure: self-esteem and well-being. Neither comes from external sources. This accounts for the frustration that, for as many hours as we work, the job just isn't delivering what we need—a sense of personal value and life satisfaction. You may get those things momentarily from performance and success, but they don't last, because these items are on shaky ground. You feel good for a couple of days, a couple weeks, and then the ground shifts and you want more. It's part of the adaptive nature of our psyches. True well-being "outlasts yesterday's moment of elation, today's buoyant mood, and tomorrow's hard time," points out social psychologist David Myers. "It is an ongoing perception that this time of one's life, or even life as a whole, is fulfilling, meaningful and pleasant. Better not to define success as the world does—by surpassing others (a neverending quest) but as fulfilling one's own potential."

You have to play your own game, one that's in accord with your view of success and happiness, one that reflects your priorities, not those of overwork and the stampede to buy self-worth that are stealing the best times of your life. Priorities have gotten seriously unhinged over the last decade. More and more of us have lost our personal identities, friends, and families to careers and the manic pursuit of success and status. We have become so caught up by the job that many have forgotten how not to work. When free time unexpectedly appears, people tell me they just don't know what to do with themselves—besides feel guilty.

It's truly bizarre that the land of the free should be so deficient in the ability to enjoy time off, the ultimate in personal freedom. But when you've never known anything different, and a ton of myth-information keeps you thinking that enjoying yourself without a productive end is evil and skipping vacations is heroic, liberty is a casualty.

I launched the Work to Live campaign (www.worktolive.info) to raise awareness about this ever-growing assault on our personal lives and to inch us toward the vacation norms of the rest of the world. The effort featured a petition drive to increase vacation time in the U.S. with a minimum-paid-leave law. We're the only country in the industrialized world without one. The proposed change to the Fair Labor Standards Act (FLSA) would mandate that anyone who has worked at a job for a year would get three weeks off, increasing to four weeks after three years.

The campaign hit a very raw nerve. The petition received tens of thousands of signatures, fanned by media coverage from *Time* magazine, to the *Today* show, to *NBC Nightly News* and *CBS Sunday Morning,* to National Public Radio and radio talk shows across the country. The E-mails that came in to Work to Live made it clear that you are not alone in the overworked trenches. The messages read like SOSs from a sinking ship:

- A nurse at a family practice office wrote: "I have seen a steady increase in the number of patients who come with depression and anxiety disorders, traceable only to the stress of trying to work the required number of hours and deal with a family. Most of these people have stomach problems, chronic fatigue, poor nutrition, and sleep deprivation. They are getting divorced, their kids are getting into trouble, and they feel there is no way out."

- And there was this from Elizabeth: "The length of working hours and lack of vacation time has been taking a larger toll on the working people in the U.S. than most are aware of. I am speaking from my own experience. After years of 'killing' myself, I finally got relief. It is not the kind of relief that I would recommend to anyone, however. After a nervous breakdown and numerous illnesses from physical breakdown, I am on permanent disability. American workers don't get any respite from stress. It's time to stop and smell the roses, and time to live!!!"

- An office worker wrote: "I worked ten years before I received even a two-week paid vacation. I started getting two weeks vacation only a couple years ago, because I threatened to leave. But it's not really even two weeks, because any sick days come out of my vacation days. The only way I will ever get additional vacation is for my boss to be forced by government law. Someone needs to wake up these tyrants."

I traveled to Washington, D.C., where Work to Live presented petition signatures collected during the campaign to labor advisors for Senator Ted Kennedy and Congressman Henry Waxman, and proposed changes in the FLSA, which would lead to a minimum-paid-leave law, among other reforms. The reception was supportive, and the lobbying process for this initiative is under way. (For more political details, see Chapter 16.)

You can start to draw your own line on overwork now. You don't have to forfeit your health and your personal life to your job—if you stop living to work and start working to live. This book will show you how to do that. You'll discover that much of the all-hours regimen that you thought you had to go through is a myth, propped up by the Office Commandments, a set of false workplace beliefs that fuel overwork. I discuss these in Chapter 3. They're not written in any company policy books; we just assume they're true and get down on our knees before them. The Office Commandments are actually inventions of fear and guilt, and since you make them, you can break them—and you need to.

The rest of the book will show you how to live by Counter-

Commandments that let you take back your time and life. You'll learn how to stop job stress in its tracks before it leads to burnout and devastating illness and death. You'll discover the psychological warpages that make us work to extremes—things such as Productivity Paranoia, Leisure Phobia, and Macho-rexia (the competitive bragging sweepstakes for the rights to the most overtime hours). You can dump them all.

The fact is, it's not too much to ask to have a life beyond the day's toil. Thomas Jefferson thought enough of this exotic concept that he enshrined it in our constitution—"Life, Liberty, and *The Pursuit of Happiness.*" The freedom to live a life beyond obligation, to partake in the feast of life's enjoyments and discoveries, is one of our "inalienable rights" as citizens. Jefferson held these things to be "self-evident." What would he think today, when people are so consumed with work and so divorced from their personal identities that women in their forties say they literally "forgot to get married," as they told Joan Williams, author of *Unbending Gender*? Or when men return to their jobs after retirement because they don't know anything else?

You'll learn how to clear more space for life, by decreasing overtime, increasing vacation time, and setting clear boundaries between work and home. And how to indulge your off-hours without guilt—through strategies such as Life Assurance, which puts you on the calendar for once, and discovering the secrets of direct experience and participant travel, one of my favorite topics. As a longtime travel aficionado and editor and contributor for adventure magazines, I can tell you that astounding adventures await you on the other side of the job-is-life box.

My dad was invited out to visit his old aerospace company a couple years after he retired. He was stunned to find two men who retired with him back on the job. "What are you doing here?" asked my father, who was never defined by his job. Forty years of work quarantine had left them with no outside interests or leisure skills. They didn't know what to do with themselves, so they reported back in for duty. In another Los Angeles office a retired multimillionaire businessman in his seventies reports to a pretend job every day at his son's company. He brings his briefcase that contains no work and spends the day checking his stocks. Money can't buy curiosity, imagination, or passion for life when you've been turned into a robot.

So act now before it's too late, as our friends at Ronco might say. Let *Work to Live* help you reclaim your inalienable right to the pursuit of happiness. To the time of your life. To a new standard of living that doesn't sentence you to forty years of chasing futile, external measuring sticks.

Free yourself up to try another standard, say, the Photo Album Index. Measure your life based on photos taken on your vacations and during off-hours enjoyments you manage to snatch from the clutches of career. The camera never lies, so what would your photo index say today? Living it up? Or time to start living?

This way to the film store. And proof of life.

PART ONE

The Office Commandments

Overworked and Underplayed

Why Your Workday Never Ends

• • •

"You can't smell the flowers / When you're working twelve hours"
—"Bring Back the Eight-Hour Day," Charlie King
© 1994 Charlie King/Pied ASP Music–BMI
(from the album *Inside Out*)

He could almost taste the salt air on his lips, feel the deck bucking beneath him. Walter Perkins was finally going sailing. He'd been counting down all year for this vacation—easy to do in a place where the rites of holiday are more important than Mom and tulips combined. As manager of a Dutch engineering firm in The Hague acquired by his American employer, Frederick R. Harris, Perkins had been watching enviously as his local staff scooted off on their ritual five- and six-week vacations. Though he got only two weeks, American style, he was going to savor them, riding the wind off the Dutch coast.

No he wasn't. Perkins wasn't going anywhere. His vacation was cancelled by headquarters. Twice. There was no sailing trip. No vacation. His Dutch staff was dumbfounded. "They knew I had plans for vacation and that it got cancelled," recalls Perkins, who, like so many Americans, felt he couldn't say no to the excessive demands of the brass. "They looked at me with this blank stare—this is crazy, totally inconceivable!" My wife and I are looking at one another and saying,

"'Hey, wait a minute, why haven't Americans caught on to the European approach to vacations?'"

Why, indeed? Perkins could see from his vantage point that it was all unnecessary—the chronic late hours at the office, the phobia about stopping and taking a break, the elusive micro vacations—all completely pointless. His Dutch employees had proven to him that you could be highly productive on the job *and* take time for your life. "The Dutch work just as hard as their American counterparts," says Perkins, "but they have that knowledge that they're going to get that one month or more where they can really recharge the batteries. Guess what? Holland and Europe get along very well. Things don't come to a halt. The work ethic in Holland is very similar to the U.S. No loss of productivity whatsoever." As a finance vice president, Perkins ought to know.

The stats bear him out: Holland's productivity rate has been higher than that of the U.S. during most of the last fifteen years, and beats it now. This, while its workweek is thirty-seven hours and its paid leave (for collective agreements) is the longest in Europe, thirty-one days.

In fact, Europe as a whole had a higher labor productivity growth rate in fifteen out of the twenty years from 1981 to 2000, according to the U.S. Federal Reserve Board. American performance jumped during the tech bubble from 1995 to 2000. But even with that, five-week vacation lands Belgium and France outperformed the U.S. in value-added productivity per hour in 2001, says the International Labor Organization (ILO). The chief labor economist for the ILO, Lawrence Jeff Johnson, told CNN.com that "American workers put in long hours to make up the gains" in efficiency of countries like Belgium and France. Research from the Growth and Development Center at Holland's University of Groningen and the U.S. Conference Board shows that Norway and Holland are also more productive than the U.S.

The evidence tells us that it's a myth that we have to keep killing ourselves with overwork or productivity will tank and the economy will suddenly crash to the level of Turkmenistan's. And that it's a myth that American business would fall apart if it offered real vacations and let people actually take them. U.S. subsidiaries thrive in Europe with all their local workers getting, by law, four- or five-week holidays, up to six and seven weeks by collective agreement.

Even better, there's proof positive among enlightened management in the U.S. that companies can provide good vacations, curb overtime, treat their employees like human beings, and thrive as a result. One of the world's most successful software companies, SAS Institute in Cary, North Carolina, has registered double-digit sales growth for two decades—it's now at $1 billion in sales annually—while offering three-week vacations and locking the gates at 6 P.M. Jancoa, a cleaning company in Cincinnati, Ohio, saw its fortunes change overnight when it adopted a three-week vacation policy. Staff turnover dropped from 360 percent to 60 percent in two months. Sales increased by 15 percent.

Tom Freston, CEO of MTV Networks, agrees that healthy workplaces make sense for people and bottom lines. "It's just good business to allow employees to have a better life balance," he told me. Freston is a believer in the need for R&R—rest and recreation, as well as rock and roll. "If you have a company where that's made known, it should be easier for you to attract people. Talent is really the precious resource. A healthy culture would be one where people's leisure and time was respected and valued. It makes people more capable to do their work."

The Europeans manage to compete and be productive *and* have a life at the same time because they see time off as a necessity, and build vacation time into the work system. They plan for their holidays, cross-training employees and making vacations an integral part of the work year. Why is it that only a few companies in the U.S. can see that stepping back and recharging is not a waste of time but critical to the health and performance of their biggest asset, the people who make them the money? The culture here views vacations as grudging interruptions in productivity, an attitude that comes to us by way of guilt, fear, stubbornness, workaholism, the insecurity of bravado—and a kind of national hypnosis that has inverted reality to make us think that not having a life is a life.

Over the last twenty years the work ethic has been hijacked by the overwork ethic, an insidious blight that has left millions of Americans exhausted, depressed, and in deep despair about what it is they're doing on this earth. The American Dream has turned into a nightmare of work without end, where 62 percent of U.S. workers report being stressed out from work overload, according to a Harris Interactive survey. When all that makes life worthwhile—family, friends, hobbies, discovery, travel, enjoyment, fun—has been swallowed up by the demands of making a living, there is no living left, which is why more and more workers today find their one-dimensional worlds frighteningly without meaning and at odds with their personal values.

Nothing illustrates the stranglehold of overwork on American lives today better than the state of the incredible shrinking vacation. While Europeans and Australians relish month-plus holidays and are extending leisure time—the Danes just added a couple more days to their five-week vacation, and the French instituted the thirty-five-hour week—we're going in the other direction: vacation starvation. American vacations average a paltry 8.1 days after a year on the job, and only 10.2 days after three years, according to the Bureau of Labor Statistics. And even getting that meager ration is a workout, as more and more vacations fall victim to approval gauntlets that result in holidays that exist only on paper.

It's a battle royale to get the time coming to you. Nancy Jones, a nurse in San Bernardino, California, put in a vacation request in February to attend her son's wedding in July. By the time July rolled around, she still hadn't heard anything. "They kept giving me the runaround," recalls Jones. "'We have to talk to the head nurse.' Then they tell you that they don't know if you can have the time, because they expect to be busy then. This happens all the time." She wound up having to corner the medical director just days before the wedding to cajole him into approving her request.

Having the time is not the same as getting it anymore. By virtue of her two decades at her company, Southern California trade show designer Victoria Criswell has accumulated five weeks vacation, but "the most I've ever taken is two weeks, and it's been a couple of years since I did that," she admits, exasperated. "They leave this threat over your head. 'We're giving you five weeks, but, God forbid, you should take it.' It's in all sorts of innuendos and comments they make. 'So you're going on vacation? Must be nice. Oh, you can afford to go on vacation? Slacker.' It's ridiculous." After *twenty* years of service.

The standard vacation unit marketed by the travel industry has now shrunk to the long weekend. Believe it or not, *half* of all travel by Americans is in two- or three-day microscopic bits. At this rate, you'll soon be able to take your vacation on your lunch hour. Vacation Deficit Disorder rules the land, as a fried workforce staggers toward the imperceptible light at the end of the fifty- and fifty-one-week tunnel. The logic here makes about as much sense as expecting the dead battery in your car or cell phone to spontaneously recharge itself.

I asked some European work-life experts how they would feel if they were in that tunnel every year. "Such a policy reminds me of the Middle Ages, when people had to work from sunrise until sunset for the owners of the land!" yelped Dutch professor Evangelia Demerouti, of the University of Nijmegen. Sweden's Orvar Lofgren, author of *On Holiday,* a history of vacations, could hardly imagine such a thing. "I would think, how could I survive? I would feel claustrophobic."

To give you an idea just how out of kilter we are with First-World norms, we are now working *eight to twelve more weeks* a year in total hours than our European peers, reports the ILO. What could you do with two or three more months of free time added to your year?

For more and more people, though, the promise of a future payday and a glorious retirement is no longer enough to take the pounding, not when you're gasping for living like the oxygen it is. There's no longer just quiet desperation in the ranks of corporate America. It's now audible. "I don't know how I can keep doing this," Julie, a manager at an agricultural firm in Knoxville, Tennessee, told me. Her voice was shaking, the desperation was clear. "I just never have any time to recover." After seven years with her company, the firm was generous enough to give her one week off a year. By the way, she also works six days a week. *Seven years, one week off a year, six days a week.* My head hurts just thinking about it. I wonder if the CEO of her company or its board members would put their daughters through that boot camp?

"It's just a frantic pace," fumes Dana Sunby, a no-nonsense guy whose ten-hour days of stocking stores around Edgerton, Wisconsin, with Frito-Lay products have left him with an ongoing back problem and now carpal tunnel syndrome. He dreams of being able to take a vacation longer than a week at a time. "We're going to *have* to pull back. It's not just me. It's everybody. It's to the point where we're not happy, and we're just to the limit. I don't know that we can be worked that much harder. I think you're going to see people either having nervous breakdowns or chucking it for some kind of simpler life."

I got a note from Vivien Keller, a secretary in Fort Lauderdale, Florida, who told me she's been with her company for ten years but gets no paid vacation time. She's seventy-four years old. This is what it has come to, holding the bottom line against potential AWOL grannies. We have to ask ourselves, What kind of nation have we become?

Hard-core work-ethic types are finding themselves questioning the very essence of who they are as Americans, as workers. It's not easy to even say the words: work isn't working. Work is identity for most Americans. But not this kind of labor, not this senseless piling on of hours to drive the stock price high enough so the brass can cash in astronomical stock options and bonuses (the ratio of CEO-to-worker pay quadrupled from 1980 to 2000, from 42 times worker pay to a boggling 500 times, according to the *Los Angeles Times*). This distortion of the work ethic doesn't wash anymore, now that we've seen where the frantic push for maximum profitability in the next quarter at all costs has gotten us—to a business culture as devoid of ethics as it is limits on worktime, to Enron, WorldCom, Adelphia, Tyco, and their sordid company. It's time to turn the con around. It's time for stoplights for a runaway workplace where the prevailing ethic is to stop at nothing and no one on the speedway to myopic, overnight gain.

The American Abduction

So how did we get here? Only a couple of decades ago a vacation was considered a well-deserved break in the action, a time for the family to hit the Great American Highway in search of campgrounds, Tasty Freezes, and the greatest prize of all, the motel swimming pool. The summer vacation was a hallowed ritual in my family. Every year my dad would pile us into the station wagon, pick a direction, and we'd be hugging asphalt from Southern California to eternity. No air-conditioning, just a windblown horizon of big skies, scenic outlooks, and busted radiators. Going without a vacation would have been unthinkable in the 1960s.

But beginning in the early 1980s something began to snap in the national R&R psyche. A recession followed by the downsizing craze began to obliterate the assumption that our ever-increasing productivity would result in less work and more leisure time. The much-ballyhooed four-day week turned into a hallucination. The ability to break free of the office and savor downtime disappeared, swallowed up by a vortex of spiraling work hours and a fixation on productivity that has devalued all that is not attached to a task or a paycheck.

Between 1967 and 1982 average hours for prime-age full-time workers were actually going down, but in 1982 they began a steady rise, according to economists Barry Bluestone and Stephen Rose. This supported what Boston College economist Juliet Schor, one of the first to spot the overtime trend, reported in *The Overworked American*. She discovered that we were working 163 more hours a year in the early 1990s than in 1967. That number jumped to 182 more hours by the end of the 1990s, according to the National Survey of the Changing Workforce. And in 2000 we reached another dubious milestone. We passed the Japanese in grindstone infamy. We now work 2.5 weeks more than the Japanese each year, giving the U.S. sole position of last place in time off among our industrial competitors.

The work binge cuts across all groups of people and all regions— particularly slamming salaried and professional white-collar employees at the top end; minimum wage earners at the bottom; and skilled hourly workers in fields such as health care, telecommunications, and information technology. Salaried employees, whose hours are unlimited and, after they hit forty in a week, free, are at the behest of employers around the clock, while the lowest wage earners get paid so little that they have to work two jobs to support a family.

Management in health care, telecom, and the computer world have found it's cheaper to pay time-and-a-half to people they already have than hire new staff and train them, which has triggered a surge of mandatory overtime for hourly workers. It has led to nurses averaging two months of overtime a year, to telecom workers forced to work seventy-hour weeks—and to successful strikes to reduce forced overtime by unions who represent nurses and communications workers.

Millions of Americans have disappeared off the face of regular life, an abduction worthy of an *X-file*. So have friends, hobbies, and bowling nights—as Robert Putnam notes in *Bowling Alone*—beamed into an overtime world of merciless fluorescent lights, to be probed to the edge of REM state. Overwork is turning us into an ever-lonelier land of strangers, on the outside prosperous and dynamic, on the inside empty and spent.

Today there is no clear agreement anymore on the end of the working day, except that, it's not over when it's over. Peter Werbie, an Indianapolis disc jockey, remembers that, "ten or twelve years ago, when I'd do a show on the weekend, there was nobody in the office but me and an engineer. Now about a third of the staff is there."

It's become so routine to work past official closing you seldom even hear the word "overtime" in offices anymore—which is part of the problem. We have euphemized a workplace without end—"I'm staying late" (as if it was your idea), "catching up on E-mail" (as if it could be caught up on), or "getting a project out" (which can never wait till tomorrow).

But no matter what you call it, it's a habit people would like to break. "A fairly significant and growing share of the workforce has longer work hours than they prefer," says Penn State's Lonnie Golden, an expert on "overemployment," as the overwork phenomenon is called by economists. Those who are getting crunched the most are working parents. "That's where the stress and pressures are building," Golden maintains, "in the dual-income or single head-of-household earners." Since the 1970s, the typical dual-income family has increased its annual total of working hours by 684 hours, or four *months* of full-time work, according to Bluestone and Rose.

That pressure is on for Dana Sunby, a single dad torn between his instincts as a go-to-the-wall American to do whatever it takes to get his job done and his need to find time for his daughter and life. The rep for

Frito Lay is caught in the vise grip of a six-day week—in theory it's five, but there's too much work for that—at ten-plus hours a day. Like so many companies in the downsized era, Sunby's vending firm is pared to the bone, which means "there's nobody to take up the slack if there's a family issue that comes up, or if you get sick. You can't wake up in the morning and not feel good. Your work will just pile up. I feel like I'm the most popular person in the world, because everyone wants more time from me. My daughter and girlfriend want more of my time than I can possibly give them."

Sunby would like to go camping with his daughter, but it would be near to impossible for him to take more than a week off, though he's seen a couple colleagues actually take two whole weeks off in a row. One thing is for sure, he says, "I know I'll never make it at this pace to retirement. Maybe the answer is to have a simpler lifestyle, to live out of a tent."

It could be a big campground. The International Labor Organization reports that 80 percent of American men and 62 percent of women work "excessive hours," or more than forty a week. A survey by the Families and Work Institute in 2001 found that 55 percent of U.S. employees feel "overwhelmed" by the amount of work they have to do, while 59 percent don't even have the time to step back and reflect on their work. The study offered this sobering conclusion: "Every employee reaches a point when increasing work demands simply become too much—a point at which personal and family relations, personal health, and the quality of work itself are seriously threatened. Today's 24-7 economy appears to be pushing many employees to and beyond that point."

Whatever Happened to the Eight-Hour Day?

The forty-hour week is now so passé, Dolly Parton's 1980 hit "9 to 5" seems almost quaint. Today's anthem for the working world is "Bring Back the Eight-Hour Day" by folk singer Charlie King (www.charlie-king.org), who chronicles a whipped workforce: "They got cellular phones for your car. / They got notebook PCs for your lap. / When ya go to sleep ya stay close to your beeper. / Now why do we stand for this crap? / Bring back the eight-hour day. / When did we give it away? / There's so much to do when the workday is through. / Bring back the eight-hour day."

The song connected some dots for Art Waskow, a New York rabbi and labor activist who runs the "Free Time/Free People" movement (www.shalomctr.org), linking the growing lack of civic and spiritual involvement, the latchkey kids, the time squeeze, and the general sense of souls adrift in the work-and-spend world. He began writing and speaking about these issues, pulling together Jewish and Christian ideas about restfulness and Buddhist traditions about meditation. He also talks about the role runaway consumerism plays in the overwork cycle—forcing people to work more to buy more. "When people feel spiritually hungry, they try to feed themselves materially," he notes. "They try to feed themselves with more goods, more products, more things to own. Working to own and buy becomes very much the real religion of the society. Then the notion of restfulness, of spending time calmly, sweetly, with family, neighbors—all that just falls apart."

Waskow compares the growing realization that something is rotten in the workplace to the dawning that came for women in the 1970s touched off by Betty Friedan's *Feminine Mystique,* which helped stifled women see that "it's not you being crazy, something's gone crazy about the society that's making you feel disempowered, alienated, and held at arm's length."

Although no one knows exactly, the eight-hour day seems to have bit the dust somewhere around the recession of 1989–92, though its demise had been building since the recession of the early '80s. There's enough blame to go around for everyone. The causes include the merger and downsizing craze, and the job insecurity it set off; employers opting for overtime instead of hiring; the stagnation of wages, which forces people to work more; runaway consumerism, which has increased the average American's spending—and need for bucks—by 30 percent and possibly as much as 70 percent between 1979 and 1995, according to Juliet Schor; technology blurring the distinction between work and private life; a cultural shift that glamorizes overwork; and the growing number of workers who are classed as "salaried" who can then be worked an unlimited number of hours.

When the law of the employment land, the Fair Labor Standards Act, was passed in the late 1930s, most of the labor force was blue-collar and very little of it was salaried. Today a third of the workforce are salaried employees. The salary has become a license for permanent residence at the office. The number of salaried employees working more than 40 hours a week has soared from 35 percent in 1983 to 45 percent in 1999, according to the General Accounting Office. Meanwhile, the number of salaried women has jumped from 33 percent in 1983 to 42 percent in 1998, which has had a big impact on the home-life time squeeze.

Not all these hours are even legit. In fact, downsizing has touched off a wave of phony salary designations, which employers use to exempt employees from overtime pay. The scope of this problem is staggering. Some experts think there may be hundreds of thousands of misclassified employees who don't fit the salary exemption, and who are working overtime for free. You might be one of them. To find out, see Chapter 9, page 171.

Once a symbol of upward trajectory in career and earnings, the salary is now the sign of a downward spiral into overwork hell. The Japanese showed how a steady diet of ten- and twelve-hour days could turn the term "salaryman" into a derisive synonym for zombie drone. Now that we have passed the Japanese in total working hours, the salary has lost its luster here, too. Now it's U.S. salarymen and women who are setting the no-life pace.

The pot of gold we seek in dollars and esteem from the salaried life looks increasingly like the fool's kind. You come in earlier, stay later, and still the to-do list and call-back stack grows. The loose ends pump up the stress and nag away at your sense of competence. Why can't you get the work done? Why aren't you better organized? Why can't you find the time for anything? What's wrong with you?

There's only one of you.

Shrink Tank

The biggest factor in the overwork madness is the wave after wave of downsizings from the mid-1980s through today that have left a stripped-down workforce doing more with less. There's more slimming going on in corporate America than at Weight Watchers. More than $1.83 trillion worth of mergers and acquisition deals were announced in the U.S. in 2000. Instead of growing companies the old-fashioned way, internally, by creating new products and marketing, corporate America took to instant gratification, buying size through acquisitions and mergers so it could get a quicker bump in share price through a lower unit cost—achieved through layoffs of the staffs of the merged companies.

"And it just kept going—merge, layoff, merge, layoff," notes John Drake, a business consultant and author of *Downshifting*. "When they 'reorganized,' as they call it, the department that had thirty-five people wound up with thirty."

This, in turn, racheted up the anxiety level by increasing the workload for the remaining workers. "Downsizing gives the people who are retained more work to do," says the University of South Florida's Charles Spielberger, who studies workplace stress. That increases stress, since one of its two main causes in the workplace, Spielberger has found, is lack of support to do your job, from co-workers, supervisors, or the organization. "With support lacking, then the pressures of doing the additional work are greatly enhanced."

The publishing industry was hit particularly hard by mergers and consolidations, and senior editors at the book houses absorbed some of the biggest punches. When a publishing house is acquired or merged, editors there who had been responsible for twenty books could easily find themselves riding herd on thirty titles. Juli Barbato found herself on the losing end of a barrage of titles and responsibilities after Disney gobbled up Hyperion Books. "At one point I was acting as copy chief and managing editor, and I had to develop a system of operations," Barbato recalls bitterly about her former stint on stress row. "So I was really doing two or three jobs without a full complement of staff. After the beginning of the third year it really got to me. I felt like it changed my whole body chemistry. I went into a true clinical depression. Hair loss, nails bitten down to the quick. My stomach hurt all the time."

She quit, but she knows plenty of colleagues still drowning today. "I can name five production editors off the bat right now in this business who are depressed. They're all on Zoloft or Prozac. They're all ill and shaky and losing hair, losing sleep. It's more than they can physically do. But production editors will try and try." Depression is a common side effect of job stress without end, and it's growing in the workplace, accounting for $12 billion annually in lost workdays, according to the Washington Business Group on Health. Given the current stress load it's probably not surprising that the incidence of depression in the U.S. has increased ten times since the 1940s. American business is throwing piles of money away by not addressing the stress crisis, since depression has been found to be the most expensive of all medical costs—70 percent higher than anything else—and stress is the second costliest.

The downsizing of America has fundamentally altered the psychology of the workplace, and more than clinically. It broke the faith in the implicit contract of hard work for a secure future that had anchored the labor-management relationship. Now the rules have changed, and no one's quite sure where the footing is. Some have decided to stick with the old routine by demonstrating more loyalty than anyone else, boosting hours voluntarily or skipping vacations in a practice known as "defensive overworking," in the hope that their extra efforts might help them keep their jobs in the next round of cuts. It's a desperate, and futile, contest to prove commitment by extreme face-time, and it adds up to another factor in excessive hours.

But more of the same isn't working. To survive the new world of slasher CFOs and forced overtime, you need to restructure, too. When loyalty is no longer a two-way street, you need to reassess old strategies. Working longer is not working smarter. And just as management will let people go when times get tough no matter how many hours they've put in, you have to look long and hard at whether you can afford to black out years of your life in massive overtime displays on the thread of hope that you'll be spared some future judgment day. And then what? For what? When do you get to enjoy the fruits of your labor? How about right now?

Guess Who's Not Coming to Dinner

If you feel like toast these days, it's because you are. You're now working 14 weeks longer each year than the folks in 1969. Technology has added to the frenzy by making it easier than ever to keep working at night, on the weekend, and even right through the vacation. Dogged by laptops, cell phones, and E-mail, one-third of employees say they work on vacation, and two-thirds of managers do, reports a Boston College survey. Longer workweeks has meant a proportionate decrease in time spent with family.

This cultural shift has come with enormous social costs—to home life, civic involvement, public safety—that we can't bring ourselves to acknowledge because work remains the Great Unassailable. Gil Gordon, author of *Turn It Off*, a book chronicling the tech overload, sums up the cost of the onslaught: "We have far too many people who never feel they're able to catch their breath, who never feel they can have any true extended quality time for themselves and their significant others, and they're always on call and always in demand. The rubber band keeps getting stretched and stretched. You can see the implications of that, from corporate performance to kids' lives. What does it mean when the parent can't focus on Johnny's homework for thirty minutes without the cell phone going off?"

What we have here is the ultimate family-values issue: missing parents, swallowed up by incessant ten- and twelve-hour days. Excessive work is robbing families of time together, and without it, they're drifting apart. Hollywood gets the rap, while most households today can't get a quorum for dinner. "We've lost in our culture this sense that business and work in general should be in service to our lives," a concerned executive, Tom McMakin, former COO of the Great Harvest Bread

Company, told the *Christian Science Monitor*. "You can't balance seventy-hour workweeks with a good home life."

One working mother who puts in ninety-hour weeks told me her kids ask her all the time if she could work less and spend more time with them. "It breaks your heart, but what can I do?" she said. No wonder that 34 percent of parents in the U.S. can't report the height, weight, and eye color of their kids when their children turn up missing.

Former CNN anchor Bernard Shaw captured the conflicted emotions of parents across the nation on his final day at the network, when he was asked by a CNN colleague to reflect on his career as one of the most respected journalists in America. His response was unforgettable: "It wasn't worth it," he said, because it had caused him to miss so much time with his family. I almost fell out of my chair. Here was one of the most successful people in America questioning the unquestionable: the success track. Shaw was articulating a deeply felt sense across America that seldom makes its way into words—that the cost of a success without limits has become intolerable. I decided to follow up with him, and Shaw told me: "Nothing conspires more against a loving family than work. After your kids are off to college, you will have spent more hours supporting them than being with them. They have the missed touches to show for it."

Family advocates need to start aiming their firepower at the real culprit: those mad doctors of the business world who created the Frankenstein that Joan Williams, a law professor at American University, has dubbed the "ideal worker." The ideal worker is someone who enters the full-time, now overtime, workforce in early adulthood, and, if he or she can, lifts their head forty years later. Ideal workers are hostages to their jobs, which makes them nonparents. Williams, who chronicles the impact of overwork on families in *Unbending Gender,* maintains that, "the ideal worker is completely inconsistent with our ideals at home, which are that children need and deserve time with their parents. That's just a profound clash of ideals, and everyone's caught in it."

The ideal worker role is a time bomb that blows up marriages, and kids are the collateral damage. The divorce rate is higher in overwork industries such as the legal profession. In the end, the kids and all of us pay, says Williams, because 40 percent of divorced women wind up in poverty, and the children along with them, since most will live with the mother.

Working mothers find themselves wracked by the conflict between work and home. Nancy, a Los Angeles attorney, started having panic attacks when she came back to the office after having her first child. "There just wasn't enough time for being a mother and an attorney," she says. She is so exhausted when she gets home from work some nights, anywhere from 8 P.M. to 10 P.M., that there are moments "when I just hope that my son is asleep by the time I get there."

In a world where parents can't make a living and be a parent at the same time, who, or should I say what, is the real delinquent when kids head south? I move that we call overwork before a Senate subcommittee.

The Job-Stress Express

Slide open the top drawer of the typical cubicle or office desk, and mixed in with the staples and Post-its and business cards of people instantly forgotten from some trade show, you'll find an archeological treasure trove, the implements used at the dawn of the second millennium to get through a working day: Maalox, Tylenol, Paxil, Tagament, Zoloft, Tums. This is the rumbling underbelly of the American office, out of sight, out of mind from the game face, the work face.

We're a gut-gurgling, groggy, cranky nation, ready to snap, and in need of a good night's sleep. The extra hours on the job have to be squeezed from somewhere, and it's the nightly shut-eye that pays the price. A majority of American adults, 63 percent, don't get the recommended eight-and-a-half hours of sleep, according to the National Sleep Foundation. The study found a direct relationship between the amount of hours worked and a corresponding loss of sleep. Compared to five years ago, a majority of us are spending more time at work and less time sleeping, with more than one-third of us working more than fifty hours a week. Sleep deprivation is no joke. It's involved in more than 100,000 traffic accidents every year, killing more than 1,500 people. Chronic sleep loss can affect brain chemistry, setting the stage for a number of health hazards, from an increased risk of developing diabetes, to male erectile dysfunction, lowered immune function, and depression.

You may think there's no time to sleep or take a vacation, but it's really the opposite. You can't afford not to. Not stopping to restore and refresh can force your body to take its own break. And it's usually others who see it coming first. After months of working 6:30 A.M. to midnight, Karen Walker, an executive for a major high-tech company in the Silicon Valley, was getting so little sleep colleagues told her that her voice messages sounded like she was drunk. She was, on work. Her hangover came in the form of insomnia, hives, and hair loss. The project she was managing was so understaffed and overwhelming that it infested her bedroom. She couldn't sleep more than a couple of hours without waking up worrying about it. She wound up calling into the office at 3 and 4 in the morning, leaving messages with colleagues that sounded like they'd come out of the bottom of a Jim Beam bottle. The feedback confirmed that nonstop stress had pushed her well into burnout, and to the brink of breakdown.

Job stress, like other kinds of stress, is triggered by a perceived danger to life and limb, when a demand, or stressor, threatens to overwhelm your capacity to cope. Your body reacts as if the stressor was a mob in search of your scalp, sending the central nervous system into flight-or-fight mode. This unleashes a flood of adrenaline that makes your heart beat faster and your blood pressure rise, forcing the body to work much harder and taxing your entire system. Some stress is part of the workplace territory and not harmful—the so-called "good stress." When the job demands are not too high and there are high levels of personal control over the job, the pressures of the job can be seen as challenge and motivation. But "when the demands are high and the individual has little control over them, the negative consequences of strain or stress develop," explains Dr. Robert Karasek of the University of Massachusetts, an expert on the link between job stress and health. "There is increased risk of physical illness and negative emotional states."

Job stress is often pooh-poohed as an affliction of wimps. Unless you're one of these pathetic weaklings, you better keep it to yourself. But more than two dozen different studies have conclusively linked job stress with heart disease. "It's not just a nuisance," declares Dr. Steven Lamm, of New York University Mount Sinai Medical School, author of *Younger at Last: The New World of Vitality Medicine* and a regular on ABC's *The View.* "It's as much of a risk factor for heart attacks, strokes and cancer as the other known carcinogens. If you go to work at 7 and come home at 10 at night, you're going to pay a price. The impact on the immune system is overwhelming."

"If you're overloading a circuit, you're going to blow a fuse," explains Dr. Raphael Kellman, of the Kellman Center for Progressive Medicine in New York. "Too much energy is coming through the system. We now know that stress can lead to thyroid dysfunction, adrenal dysfunction, immunological problems, coronary heart disease, lower back pain . . . Stress can lead to just about everything." It's the leading cause of insomnia, and can also trigger stroke, ulcers, chronic fatigue syndrome, irritable bowel syndrome, ulcers, and chronic headaches.

Job stress doesn't just assault bodies; it also wreaks havoc on business, costing $150 billion a year in absenteeism, lost productivity, and health bills, according to one study. Some 75 percent of visits to primary care physicians come from stress-induced problems. And it's all preventable, if we can acknowledge the stupidity of the workstyle that maintains it.

Burnout: The Hostile Takeover

The last act of the stress cycle, burnout is a fitting epidemic for the overwork age. Its total colonization of the mind, body, and spirit mirrors the complete takeover of life by the job these days. Unlike periodic stress that comes and goes with specific events, burnout develops from a condition of endless, chronic stress, where emotional resources are stripped away until there is nothing left to counter the drain. It's a "gradual depletion over time of individuals' intrinsic energetic resources," points out Tel Aviv University's Arie Shirom, a leading authority on job stress. The result is a three-way, mind-body shut-down, characterized by "emotional exhaustion, physical fatigue, and cognitive weariness." It's more than being tired. You have been sucked dry. Motivation, pride, ambition, drive—it's all gone, and hope along with it. Numbness and cynicism set in, and along with them a sense of depersonalization and a lack of accomplishment. Withdrawal and symptoms of depression mark the advanced stages of the cycle. "You detach from work and other significant roles and relationships," explains Washington, D.C.-based Mark Gorkin, a psychologist known as the "Stress Doc" to his clients in the business world. "The result is lowered productivity, cynicism, shame, doubt, confusion, the feeling of being drained, having nothing more to give."

Stress morphs into burnout when we suffer a loss of physical and emotional resources too great to replace. If coping efforts fail to restore the loss, and there's no interruption of the stress response—like, say, a solution to the stressor, or a vacation, we crash into burnout. Typical burnout stressors include an overwhelming workload, a lack of support or reward, interpersonal conflict, loss of control, and a sense of impotence, the feeling that nothing you do makes a difference—all features of a downsized workplace.

Because burnout is at its core a story of emotional conflict, the stress can often come from ongoing strains with co-workers or a "dysfunctional managerial relationship, where you become like a battered employee," notes Gorkin. "This saps your energy, saps your confidence, which then makes it harder to leave the company, so it becomes a vicious circle."

It's an eery, mystifying transformation for the typical burnout victim. "These people have been going, going, going for a long period of time, and they can't understand why they can't go anymore," says Dr. Tod Loring, a physician in Culver City, California, who has seen many a burned-out case. "When I get into the history, I find out about heart palpitations, shortness of breath, hot flashes, sweating without any reason. The patient just thinks that's part of his day."

This adaptation is why an alcoholic will outlive a workaholic.

"Workaholics die faster because adrenaline provides a certain masking that the body is going down," explains Diane Fassell, author of *Working Ourselves to Death*. "An alcoholic can live for years with cirrhosis of the liver, but it's often a stroke or heart attack that kills the workaholic."

There are plenty of flares sent up if we're paying attention—fatigue, frequent illness, upset stomach, frequent headaches, muscle tension and pain, rapid heartbeat, forgetfulness, being late to work, alienation, aggravation, frequent mistakes, and sleep difficulty.

As a disease of accumulation, burnout is a particularly insidious fit for American workers. We're raised to take the hits and keep on firing, and never let on that we're wounded. Men, in particular, are taught that admission of any weakness—even, idiotically, the physical reality of your body falling apart—is tantamount to wimpdom. So we ignore the gastric volcanoes, the head that feels like there's a WWF match going on inside, the grinding fatigue, and soldier on, because if we don't, we're weak, which means we don't cut it as red-white-and-very-blue pile drivers. The adaptive process of burnout thrives on the warrior mentality. The adrenaline racing through our body masks the damage to overloaded internal organs. The adrenal glands are working overtime like you, even while you sleep. Tom Row, a Tennessee scientist, drove himself to 12-hour days for two decades, burning up weeks of untaken vacation time, without giving it a second thought—until he wound up on an operating table, calculating his odds of surviving a heart attack. "I had no idea I was stressed," he says. "It wakes you up real fast. I had to look at where I'd been and where I was going for the first time. It changed my whole outlook on life. If I had to do it over again, I'd set limits on the work."

The macho streak that dominates the workplace would have us believe we are invincible. Any physical or mental signs to the contrary could be interpreted as our not having the right stuff for advancement. We don't even want to admit any strain to ourselves—that would be weak. We can't have that. The lengths we go to to ignore pain, exhaustion, and life implosion to prove to bosses and ourselves that we can take it is truly astounding. Case in point: Susan, an editor who found herself in a dungeon of eighty-hour weeks doing three people's jobs, producing annual reports for the World Bank in Washington, D.C. A self-confessed "workaholic," she tried to get all the work done, even if it couldn't be done by one person. Her life disappeared, and along with it her health. She suffered a major back problem, "scoliosis with a twist" from hours of sitting hunched over on her marathon until the pain was so excruciating she could no longer sit or even stand up.

But Susan was not a quitter. She would take it—for three long years. "There were days and days on end where all I could do was sort of hobble into the office and lay on the floor in my cubicle with one of those blue ice things on my back while people came in and out of my office," she recalls. Her bosses wouldn't even acknowledge that there was anything weird about an employee stretched out on the office carpet like a corpse. It's a perfect metaphor for the state of overworked America. That's us—flat on our backs—mentally, emotionally, physically, spiritually. Yet everybody acts like nothing's wrong, and the charade goes on.

The battering is a distortion of the nature of real courage, which lies not in masochism or martyrdom but in the path that counters that herd. As Lao Tzu said in the ancient Chinese book of wisdom, the *Tao Te Ching,* "He who is brave in daring will be killed. He who is brave in not daring will survive." In a work culture driving society to the brink, opting out of esteem-based workaholism is the real home of the brave.

Assess Your Stress

To prevent yourself from being another sudden medical statistic, you have to remove yourself from the hype of adrenaline and recognize the stressors in the workplace that are setting you off—and then do something about them. Don't "take it," out of a fear that you'd be a gelatinous wuss if you spoke up. Find the source of the stress, communicate the problem to the appropriate parties, and reach a solution.

The fact is, the quickest way to be truly weak, if not stone dead, is to go the stoic route. This self-sabotage prizes others' opinions over your own life. It's not weak to admit to a problem so you are able to solve it.

That's strength, not to mention intelligence. To get off the overwork treadmill and reclaim your health, you have to free yourself from the superstition of weakness. Whenever the words "weak" or "wimp" pop into your head when you try to take care of yourself, imagine where you will be if you follow this hoax: in a delightful paper gown or a wooden box.

So as a first step to avoid ultimate weakness, take a few minutes to complete the following burnout test, kindly made available by Dr. Shirom. The Shirom-Melamed Burnout Questionnaire measures stress on the three levels that comprise the burnout condition, emotional exhaustion (EE), physical fatigue (PF), and cognitive weariness (Cog). Respond to each of the statements by indicating how often you have that feeling during working hours. Almost always = 1 point; very frequently = 2 points; quite frequently = 3; sometimes = 4; quite infrequently = 5; very infrequently = 6; almost never = 7. Add up your scores for each of the three categories. To find your stress range, see the ratings printed below the text.

It's not easy to be self-reflective when you're in the belly of the beast. You can only see the damage of overwork and stress by stepping back. You need to make the time to ask yourself the questions: Is this the life you want, risking your health and sealing yourself off from family, friends, and the experience of living? What's really important in your life? What do you need to change to get more of it?

Paychecks have a way of stifling critical thought, and before you know it, you've burned up ten, fifteen, or twenty years on the live-to-work treadmill, if you last that long. That time is not coming back. But you don't have to be played by the job like an organ grinder's monkey anymore. You can make a commitment that the rest of your life is going to be different—by setting a course for new priorities, ones that focus on life as well as career. This starts by freeing yourself from a mind-set that says you are worthless unless you're buried in work. So let's get to the root of that warped ideal, the psychology that keeps you at the heel of the Office Commandments, and give it the boot.

THE BURNOUT TEST

Physical Fatigue

_____ 1. I feel tired.

_____ 2. I feel physically fatigued.

_____ 3. I feel physically exhausted.

_____ 4. When I get up in the morning to go to work, I have no energy.

Emotional Fatigue

_____ 5. I feel fed up.

_____ 6. I feel like my emotional batteries are dead.

_____ 7. I feel burned out in my job.

_____ 8. I feel emotionally fatigued.

Cognitive Fatigue

_____ 9. I am too tired to think clearly.

_____ 10. I have difficulty concentrating.

_____ 11. My thinking process is slow.

_____ 12. I have difficulty thinking about complex things.

_____ TOTAL

(Dr. Shirom advises that men whose scores average 3.0 to 3.75 and women who average 3.6 to 4.0 are at the high end of the burnout range and should seek expert help for preventative measures.)

2

Who's Afraid of a Day Off?

The Fears That Keep You Overdoing It

• • •

"I wish that they would try a little more to make great men; that they would set less value on the work, and more upon the workman; that they would never forget that a nation cannot long remain strong when every man belonging to it is individually weak."

—Alexis de Toqueville, *Democracy in America*

One of the tip-offs of low self-image, psychologists tell us, is the need to boost your standing by inflating yourself in front of others. The braggart tries to prop up weak knees by saying his knees are stronger than yours. Of course, what it says is just the opposite—they're wobbling—which should tell us something about a workplace where this defensive behavior is as epidemic as the overtime. It's turned the job for some into a game of Ultimate Zombie, in which competitors vie for bragging rights to the longest hours on the job. "I worked till 10 P.M. last night," Johnny Workaholic will bluster. "I didn't get out of here till midnight," a fellow blowhard will boast. "I did an all-nighter last week," goes the next bag of wind. And on and on. "I put in 14 hours yesterday," "I came in on Saturday."

If it wasn't so tragic, it would be high comic action, the idea of competing to have less of a life than the next guy. And shouting it to the world. Yet our work culture is so skewed to excess that hours are worn like notches on the holster to cover the racing insecurity behind the trigger. Some brag about the time they've done like ex-cons, trumpeting their skipped vacations or how much holiday time they've accrued. They may as well get on a local rooftop and scream, "I DIDN'T DO ANY LIVING THIS YEAR! NONE!"

Others score points via E-mail. A manager at the New York headquarters of a national clothing retailer likes to let co-workers know, "I was here," with the time posted on E-mail dispatches in the wee hours. "She'll send E-mails at three o'clock in the morning, like it's evidence she was here that late," reports Cristina, a flabberghasted Australian who was working until after midnight her first weeks on the job to keep up with this insomniac boss. In Australia, "if you worked till 7 or 7:30, your manager would sit you down and say, 'Okay, what's wrong? What are you doing wrong with your time management? Is it too much of a workload?'"

Work martyrdom is seen as equally dumb by the European Union, which has a cap on overtime of forty-eight hours per week. Workaholism is considered stupid, not only because it's a threat to personal health and family, but also because it's counterproductive to quality performance in the workplace. The belief is that workaholics drive, not profits, but the stress of everyone else around them, which causes frayed interpersonal relations and reduced productivity. One firm in Belgium has a program that identifies and roots out workaholics and then guides them through a course in simmering down. The company, ironically enough, is American, a division of Hewlett Packard. Would such a program ever make it to the Silicon Valley headquarters of HP? No surprise, a human resources spokesperson for the company told me that there is no such program in the United States.

That would be like Budweiser enforcing a one-beer limit per customer. The whole idea is to get you to always do more and show you can hold your overtime like a pub crawler holds his ale. We celebrate working longer than anyone else or even you can stand it because of a tangle of guilt and fear that keeps us feeling we are never enough. We have to keep working. Or we'll fall behind. Someone might pass us on the totem pole. The company would crumble without us. The boss might not consider us promotion material. We'll be worthless. In this twisted logic all value is derived from work, and so we are valueless unless we're grinding away on some productive task every waking breath. Leisure is seen as unproductive, an alien realm that is a diversion from our prime goal, making money. Add this to the nods, winks, and not-so-veiled threats from supervisors suggesting it would be a good idea to skip your holiday, and you've got 26 percent of workers who don't take a vacation each year.

Tom Lewiston, a longtime American musk oxen in Seattle, didn't take a vacation for nineteen years straight as a sheet-metal foreman for Lockheed Shipbuilding. He didn't need time off. What for? Every year, instead of taking a vacation, he pocketed his holiday pay and kept on working. "That was the norm," he admits. "That's just what you do. It's like, This is why we're here: to work. We're not here to enjoy life. You feel like you're cheating somebody by taking your time."

Then just before his twentieth year on self-appointed iron-man duty, a flash of regret popped into his hard head. Here it was, two decades later, and he hadn't "gone anywhere, seen anything." So he took off on a trip to Europe, where he spent a month in Spain, discovering new taste delights like paella, late-night gabfests with locals, and a lifestyle where work was simply a means to play and enjoy life to the last drop of Sangria. "It didn't take me long to realize," he says, "that for twenty years I had it all wrong. I quickly came to the conclusion that there was more to life than just working. There's a whole world out there to explore. Aside from that, it's relaxing. I can come back after a month off and feel reasonably refreshed and rejuvenated. It's a life-altering experience."

Once he could see what was out there beyond the Great Wall of work, Lewiston was sold. Like so many Americans, he had been swept up in the idea that only one thing mattered in life: his job, and that all sustenance would flow from there. Money. Esteem. Success. Toys. Manhood. And thus: happiness. He lived to work, piling up as much overtime as his body could withstand. Six-day weeks were routine. He was proud that he could "take it," the most vaunted virtue of a culture defined by its labor. Until he discovered that, much to his surprise, a life of "taking it" had taken him. He was exhausted, stale as an old Saltine, totally out of balance, cut off from a social life, the world of the spirit, joy. Until he found himself on vacation.

Lewiston needed time to step away from the marathon grind, not only to refresh and recharge his overloaded system, but also to reflect on how unbalanced his life had gotten from a single-minded focus on work, on the stampede to money, success, and busyness to the exclusion of all else. He discovered something we're going to be exploring at length in the pages to come: We've got it Ass Backwards.

We're led to believe it's all going to happen tomorrow. If we just work harder and longer and give up more nights and weekends and bang our heads just a little more we'll get that promotion, money, status, spouse/house/car of our dreams, and then we'll be "there," where the struggle and sacrifice will have been worth it. We live for a future that never quite arrives, and in the meantime, life goes on without us. We lose touch with friends, and have no time to make new ones. Relationships and kids are sacrificed to prove our career mettle. Passions and hobbies are lost in the race. We miss out on scores of experiences to learn and explore and keep life new. We forget what fun is. The months turn into years of postponement.

We're left with a nagging exhaustion and emptiness that is trying to tell us the picture is upside-down. In the all-consuming drive to prove worth through fickle external measures of esteem like work, productivity, and status, we wind up excluding the very parts of life that can deliver the more lasting inner validation we really want. The real scorecard is inside, as is all the stuff that prevents you from seeing that, the fears and misconceptions that create the life-killing Office Commandments we think we need to obey. So let's get the culprits all out in the open right now—Job Title-itis, Macho-rexia, Productivity Paranoia, and Leisure Phobia—and see how we can dismiss them for being the useless time-wasters they are.

Job Title-itis: You Work, Therefore You Are

It's question number two for strangers at any American social setting—right after "What's your name?" and within the first two minutes of conversation or your passport is revoked: "What do you do?" We ask this instinctively and unself-consciously, as if the job is an appendage of family name. But pop this same query off the bat at a Swiss, English, or Spanish gathering, and it doesn't go over as well. In fact, "it would be quite a shock and even impolite to rush into that immediately," admits Steven Poelmans, a Belgian work-life expert and professor of organizational behavior at the IESE Business School in Barcelona, Spain. "Europeans identify themselves more in terms of their private life—family, where they're from, social activities."

You are what you do for most Americans. In a classless, rootless society, the job has come to define the person and the pecking order, one based on professional status and the toys that come with it. Being the youngsters that we as a culture are, we don't have the anchors of older societies, such as long social/regional traditions that define the individual by his or her place within the group and geography. As rugged individuals, we're on our own to try to figure out who the heck we are and where we belong. The blessing in that is that we have more choice and are free to constantly reinvent ourselves. The curse is that we select our identity only from column A: what we do, ignoring the several other columns that make up the full measure of who we really are—and have to be to feel good about ourselves. When the job is the sum total of identity, it makes you a pushover for sixty-hour weeks, because your entire being is riding on your worth as a worker.

As Mark Liechty, a professor of anthropology at the University of Illinois, Chicago, explained it to me, "Americans compared to almost any other society are encouraged to achieve and display identity through labor more so than other domains in life. Most Americans labor in order to consume and construct the self. Europeans have much more of a sense of sociality than Americans. They take social relationships and friendships more seriously."

There's no doubt about who's the boss here. Work is the puppet master. Our existence rises or falls depending on the play-by-play at work, which doesn't stop there. It's replayed over and over again once we get home to the eternal boredom of significant others and friends. We suffer from a bad case of job title-itis, such intense identification with profession that, if you got laid off, you'd have to report yourself to missing persons.

For many the work ID is the only self in town. "Our culture explicitly states that your identity can be found in what it is that you do," explains Dr. Scott Stacy, a psychologist at the Professional Renewal Center in Lawrence, Kansas. "From a very young age we begin on this journey, looking for the treasure of finding and holding on to a cohesive sense of who we are. We're told that the treasure is to be found in what we do, our work. Many people will go after that at the risk of compromising their health, their family life and their psychological life. Some will go after it with so much incredible hunger for self that they wind up losing themselves in the process."

They validate at the office, punching your ID ticket with proof that you are needed, and thus have worth. Work provides the affirmation of self that might have come from family and community in another era. In a time of fragmented social units, work has become a kind of surrogate family for many, which can be hazardous to your health. It can create a familial sense of duty that may make you work beyond the bounds of capacity and sanity to get the daily dose of validation.

It's a chase that never ends, for more strokes, status, money—all of it about getting more approval from others. But all the promotions and compliments can't make you feel what you don't already believe. Social psychologist Mihaly Csikszentmihalyi described why in *Flow:* "People keep hoping that changing the external conditions of their lives will provide a solution. If only they could earn more money, be in better physical shape, or have a more understanding partner, they would really have it made. Even though we recognize that material success may not bring happiness, we engage in an endless struggle to reach external goals, expecting that they will improve life . . . The reality is that the quality of life does not depend directly on what others think of us or what we own. The bottom line is, rather, how we feel about ourselves and about what happens to us. To improve life one must improve the quality of experience."

Having a clear sense of self is a basic need for everyone. It's the system software, the MS-DOS, of our personal operations. If you don't know who you are, you're going to be smothered by the identities others choose for you, and your capacity to function in the world will be stunted. That's what happens when you focus all efforts on your job ID, and none on the requirements of genuine identity—social relations, personal values, a sense of meaningfulness and contribution, love, creativity, growth, play, spirituality, and "individuation," as Carl Jung called the insistent drive within us for self-discovery and realization of all our potentialities. These are the aspects of the self that determine your state of contentment and fulfillment, and provide balance.

In quiet moments we can sense the stirrings of that path, something closer to our real essence, to "an inherent fearlessness, connectedness, integrity, and belonging," as Jack Kornfield puts it in *A Path with Heart.* Pulsing through the fog of overwork and business like a lighthouse beacon in a pea souper, this interior homing device is where those signals come from that tell you something's off in your life, that you're not in alignment with your values or heart's true course. It's authenticity, calling. You.

Mistaken Identity

The job is, in actuality, just your social face, what the psychologists call your "persona." The term comes from the masks actors wore in ancient theatrical performances to indicate their various roles in the play. Jung described the persona as "a compromise between the individual and society as to what a man should appear to be. He takes a name, earns a title, exercises a function." The persona is a mask you need to function in society, but it isn't the real you. When you think of yourself as your persona—an accountant, a scientist, a teacher, and nothing else—you have only part of the ID equation.

Confusing persona with self can cause emotional and psychological

meltdown, resulting in "inexplicable failure in job performance or relationships . . . a nagging sense of something missing from one's life, a
diminished or even nonexistent capacity for intimacy and vulnerability
with others, and a lack of creativity," psychotherapist Robert Hopcke
notes in *Persona.*

Overwork inflates the ego's mask, while the true regulator of esteem under the costume is ignored. It's so instinctive, you don't even
know you're doing it, and if anyone were to point it out, you'd think
they were out of their mind, quite possibly a communist to question
that work was not the end-all and be-all of life. It's a fantastically real-
appearing delusion. The persona is the tail that wags the dog.

When your identity is dependent solely on your job, you're conditioned to feel as good, or as bad, as your latest performance, your worth
always hanging in the balance. You have to prove yourself all over again
with every task. The strain of always being on the line, having to re-
manufacture your worth every day, is enormous in today's multitasking
world and can lead to the breaking point. "Many of the people I see are
working way beyond their emotional, psychological, and physical resources," reports New Jersey psychotherapist Carla Natalucci. "They
have heart issues, high blood pressure, 'nervous skin' issues. But the underlying issue is: I identify myself as a productive individual by these
criteria, and if I'm not meeting them all the time, then I'm not worthy.
I'm worthless. The underlying structure is not being dealt with, so
physical or emotional disorders pop up."

It's not easy to admit that everything you know in life—that work
is the answer to all esteem and worth needs—is a crock. The water in
your sink might just as well go down counterclockwise, north turn to
south, or Bill Gates join an ashram.

You're looking for love in all the wrong places when the persona is
directing the show. The hits of job success are momentary and can fade
by the next sunrise. With so much effort being expended on a route
that can't deliver, the frustration and emptiness grow. It's hard to pass
off an imitation. Persona lives are a bit like one of those old black-and-
white films that's been colorized. They feel off, fake. The form is there
but not the content. Depth and richness have been flattened, author-

ship altered, mood painted on. You long for the original, as your inner makeup does for the real you.

When your identity is based on the resilient corps of inner attributes—you're smart, competent, generous, fun, resourceful, a cyclist, a father, mother, good friend, jazz lover, a great cook, a soulful spirit—you're calling the tune. You're not at the mercy of outside approval, what Mark Twain once called "cornpone opinions." You don't have to live and die every day based on a supervisor's comments or how fast or slow you got a phone call returned.

If you want to get time for life and real vacations, you have to play your own game. That starts by separating your identity from the job. Then you can make room for the things that give purpose to the work— the fruits of your labor. When you have a fulfilling life outside the office, you're less likely to tolerate it being frozen out. You can start down that path by innoculating yourself against the scourge of Job Title-itis.

Rx FOR JOB TITLE-ITIS:

1. **Get to the Core.** Take time to reacquaint yourself with your inner ID. Assess what values and goals you want to achieve for yourself outside of career. What is success and happiness for you beyond the job? Where is your joy? Passion? Curiosity?

2. **Create a Nonwork ID.** Draw up a list of the interests, talents, and personality traits that make you unique—generosity, humor, science fiction buff, candor, dancer, runner, garden designer, eBay auction maven. Use friends and associates to help you find your true identifiers.

3. **Play Your Life Card.** Put together a business card for your nonwork ID, a life card. You can give yourself whatever title you like, but it has to be related to a hobby or personality trait— i.e., John Smith, "Wilderness Explorer;" or Jane Jones, "Soulful Gourmet." Pull it out often as a reminder of your real business: to partake in as much of this planet as you can while you can.

4. **Change the Conversation.** Scrap status-digging small talk. Change "what do you do?" to "what do you like to do?" Or, as the Tarahumara Indians of northern Mexico say when they greet each other, "What did you dream last night?" Now there's an ice-breaker.

5. **Get Out of the Manufacturing Business.** Don't let your ID and esteem hang on the latest job performance. You don't need to re-manufacture yourself every day when you have your non-work ID to bolster persona.

6. **Price Out Prestige.** Calculate the true cost of a job title or promotion that leaves you no life. We all want to be respected but does a high-status position that leaves no time for living add up?

7. **Reposition Your Gig.** Here's a good idea on how to separate work and personal life that came in to Work to Live via E-mail: "I have been thinking about the language I use to describe what I do for a living and have decided to insist on calling it a 'job,' rather than a 'career.' The word 'career' seems to blur the distinction (already too blurry) between my life and my work (how I pay for my life). I find it easier to keep my 'job' and my 'life' separate."

Macho-Rexia: My Ulcer's Bigger Than Yours

At six-foot-five, 338 pounds, Korey Stringer was a Paul Bunyan of a man who worked not too far from the home of the mythic strongman as an all-star guard for the Minnesota Vikings. He personified strength and toughness, putting his body on the line in hand-to-hand combat with other 300-pound warriors so that the armchair gladiators of the land could butt heads vicariously—until he died of heatstroke after a punishing workout in hundred-degree weather in August 2001.

Stringer had been pulled off the field the prior day after he vomited several times during practice. Like so many athletes, Stringer was extra determined the next day to prove that he was man enough to take it, even if it was one of the hottest days of the summer. Though he sweltered in full padding in the searing heat and high humidity, he kept pushing. In the macho world of football stopping for water breaks can be considered "weak," either by your peers, the coach, or by yourself. So Stringer kept driving himself onward, not taking the hydration he needed. His body temperature soared to 108 degrees, then he collapsed and died within the hour. He was just twenty-seven years old.

This needless tragedy is a potent metaphor for the macho marathon of the workplace. Heatstroke may have been the official cause of death for Korey Stringer and other football fatalities, but the real culprit was insecurity—players trying to out-macho each other, and coaches with testosterone doubts of their own pushing players beyond their capacities. As on the gridiron, wage warriors refuse to acknowledge mortal limits, shunning vacations and stress breaks like water at a football training camp. Thousands die of heart attacks from job stress every year, making football deaths a blip in comparison. They are brought down by the same Neanderthal mentality: Mine is bigger than yours. That is, my ulcer, my back problem, my cholesterol count. It reminds me of a line by John Milton: "What is strength without a double share of wisdom?"

What drives this insanity? "It gets back to that core," notes Dr. Steve Sultanoff, a psychotherapist in Irvine, California. "I'm valuable, I'm powerful, I'm greater than life. I'm overachieving. I can stand more pain than you can."

When the boss boasts that he gets into the office at 4:30 A.M., as does one media mogul, or the chairman of a national retailer trumpets that he doesn't take a vacation, it all strikes me, not as manly, but as something out of the realm of boys, say, from junior high or high school. Methinks thou doth proclaim manhood too much. Wes Patterson, a psychotherapist in Coral Gables, Florida, confirms the juvenile connection. "It starts in elementary school, and goes all the way up," he says. "I'm stronger than he is, I'm better than he is. It's fostered by so many forces—parents, teachers. If you are a more macho worker than the next guy, you become admired, you have status."

We all contribute to reinforcing the ironman myth, marveling at our overdoing-it colleagues. Mathew Beck, a computer technician in

Massachusetts, points to a guy in his company "who wants to be an ironman. He smokes and drinks coffee constantly and puts in all-nighters—and he's proud of it. And we all express our admiration for him, because he gets the job done, and he finishes things we don't want to finish. Trying to express disapproval of a behavior like that is hard—you don't want to hurt the guy's feelings, because this is how he gets his social perks."

The testosterone ethic is highly contagious and sets the tone in the office, as it did in the high school lunch room. Overworkers are the jocks of the company, a sign that you're a competitor, a winner. The strutting pulls in women, too. Connecticut-publicist Andrea Obston, all five-feet-two, one hundred pounds of her, was proud of the fact that she could outwork anybody in any weight class. "That Clydesdale mentality, that I could pull more hours than the next guy down the block, really turned me on," she admits. "I loved that tough-guy image. It was a way to get respect. Now that I think of it, it's very much like anorexia, because the more you do it, the more people marvel at it and the more you can go, 'Wow! I must be something.'"

Call it "macho-rexia," an affliction that starves the life and soul out of you, so you can look good to others. In the effort to appear strong, you become physically, emotionally, and spiritually feeble. Like the anorexic, extreme workaholics can't even see the problem, though their ulcers and back problems beg to differ. Macho-rexics are just following orders. The culture tells us to be an ideal worker, so that becomes the image that rules, as ideal body image rules anorexics.

Macho work culture is about proving over and over that you're man or woman enough, tough enough, to be worthy of adulthood and existence. In traditional cultures there were rituals that proved it early and conclusively, marking a clear passage to adulthood. Boys became men in aboriginal Australia through a rite known as a "walkabout," a test of survival alone in the wilderness. After proving their hunting and navigating skills, they came back no longer teenagers but adults. In our culture grown adults go out every day on their test of survival at the office only to return as teenagers, having to prove their virility again the next day—women, too.

You can get the upper hand on this mentality when you realize that you've been there, done that—high school is over, and the adolescent proving ground along with it. Extreme hours and skipping vacations prove only one thing: You don't value yourself. Increase your valuation by heading off bravado behavior.

Rx FOR MACHO-REXIA

1. **Flex Your Mind.** Toughness isn't about bicep size or notches on the hour belt; it's an inside job. Work smarter, not longer or faster, relying on the strength of your inner resolve, not the testosterone sweepstakes.

2. **Leave the Proof to Stolichnaya.** Vodka may need the proof; you don't. Make a list of key times you've proven your abilities and competence. Make those a quick reference point when you start to overperform. The only proof you need is of life.

3. **Abuse It and Lose It.** The strongest among us can be brought down by abuse and overuse. Many of the biggest, baddest NFL players face a life of infirmity or worse after their football careers from years of punishment on the field. Former Oakland Raiders center Jim Otto has had forty surgeries, thirty on his knees, and can barely walk. Ex–Pittsburgh Steeler Mike Webster, known as "Iron Mike," because he was tough enough to play ten years straight without missing a game, retired with a brain as battered as a boxer's, a doctor said. He died in 2002 at the age of just 50. You are not immortal. Identify the excess in your work life and start pulling back.

4. **Tout Living Time.** The rutting contest doesn't get you anywhere except closer to a plastic bracelet with your name on it. Try bragging about things you did for yourself outside the job: "I had a great bike ride yesterday," "I heard an incredible band last night," "I did something I've never done before: I went parasailing."

Productivity Paranoia

How many times has someone asked you how it's going, and you've told them "busy," but you weren't? Come on, admit it. I've blurted out a few unwarranted b-words in my day. It's so automatic, it's reflex. We certainly don't want people to think we're not happening—a cardinal offense in the United Hives of America. Nonstop worker bees equate to productivity, success, popularity, and more money, honey.

There is just about nothing better than being busy. "I'm so jammed this week," we say with delight. "I'm up to my eyeballs," we complain rapturously. "It's so hectic," we squeal. Our protestations are bogus, because we love it. We love the attention. What we're saying is "I'm popular," "I'm productive," "I'm making money." The action, real or otherwise, suggests motion, forward progress, respect, and all that is good in the world, while the opposite, downtime, means all that is frowned upon—laziness, stagnation, suspect earning ability, unpopularity, and worst of all, no production, you slacker.

Busyness is the nation's real business. It has become a goal in and of itself. Many of us live to be occupied, and whatever business takes place along the way, great. Filling every moment of the day with tasks is part of the constant commotion that seems to be needed to reinforce our fragile IDs and distract us from deeper issues—the conflict between what we do for a living and how we really feel about it, the sense of emptiness that rears when the action stops, the relationship that's on the rocks or nonexistent.

Chronic busyness is rooted in "the belief system that I have to perform in life to be okay," according to Dr. Sultanoff. "People who are driven to perform all the time are saying, 'Look at me, I'm performing, I'm okay.' The problem is that in their core, they don't really believe they're okay, so they have to constantly be working to fill the void. No matter how hard they beat themselves against the wall, no matter how hard they work, they only fill themselves up temporarily."

Overperformers plow ahead with 12- and 14-hour days, one hundred percent convinced that they are doing exactly as they should, even though their bodies and families are falling apart. The consequences of overwork don't matter, because they have to get that fix—the pat on the back—of others' approval. It's such an intense craving that all the moderating signals—back pain, heart palpitations, knot in the stomach, bowels on the loose—are squelched. The workaholic remains oblivious to all but the gush of adrenaline and the next sweet sound of approval—"Awesome that you stayed up all night," "Great flow chart."

The pattern is very much the profile of a substance abuser. As Dr. Raphael Kellman of the Kellman Center explains, "Work is really a subtle addiction. It has the same physiological consequences. There's a fine line between making a living and an addiction to work, an addiction to making money, an addiction to success."

Diane Fassel, author of *Working Ourselves to Death*, believes we're hooked alright, buzzing on "an addiction to incessant activity. Many of us may feel we're not enough," she suggests. "We don't want to face that terrible void. One way to avoid it is to be constantly busy."

Busyness books up your life until you can't remember anything else. "If I have free time, I never know what to do with it," admits Maureen, a Washington attorney who does 80-hour weeks regularly. "I used to be good at exercising, but that's gone out the window."

When the action stops, there's the fidgeting. It's weird to stop. Shouldn't you be doing something productive? Welcome to Productivity Paranoia, the nag of American Dreamers. You can't sit still, because you know you should be doing something, something useful, that is. This is the cultural piece of the overwork puzzle, and it's a major factor in our attitudes about work and play. When you've got a shadow commander constantly badgering you to do more, telling you that value lies only in productive tasks, you are going to be easy overtime prey. It's also going to be very hard to see nonwork and vacations as anything but insignificant and frivolous.

This all comes from the belief that free time, or as it's usually referred to, "idle" time—i.e., not busy time—is a waste, because it pulls us away from the only time that's valuable, productive time. You can never enjoy your free time if you have to justify it by the productive measures of the job, which is what we've been doing of late. The reason why so many of us have forgotten how to enjoy life, or have even become afraid to enjoy it, is because the cult of productivity has become the gauge of our personal lives. We are ruled by a need to fill time, instead of finding ways to make the time fulfilling. Anything unproductive, done simply for intrinsic pleasure and edification—reading a book, lingering at a café, wandering aimlessly, quiet time on the weekend—is cause for twitchiness and guilt. You're not getting anything done.

Yet this supposedly "unproductive" part of your life happens to be where you live. As a result of not trying to produce anything, it yields such trivial things as friends, hobbies, families, love, learning, discovery, and spiritual well-being—nothing that provides quite as much of a drumroll as getting those ten E-mails returned, I realize. The productivity compulsion dupes us into believing that value only comes from external accomplishment, not from living! How twisted is that? Who needs Big Brother when we've got us?

Productivity Paranoia abducts you from your own life, imprisoning you in a mechanical world of perceived duty and guilt. You can never let up, never relax, because there's always something next on the list clouding the horizon. You are never here; you're always there with the next project, and that's one of the most life-robbing aspects of the obsession. "You're never in the moment," agrees publicist Andrea Obston. "When you're here, you want to be there. That's the best lesson my son taught me, to live in the moment. The pile will always be there tomorrow. Your son will not always be 8. He won't always be able to look out the window and say, 'Hey, Mom, look at this.'"

Workaholism, chronic busyness, and productivity mania hoodwink us into believing that we are making the most of our time with all the action, when, true to Ass Backwards, we're actually squandering it. We miss the whole point of our stint here. As the Dutch philosopher Van der Leeuw phrased it, "The mystery of life is not a problem to be solved, but a reality to be experienced." In the frenzy to stay locked on output, we miss the input—the experience of participating in life.

Rx for Productivity Paranoia

There's nothing wrong with working hard, wanting to get things done, or taking pride in accomplishment. In fact, if you can feel good about what you've done for longer than a millisecond, you probably haven't developed full-fledged workaholism—yet. Workaholics can't take any enjoyment from their work, because they're already on to the next task. They have to constantly be in motion, or their self-image, which depends entirely on external validation, wilts. Besides, enjoyment isn't allowed. That's for wimps (since they're not terrified by it). To keep productivity paranoia from turning you into a no-life workaholic, start gearing back from overperformance compulsion here:

1. **Don't Count Yourself Out.** When all that counts are tasks, you and your life don't count. It's not how many items you check off the to-do list every day, but how well you do them, and how that stuff affords you the chance to partake in the point of it all, the fruits of your labor.

2. **Recognize Withdrawal Symptoms.** The fidgeting and edginess you feel when the work slows or stops are symptoms of more than work ethic guilt; they can be signs of withdrawal. The drug in this case is adrenaline, fueled by incessant productivity compulsion and the stress it unleashes. Overwork is an addiction, and the biggest withdrawal it sets off is the one from life. See the habit, and you can begin to kick it.

3. **Wake Up and Smell the Ammonia.** When we're flying on mechanical busyness, we're missing in action. We've lost consciousness and are operating in wind-up robot mode. To resuscitate sentient faculties, such as actual thought and awareness, keep a vial of smelling salts, real or symbolic, handy. Take a whiff when you catch yourself overdoing it, feeling anxious in a quiet moment, or paranoid that you're not getting enough done. Welcome back to the planet.

4. **Go to Intermission.** Just as your favorite sports team or concert performer can come back from time-outs and halftimes to finish the show, so can you. See pauses in the action as time to gather strength and adjust strategies. Stillness isn't the enemy; it's the condition that informs all true forward movement with intention and meaning.

5. **Fill Your In-Box.** Don't let your self-image be strangled by an obsession with the tally of out-box items each day. It's what goes into your in-box, as in intrinsic experiences, not external approvals, that creates strong self-esteem and life satisfaction.

6. **Give Yourself a Nonperformance Clause.** Ease up on the production bullwhip and allow yourself to have your official permission to indulge in some nontasks. Review those at the end of each day, and consider them accomplishments of living.

Leisure Phobia

It's hard to relax when you're programmed not to. The programming comes by way of our original taskmasters, the Puritans, whose influence on our work habits would come to be known as the Protestant work ethic. German sociologist Max Weber identified it as the driving engine of capitalism, but also noted that it could be an "iron cage," trapping people in all-consuming work. Weber theorized in 1904 that the religious doctrines of the Puritans and Calvinists, in particular, led people to work not simply to make a living, but as an end in itself. The job was a divine vocation, "the expression of virtue and proficiency in a calling."

Work was a means to glorify God and keep busy, because idle time was the devil's time. It's stunning how much of that mentality, converted to secular use, affects the way we think about work today. Weber described a very familiar mind-set, such as the Puritan's "acceptance of his life in the world as a task," and "the strict avoidance of all spontaneous enjoyment." He could have been talking about us today. The motivation is different now—money instead of divine inspiration—but the mentality is identical. We're every bit as proficient in life denial, particularly when it comes to the attitude about free time.

Distrust of leisure was the central tenet of Puritan life. Wasting time was "the first and deadliest of sins." Work was its antidote. Idleness was despised. "Not leisure and enjoyment, but only activity serves to increase the glory of God," reported Weber in *The Protestant Ethic and the Spirit of Capitalism.*

There were to be no illicit weekends bobbing for apples in New Amsterdam (New York back then). Leisure was branded with a scarlet "L." The rap stuck even as the theology gave way, and leisure today is still seen through a prism of guilt and unease. The guilt has been translated into a secular angst just as effective. It makes you feel guilty when you ask for a day off to attend a daughter's graduation, when you take your vacation, when you leave the office after eight hours and co-workers are still there, even when you're at home on the weekend not doing anything "productive."

Enter Leisure Phobia, the fear of free time, a condition that causes you to have an irrational fear of nonwork. The prospect of time not on task makes you restless and frantic to try to fill the time with busyness. You've been so wrapped up in the drama of work that you don't know how to behave in civilian life anymore. Take away the job action, and you're as lost as a man in a women's clothing store, marooned while his girlfriend or wife shops.

On automatic pilot, we use the office yardstick of performance to judge our leisure time, when, in fact, there's no yardstick needed here at all. It's about *being* rather than *doing*, about process and the intimacy of the present tense. Work-ethic guilt tags "downtime," as the word itself suggests, as a downward descent from the pedestal of work, which dooms our half-hearted attempts to break free.

Productivity obsession leads to the final abject terror of retirement. When you finally get to the life you have deferred, you're scared to death of a realm where productivity can't play. You have no nonwork interests or leisure skills to fall back on. You don't have a clue how to live. Yale University Medical Center's Dr. Mark Cullen has seen the fright on the faces of ex-productivity machines now afraid to live. "Some men who retire have a hard time moving from the constant motion to doing things for themselves, because the things they're in motion about are usually for other people. The minute they stop, twenty or twenty-five years of accomplishments all leak out. In this moment they're not accomplishing anything, so they feel they are nothing."

Can we really be that fragile? Yes. If we put all our eggs into one basket. But we can be strong and resilient with a balanced life portfolio. Start broadening your base here:

Rx FOR LEISURE PHOBIA

1. **Get Out of Court.** When you start to feel fidgety with time off, cut off the court proceeding. There is no transgression to feel guilty about. View "free time" as short for freedom, which never needs a justification.

2. **Toss the Job Gauge.** Leisure time can't be measured by work standards. Life satisfaction can't be quantified, only felt. Go for quality of experience in your off-hours, not quantity of accomplished events.

3. **De-Program.** Don't let the false stigma on leisure scare the life out of you. Counter the brainwashing by linking leisure with another word, *life,* which truly can't be accessed without it. When leisure moments crop up, see the life in them, and you trump the task treadmill.

4. **Don't Just Do Something, Sit There.** Rid yourself of the unease that comes with sitting quietly and calmly. It's quite relaxing when you get used to it. Practice the art of nondoing a few minutes every day. Put on some relaxing music, and drift off, celebrating your freedom to do nothing. Or find a relaxing spot outdoors, in nature, to muse, reflect, and get connected to the essence inside your skull, buried in chores for too long.

5. **Have No Purpose.** Make a list of what makes you happy, things that are instrinsically rewarding. It can be anything from taking a Jacuzzi to reading a favorite author. Make sure that whatever it is, there is no objective other than the experience itself. Set aside time for these purposeless pleasures at least three or four times a week.

Let Freedom Ring

The fear generated by the overwork culture obscures the irony that what we run away from when we skip vacations, cut them short, or let others browbeat us into feeling guilty while we're on them, is what we're supposed to be about: freedom. The word "vacation" comes from the Latin root, *vacatio*, which means "freedom." And that's the operative feeling for me whenever I'm on one. A vacation is emancipation from all the ties that bind—the same old job, folks, geography, and personality code that keep us locked in the rut race. It's surprising to me that freedom-loving Americans would opt out of, or prevent others from enjoying their freedom. But then fear is a specialist in strangling independence.

The overwork culture has spawned a self-defeating, adversarial relationship between the job and the vacation, which is thought to be an enemy of productivity. But, like so many of the unspoken commandments that rule workplace behavior, that perception is a myth. The reality is that work and time off go hand in hand. A decent bout of time away from the office recharges the batteries so you can work more effectively when you return. It's self-evident that fried workers do not produce as well as rested ones without zombified gray matter, capable of clear thinking. As you will learn in the pages ahead, all the extra hours and nonstop busyness don't make us more productive, they make us less. We mistakenly equate the way we work, specifically, the degree of difficulty—long hours, much straining, pain and suffering—with performance outcome. That's not surprising given the incessant emphasis on "hard" work as the centerpiece of our lives. But when the hardness of the work, instead of the content of the work, becomes the focus of competition and self-worth, enough work is never enough, because someone is always upping the ante on what's harder than thou. When we're caught up with the adjective—hard—we miss the point of the noun—work, which is how well you do it, not how long or how torturously. Studies have shown for eighty years that long hours and unrested workers provide diminishing returns, ever since economist Sir Sydney Chapman observed that output declines as the standard day becomes too long for the worker to recover sufficiently from fatigue. Time off is even more critical in the knowledge workplace. The main tool today is the brain, which can't be run like an assembly line. It needs time off task or it gets overtasked.

The key to productivity in the information age is not more overtime but more free time, argues business consultant Dan Sullivan, cofounder and president of the Strategic Coach, a $25 million firm that, believe it or not, has been persuading entrepreneurs, the most workaholic people in the nation, that time off is good for business because it's a precondition to achievement. This is like telling a roomful of sex addicts that abstinence is the secret to being desirable. "We gradually inch them up," says Sullivan, whose company has offices in Toronto and Chicago and whose employees all get six weeks off. "You have to crawl before you can walk."

The central problem is our self-defeating belief "that you have to work very long and very hard before you deserve free time." Sullivan calls this the "Justification Model," an approach that always puts us in the position of having to justify time off, because it's taking us away from our purpose: work. So we spend our vacation feeling guilty and anxious, and come back feeling like we've lost stride and have to work even harder when we get back to catch up. In the justification model, free time comes last. Sullivan's counter to that, the "Achievement Model," puts time off first, starting a cycle of rejuvenation and creativity that dramatically increases productivity—and profits. Companies in the Strategic Coach program have seen sales increases from 15 to 30 percent, according to Sullivan.

"The more tired you get, the longer it takes to do things," he explains. "When you're working seventy hours and pushing deadlines, everything takes an eternity. During a vacation, your brain re-forms itself, reorganizes. The same assignment that would have taken you twenty hours before, takes you five hours."

Formerly workaholic business owners are now taking month-plus vacations and passing that on to their staffs. Ron Kelemen, who owns a financial-services company in Salem, Oregon, used to hardly ever take a day off. Now he gives himself a month's vacation and his staff three-and-a-half weeks every year. "Now I work more smartly when I work," says Kelemen. "If you take more free time, it forces you to be more productive when you're working. Your whole attitude about life changes, and the people you work with change, when you have a chance to get away from it all. I've accomplished more in the last seven years than I have in the last twenty." By putting free time first Kelemen, 50, has become an ace snowboarder, visited Costa Rican rainforests, and, oh yeah, he's doubled his income.

But vacations can do even more than that. They can bring you back to life. Numerous studies (for more vacation research, see Chapter 10) have shown that vacations can reduce stress, stop burnout, and facilitate critical regrouping of lost physical and emotional resources. A study by Dr. Brooks Gump and Dr. Karen Mathews of the University of Pittsburgh at the State University of New York, Oswego, found that men who took a regular annual vacation lowered their risk of heart disease by 23 percent and were 30 percent less likely to have a heart attack. Researchers using data from the Framingham Heart Study found that frequent vacations for women aged 45 to 64 cut the risk of death in half. So for something supposedly nonproductive, vacations can get pretty significant results. Just think of all the things you can get done at the office if you're alive.

To let free time ring without guilt, you need to change the word in front of the famous ethic that is pinning you to the wall. The operative ethic in your life should be the Worth Ethic. Measure the madness around you by whether it has worth for you, instead of whether you are worthy enough to take the ceaseless beating. Does it bring you significance, satisfaction, a sense of accomplishment, contribution, challenge? Or does it cut you off from sources of internal worth, isolate you, and sabotage your health? That's not worth it, no matter the dough.

The evidence shows that life satisfaction doesn't come from where we think it does—wealth, job titles, material goods. The thrill is gone for a lottery winner or a newly promoted executive within two months, say researchers. Because of our talent at habituation, we adapt to the new state, and then want more. Increasing levels of possessions or wealth don't equate to increased happiness. But the belief that they do can put you on a "hedonic treadmill," as social psychologists call it, where you can never catch up to your wants. An Illinois study found that lottery winners wound up not only no more happier than nonlottery winners, their increased expectations (due to the treadmill effect) now made it difficult for them to enjoy life's everyday pleasures, such as reading a magazine or socializing with friends. Another study, by psychologist and subjective-well-being expert Ed Diener, measured the happiness of forty-nine members of the Forbes 400, the richest people in America. He found that they were only slightly happier than the average American and that a number of them were unhappy to downright miserable. Social psychologist David Myers reports in *The Pursuit of Happiness* that, though the buying power of the average American has almost doubled since the 1950s, self-reported happiness hasn't changed. "Once we're comfortable, more money provides diminishing returns," points out Myers. "The correlation between income and happiness in both the United States and Canada has now dropped to near zero. . . . The river of life is fed far less by wealth than by the streams of ordinary pleasures."

Life satisfaction comes from a host of things that don't have price tags or prestige attached to them—close relationships, a sense of belonging, positive attitude, managing expectations, strong self-esteem, working for goals that are consistent with your values, and, yes, the studies show, an active leisure lifestyle—from the stuff eviscerated by overwork: family, friends, play, discovery, participation. From the here and now, not living for tomorrow.

The premise that we have to work at the threshold of pain to be doing anything worthy at all in order to get security and well-being someday is Ass Backwards. "It's not about beating your brains out to go on living," noted philosopher Alan Watts, who found life more like a concert than a contest. "No one imagines that a symphony is supposed to improve in quality as it goes along, or that the whole object of playing it is to reach the finale. The point of music is discovered in every moment of playing and listening to it. It is the same, I feel, with the greater part of our lives."

You're not here to sit on the bench. You came to play. And you can—by putting what you want in life, not what anybody else wants, Front Forwards.

3

The Office Commandments

The Unspoken Rules of Working Life

• • •

"Do the thing you fear the most, and the death of fear is certain."
—Mark Twain

W e're born with only one fear, and it's not programming the VCR or even ring-around-the-collar. It's the fear of failing. All the rest of our anxieties are learned. You might have noticed, for instance, how most kids are fearless when it comes to public speaking, quite comfortable with all of their upper decibel range. But it's the number one fear in adults. It's the social conditioning from parents, teachers, and peers over the years that supply us with our various dreads. Many of these acquired worries have to do with how we are seen by others.

We look to the group for guidelines about how to behave, because unlike for aardvarks or ferrets, they don't come with the biology. So we're always trying to conform to what we think the majority has defined as the way to be, says H. Wesley Perkins, professor of sociology at New York's Hobart and William Smith Colleges. By the time you are a gainfully employed adult much of your workaday behavior is based on life as defined by the cues of office culture, which are not always in your own best interests or even the company's. Herd instinct leads you to work more than you want to or skip vacations in the belief that it's the norm, that others are doing it, that the boss demands it, and that if you don't, you will be met by fear incarnate: boss and co-worker disapproval. We learn to operate by a code of conduct that everyone follows but nobody knows, a set of rules you can't find in any company handbook, but that are taken as gospel: The Office Commandments. You might not be consciously aware of these shadowy regulations, but they're running you ragged just the same. The Office Commandments undermine all attempts at balance or a personal life by forcing you to overwork.

Perkins told me about a study he performed on college campuses that were having a problem with binge drinking. The perception was that most students were drinking alcohol to excess, a notion that made it cool to get drunk because everybody was. But when Perkins surveyed the students, he found that a clear majority of them were not getting plastered and did not approve of those who were. Once the results of the survey were known by students, a surprising thing happened: The drinking rate at those colleges nosedived. The majority didn't think it was cool to drink, so it wasn't anymore.

It's a similar misread in the workplace today. We have the impression that success depends on abusive hours—because everybody loves it, thinks it's heroic. To keep up, we have to do it, too, and so we get sucked into this socially admired regimen. But the majority of U.S. workers say in surveys that they don't want to be working so many hours. Most Americans, if they had their choice, would prefer a workweek a little over thirty hours, says Penn State economist and work-family expert Robert Drago. Studies by recruitment firm Robert Half and the Families and Work Institute show that two-thirds of employees would even take time over money. A Xylo Report study found that 93 percent of working adults believe that time off is necessary for productivity, and that it increases it, while another Xylo Report survey done in 2002 tells us that 77 percent of U.S. employees plan to take a vacation in 2002, the highest that number has ever been. Most of us want to have a life as well as a job, but we keep postponing it, because we fear that we will be out of step with the norm of what we "should" be doing—working ourselves to a pulp—which isn't even the true norm the majority aspires to.

The norm you have to start paying attention to, if you want to escape the straitjacket of overwork, is the one in your gut—what's right for you, not what's right for your perception of what the majority is doing. That's the only survey that counts. When you look within, you end knee-jerk adherence to comparison fear. You realize that what appear to be the rules of the working game are really no more than assumptions, and that you are the one who controls whether you want to be manipulated by their projected outcomes or not. We're going to expose those rules—the Office Commandments—to the light of day in this chapter and, as we point toward their Counter-Commandments in the chapters that follow, you'll discover that you are at the wheel more than you think are. You decide whether you want your health to be jeopardized by ceaseless work or not, whether you see your kids only when they're sleeping or not, or whether you give up friends, hobbies, and vacations because you're too embroiled. Because you can beat the commandments. They are acquired fears, and you can off-load them one by one.

The Ten Office Commandments of Working Life

Like other commandments we know, the Office Commandments carry the graveness of unshakable moral duty, yet they are surprisingly optional, because they are self-imposed. Until you put your foot down, the Commandments are a green light from you to the workload universe that says, "pour it on." They turn you into a piece of work with these instinctive, unspoken commands.

1. Thou shalt not be among the first to leave the office after closing time.

2. Thou shalt not take breaks or a lunch if there is too much to do.

3. Thou shalt not turn down overtime or extra responsibilities.

4. Thou shalt not work less than full blast all the time.

5. Thou shalt not be a work wimp and take your sick leave or personal days.

6. Thou shalt not have any legal rights as an employee.

7. Thou shalt not take your entire vacation, or any vacation, when there's too much work at the office.

8. Thou shalt not broach the subject of fewer work hours or more vacation time with the boss.

9. Thou shalt not be out of contact with the office.

10. Thou shalt never quit your job.

Each of the commandments contributes in its own way to always increase your workload, never reduce it. They rob you of time to recharge. They pump up the stress, eliminate recreational outlets, and squeeze out family life—all the while deluding you into thinking that it's your duty, a sign of great success, in fact, to be so consumed. The commandments force you to work ridiculous hours to keep up with workaholic colleagues and deny that you're stressed from doing it, because you're not a wimp. They've got you under your thumb. Perhaps it's time that you got acquainted with the taskmasters behind the whips.

FIRST COMMANDMENT
Thou shalt not be among the first to leave the office after closing time.

It's an undeclared sweepstakes at many companies, a contest to see who has the most stamina or least personal life to stay the latest after official closing time. While some overtime is tied to project deadlines or explicit demands from supervisors, a lot of it falls into the gray zone of office etiquette that no one knows how to deal with. You wind up playing tennis with the clock as you try to look busy for an extra hour, or you get caught up in E-mails you don't have to answer, or face off with other competitors and go all night in a self-destruction derby to demonstrate commitment to the company.

Why do we do keep up this charade? Because work-ethic guilt tells us enough isn't enough. We have to do more, particularly if others are staying late. If we left at six, we could feel like we're letting the side down, or we don't want to see those deadly raised eyebrows as we leave on time while others stay. The drive for success ups the ante. If we work longer than anybody else, we'll get the promotion. Though hours have always been a way to score points for advancement, it's a game that too many play too much for too few results. The layoff rolls are jammed with employees who "gave their all," shocked that ten, fifteen, and twenty years of sixty-hour weeks meant nothing in the end.

SECOND COMMANDMENT
Thou shalt not take breaks or a lunch if there is too much to do.

Studies have shown that continuous time on tasks creates fatigue, mistakes, and accidents on the job, lowers productivity, and is, in four words, not Phi Beta Kappa. Our frazzled nerves and growling stomachs could tell us that. Yet we allow ourselves to get caught up in the racetrack mind of productivity mania and convince ourselves that we can't stop for a second. A study by Oxford Health Plans found that 32 percent of workers today inhale their lunches at their desks. While that's good for those who own stock in Mylanta, chronic inability to take a break intensifies stress, fuels habitual overwork, and robs you of moments in the day to know you *have* a day.

A walk in a nearby park or discovering a new author at lunchtime not only helps you recharge, it allows you to reconnect with yourself and a world beyond yesterday's office politics and tomorrow's spreadsheet—called Right Now. There's very little work that can't wait a few minutes or an hour, and when you realize that, you're on your way to countering knee-jerk busyness and the other delights of this commandment.

THIRD COMMANDMENT
Thou shalt not turn down overtime or extra responsibilities.

Doing your job is often not enough these days. In downsized times, you can suddenly find yourself with a job and a half, or two. There are also the growing demands to work overtime, some explicit, others pressured by guilt and insecurity. The American tendency is to take on the challenge and go the extra hour or four until the trips to the doctor's office start mounting or your family puts out an all points bulletin for your whereabouts. A certain amount of off-the-clock work and additional job descriptions might be unavoidable, particularly for salaried workers. But you don't have to be a dump truck.

Sometimes you have to say no, even to promotions. There are ways to do that to let the boss know you are on the team, but that you also have boundaries that need to be respected. Establishing boundaries is a critical step on the way to work-life balance.

FOURTH COMMANDMENT
Thou shalt not work less than full blast all the time.

The race-pace of the twenty-first century has given this commandment more authority than ever. More and more of us find ourselves competing with the machines, frantically working all day, into the night and even on vacation. Sprinters don't see much along the way. They're only focused on the finish line. But the race is addictive, fueling a flood of adrenaline that pumps up the illusion that ability to go fast is itself part of the accomplishment. Yet it's a mirage of commotion, making you think you're going somewhere when you're really running in place. It's not a sprint you're on, it's an ultramarathon, and you have to pace yourself or you'll blow up, as any marathoner does who goes out too fast.

The rush to be on time, save time, and find time hangs over our every move. In the panic to do more faster, we kill the trip, always trying to get somewhere we aren't. When the journey is irrelevant, so is waking up in the morning. But it doesn't have to be when process can become as important as objective. The best way to truly save time is the one we never choose: slow down. And, believe it or not, you get more done.

FIFTH COMMANDMENT
Thou shalt not be a work wimp and take your sick leave or personal days.

Overheated bravado can turn your days into long nights and weekends, when you're at the beck and call of this commandment. It forces you to work longer than your rivals, come in on your sick days, never let on about stress, and scoff at vacations. The cult of the martyr-gladiator grows, and suddenly any activities that aren't pinning you to the mat with work smack of effete idleness. All ego strokes come from the job and from having people know you've turned your office into a motel.

Insecurity is the commander here, having to prove your worth by putting your hours and health on the line and treating any departure from the head-banging as weakness. This commandment leads to perpetual postponement syndrome, writing off today for the next hero's salute, painting yourself into a very dull corner.

SIXTH COMMANDMENT
Thou shalt not have any legal rights as an employee.

The upheaval in the job market over the last decade and the demise of unions have many people believing that employees have no legal protections whatsoever. While it's true the boss has a lot of power, it's also a fact that you do have rights in the workplace, some you might not be aware of. You're entitled by law in most states, for instance, to take two breaks each day. When you're told there's not enough time for you to take a vacation, you can say, No. You have a legal right to your vacation, if your company offers one, whether it's written down or a verbal agreement. You also have a right to overtime pay if you are being called a salaried employee but your duties don't match the designation. There is a rash of this going on right now. It pays to know what your protections are at the office.

SEVENTH COMMANDMENT
Thou shalt not take your entire vacation, or any vacation, because there's too much work at the office.

This commandment comes by way of poor planning, guilt, and the compulsion of busyness. Many are afflicted. I know a guy who hasn't taken a vacation in ten years out of a generalized fear that he might miss something in his industry while he's gone. Others are afraid if they take off for two weeks, someone might pass them up back at mission control. Some people think they are so irreplaceable that the company will fall apart while they're gone. It can be exhausting having the weight of a whole firm on your shoulders, completely self-inflicted.

Of course, there's plenty of guilt being foisted from the company side, too. You try to fit your vacation into the company's schedule, and your supervisor can never seem to find the time for it. But if your company has a vacation policy, you're entitled to it. That's the law. When you can see the value of vacations, you'll be able to get past: 1) company stall tactics and smokescreens, and 2) the false urgency that makes you think you have to do now what you can just as easily take care of when you return from your holiday.

EIGHTH COMMANDMENT
Thou shalt not broach the subject of fewer work hours or more vacation time with the boss.

The secret to the universe that top salespeople know that most employees don't is that everything is negotiable, or at least more than you might imagine. The assumption of this commandment, fueled by a fear of the boss or being perceived as weak, keeps you taking a lot more than you have to. Chronic stressors on the job don't have to stay that way. It's to the company's benefit that you are not burned out and racking up medical bills. Letting your supervisor know what's draining you can help efficiency as it cures your heartburn and lightens your workload.

Most people assume that there's nothing that can be done about company vacation policies. Wrong. With the right pitch and appropriate boss psychology you can negotiate more time off for yourself. All is not as it appears that it will be when you break this commandment.

NINTH COMMANDMENT
Thou shalt not be out of contact with the office.

Thanks to the wonders of technology, the need to stay in touch with the office has reached epidemic proportions. How many times do you check your E-mail a day? Your discretionary time can be sliced and diced to bits by this commandment, which intrudes into your vacation, home, car, garage, or bathroom, without a qualm. It's a new communications world, and you've got to lay down some new rules for it or your entire life will be under job arrest. Sure, it's nice to be popular, but cell calls late at night or E-mail checks on vacation are a fool's seduction.

There are other people who want you, too. Family, friends, lovers, and acquaintances-to-be. You don't have to be available at all hours of the day and night, if you make it clear when you don't want to be. This commandment relies heavily on your consent, guilt, and busybody quotient, all of which are optional.

TENTH COMMANDMENT
Thou shalt never quit your job.

The idea of quitting runs counter to the can-do spirit of the land, but sometimes enough is enough. When your health or spirit is being assaulted by a job that you've tried everything you can to make work, this commandment needs to be violated. Overstaying your presence in a toxic, workaholic environment can literally kill you. You don't have to stay trapped out of misplaced company loyalty. To move forward you need to get past the stuff that keeps you stuck—anxieties about security, resumes, and your overhead. You won't be alone. Every year, millions of Americans quit their jobs to take other, usually better, ones.

How to Break Through Commandment Fear

The Office Commandments thrive on a quality not usually associated with American Dreamers: inertia. They play off fear and fatalism—you have to take what's meted out because you think there's nothing that can be done. You need your job, you don't want to jeopardize it. You're afraid to speak up. What can you, as a lone employee, do to improve your working conditions?

Depending on your determination and willingness to take some control over your life, a lot. You have more influence over your time than you think. The cost of replacing personnel is increasingly more expensive in the knowledge economy. According to the Employment Management Association, it costs your boss an average of $10,500 to replace the average salaried employee, plus another $89,148 in opportunity costs because it takes an average of seventy-six days to find a new hire. That's a grand total of $99,648. Does your boss want to drop a hundred grand by firing you, just because you raised concerns about your schedule? No way. Every human resource person and headhunter talks about how difficult it is to find quality personnel. If you're one of them, your boss wants to keep you. As a result, your needs have to matter. And they do. "Employees have to understand that they are in the driver's seat and that they are the ones who can really dictate what they want," says Joyce Gioia, a management consultant and co-author of *How to Become an Employer of Choice.* "There's a lot of fear about asking for what you need, but it's unfounded fear. The more communication you have with your supervisor, the better."

Most of the commandments are about appearances. They cleverly play our work ethic and competitive drive against our fear of being seen as less than committed to work, or weaker, than others. They run a very effective self-policing operation, directing us as surely to excess work as if the boss concocted them him or herself. The commandments are so ingrained, we're not even aware we're following them. It's all very instinctive, as fear usually is.

Fear gives the commandments their authority and keeps us on the burnout track, because we're afraid what might happen to our job or self-image if we speak up. But fear isn't a very reliable barometer of what will happen. It's simply the anticipation of an unknown outcome. Once you act despite the fear, and live to tell the tale, the fear is revealed to be what it mostly is: unwarranted. Is there a risk? There isn't a single human behavior that has total certainty of outcome, according to risk experts. You could choke on your bowl of Wheaties tomorrow. There also isn't much in the way of reward or forward progress that gets accomplished without taking a risk. As Alan Watts put it, "When no risk is taken, there is no freedom."

The antidote to the helplessness that breeds fear is action. Good things happen to your health and life when you move past fear and inertia and take some control over your work life. Let's plunge in.

DEFANGING FEAR

Getting the upper hand on work fears requires that you do something you'd rather avoid: move toward the fear. The fright of fear comes from trying to run away from it. You can rob it of its power by sitting with it, and developing ways to counter it, and then acting despite it. Here are some things you can do to knock down anxieties that fuel the Office Commandments:

- **Name That Angst.** Opponents are easier to defeat when we know who they are, and when you can admit their hold over you. Itemize the chief fears that keep you at the whim of the commandments—they might be boss disapproval, getting fired, being seen as weak, spouse pressures, articulation anxiety. Dig out the dreads and expose them to the light of reason.

- **Apply the Reality Test.** How legit are these fears? How much of it is in your head? Are you really going to be fired if you communicate thoughtfully how you could do your job better if you were more refreshed from an extra week's vacation or had the time to take care of family needs? Those who work hard but also make their needs clear in a diplomatic but firm way are almost always respected for it.

- **Do the Advance Work.** Work up to your requests for more balance by communicating regularly with your boss and building a pattern of candor. The more you practice, the more you'll be able to ask for what you need and have a relationship basis to get it.

- **Forget the Peanut Gallery.** Who cares what the rest of the work-aholics at the office think? Your mission is to do a good job *and* to have a life, one that lasts longer than the next quarter. If co-workers don't want to take their vacations or go home at a decent hour, that is their affliction. Only you can control your life. Nobody else.

- **Make Small Changes.** The more you feel helpless, the more fears and stress run you. What things could be done to help you feel like you have more latitude in your work schedule and duties? Start with small things. Come in earlier or later one morning a week. Set a lunch date once a week with a friend, or turn lunch into a yoga class on hump day to get you through the rest of the week. Think of two things you can change about your daily assignment that will make you feel you have more authorship, more influence in your day.

Your Life is in the Balance

When we blindly follow the Office Commandments, we consign ourselves to be bit players in our own life story, leaving the choices to others. The problem is we weren't designed to be walk-ons. "The key to psychological health is to be able to do what you want to do and be self-fulfilling," explains Dr. Wes Patterson, a psychotherapist in Coral Gables, Florida. "When the job doesn't fulfill your needs and your goals, that's when you develop physical symptoms."

We know from the social scientists that what we're supposed to be doing on this planet involves more than being welded to a workstation. Psychologist Abraham Maslow's famed Hierarchy of Needs, demonstrated that we are all compelled to grow toward our highest potential. Our needs evolve in ascending order as basic wants are satisfied, rising through five different levels. At the bottom are the survival needs, such as food, clothing and shelter. When those are met, we move up to safety needs. Next come love, affection and belonging needs to take care of our social animal side. Just before the top we reach for esteem needs, which drive us to seek a strong sense of self-respect, competence, and confidence. If esteem needs are not met, we feel insecure, weak, and worthless. Then, with esteem at our backs, we seek out the top of the pyramid, the crowning glory and the ultimate prize of our journey, self-actualization, which Maslow called "the desire to become more and more what one is, to become everything that one is capable of becoming." It's in this state that we can enjoy what he dubbed "peak experience," moments where we can fully immerse in our surroundings with optimum involvement and satisfaction.

Our mission, then, as laid out in our very biochemistry, is to move up the pyramid to the top, to become who we really are. Another eminent psychologist, Alfred Adler, boiled it down to three main tasks in life: work, the social task of getting along with others, and the intimacy task, or love. Some argue for a fourth task as well, the spiritual quest. Your level of life satisfaction depends on how you are solving all these pieces of the puzzle, says Dr. Les White of the Adler School of Professional Psychology in Chicago "by being balanced in all these areas—the social area, doing things for other people, having a sense of community, and having an intimate relationship."

Yes, work is important. It's one of the ways we can demonstrate our competence and talents, develop skills, get a sense of accomplishment, and make a contribution. But focusing only on the work task is like a jazz quartet with one musician, or playing baseball with one base. It's not the whole song or game, and we know it at some level. We might be oblivious to our internal needs or try to ignore them, but they have a way of making themselves known, in the form of burnout, heart attacks, ulcers, or a nagging void that shadows you like a vulture and won't go away no matter how busy you are. If you can't access the realms of enjoyment, social engagement and growth that are a part of your biochemical mandate, you feel the holes.

But you can feel *whole,* instead, when you off-load the guardians of the darkness, the Office Commandments. Break through the false authority of the commandments with the Counter-Commandments, and the light returns to the world, not to mention your own true nature, on the other side of fear. Coming up in Part II.

• • •

PART TWO

The Counter-Commandments

4

Plead Not Guilty As Charged

Dump That Work Guilt

• • •

"Man's main task in life is to give birth to himself."

—Erich Fromm, psychoanalyst/philosopher

When you see a patrol car a few vehicles back in your rearview mirror, lights flashing, what's your initial response? Do you: 1) immediately flush with adrenaline, assuming you've done something wrong, and plead guilty? 2) calmly drive on in the assurance somebody else has screwed up? Or, 3) start getting an alibi ready about that broken speedometer? For many the answer is number one. You feel guilty, even if you aren't. The false confession is similar to the kind of guilt we feel at the office, proximity to authority causing assumptions of guilt that the facts don't bear out.

It rears its head on a regular basis around departure time each night. The dilemma: When can you leave the fort without seeming like you're in a hurry to do so? There are many variables that must be taken into account. How many of your colleagues are still hanging around? Is the coast clear of supervisors and busybodies? When did you leave yesterday? Did you put in only twenty minutes extra? Or did you fill space for a more respectable hour beyond the call of duty? Was the boss in a good mood? If you go out the door first, you'll be the odd one out, like an introvert in Italy. The tension builds as a Spanish Inquisition of guilt descends upon you. You feel the unmistakable angst of an Office Commandment: *Thou shalt not be among the first to leave the office after closing time.*

We burn up a lot of hours playing the extra-innings game, staying a half hour here, an hour or two and more there, not always because the work or boss demands it, but because we're trying to score points, fit in, jockey for position, avoid looking like we've got another suitor beyond our one true love, the job—and because we'll feel guilty if we don't. It's one of those things we've all done on the assumption that it must be done to keep in good graces with the boss and fellow staff. But all we wind up doing is shaving precious hours off our life-leisure ration.

To show you just how absurd these assumptions of guilt can be, the top executive of one large company told me that he goes through the same waiting rituals as his staff. "I'm waiting for my managers to leave, so I can leave, and they're waiting for me to leave, so they can leave," he confided with a laugh. "It's a standoff."

Everyone's waiting for someone else to give the exit cue, but it turns out we can make the call ourselves—if we can get the monkey of guilt off our backs. As with most guilt, the heartburn of when to leave is for nothing. In this chapter we're going to find out how to sack this useless workmate, and free ourselves from ourselves, our worst taskmaster. We'll explore the hold that guilt has over our working lives, how it makes us work when we don't have to, and causes a host of other emotional issues in the workplace that drain our energy, efficiency, and spirit, and sap our personal lives. You can lick this commandment by pleading not guilty as charged!

Where does closing time guilt come from? From inside our heads. How it gets there is a little more complicated. We're not born guilty. We learn to agonize about what we've done, or want to do, once we have a sense of self and have absorbed a set of rules and values. Guilt occurs when we believe we have committed some infraction of those values—or thought about it—against someone or a principle we hold dear. The closer we are to someone and the more we respect them, the guiltier we feel when we make them unhappy.

We experience guilt whenever there's a conflict between a rule, either real or imagined, and a desire, explains Dr. Steve Sultanoff. "The first thought is the rule, something you've incorporated as a belief system," he says. "For example, you might feel, I should go to work. The conflicting thought is one's desire. So if I believe I should go to work, and I don't want to, I now have a conflict. When that conflict exists between what someone believes they should do and what they want to do, then they either feel guilty if they don't do what they should, or they feel resentful if they do."

"There are three main realms of guilt—the work sphere, the home sphere, and the self sphere," notes Dr. Ellen Ostrow, a psychotherapist and coach who advises overworked attorneys at Lawyers Life Coach in Washington, D.C. They play on the central dilemma of the modern worker, "'I can't take time for myself.' Even the literature calls these conflicts work-family. There is no self there."

So the national phobia about weakness—which we try to avoid by working around the clock—is very much alive and well in the form of anemic self-image, which doesn't permit us to assert our needs on the work versus family versus personal-time battlefield. This allows the ritual we know well to get under way. The voice in your head pops up, telling you you've done something wrong, even if you haven't. Because we tend to take the flittings of the mind as gospel instead of as the random noise they usually are, we wind up sweating out a lot of false guilt alarms.

Lucy Freeman and Herbert Strean, authors of *Guilt: Letting Go,* explain these all too frequent eruptions, "Most of our guilt is a result not of fear but anxiety. No one menaces your life when you feel anxious. There is only ephemeral danger, one that does not exist in the real world but in your fantasy. You have created the danger within—you are both victim and villain."

Psychologists call these imitation pangs "unreal" guilt. Like the imagined dreads of a blind date, unreal guilt is an anticipatory anxiety. Our willingness to be manipulated by this artificial guilt results from the confusion we have in distinguishing it from the other brand of guilt, "real" guilt, which forms the basis of the conscience we need to be able to function in society. Real guilt helps you to show up on time to work, be trustworthy, and not strangle parking ticket officers. But unreal guilt is a pretender, passing itself off as bona fide as it inflicts your life with needless agonizing. It's the driver of all the Office Commandments and, though fabricated, feels plenty real.

Unreal guilt is the silent slave driver, pushing you to stay at the office longer, skip vacations, and overwork to the breaking point. So maybe it's not so surprising that guilt is also a major stressor, touching off the same flight-or-fight adrenaline response as other work triggers and gradually undermining your health. The expression "sick with guilt" is an actual occurrence. Guilt is a contributing factor in illnesses from heart disease to ulcers, and drug companies and HMOs are only too happy to have you do them the favor.

Overwork pushes all the guilt buttons, because it forces us to choose between a host of competing demands—various bosses and coworkers; work and family responsibilities; and work and personal life; which puts us in the position of denying our time or services to many who want them, particularly ourselves. "I feel guilty when I'm at home and not at work, and I feel guilty when I'm at work and not at home," declares Maureen, an exasperated Washington attorney. "I'm the Paxil commercial. Everyone I know is a Paxil commercial. We're all torturing ourselves."

Bosses get it as bad as employees. Dan Storper, founder and president of Putumayo Music in New York, has had many years where he's taken off only a handful of weekends the whole year, logging twelve hours a day. "When I didn't work on a Saturday that I thought I could accomplish a lot, I'd be sitting there guilty, feeling as if I'd deserted my business," recalls Storper, who's doing better now, having cut his week down to five days.

As wracked as we get by nonperformance anxiety, most work guilt falls into the unreal category, infractions committed only in your head. They're little more than irrational neuron burps that say you're less of a hard worker if you walk out the office door at 6:15 P.M. instead of 7, not as good as stalwart Neil or Sally if they stay longer, or that you'll be a self-indulgent sloth if you thoroughly enjoy yourself on your vacation. These projected anxieties have no basis in fact. They're all concocted and enforced by you. We let this unreal guilt run us disguised as our real conscience, causing us to hand over the reins to a rank pretender, the slave driver.

To understand just how unreal most guilt is, it helps to know the bizarre way some of these bouts of optional angst come to us. One of the quirks of the way the mind works is that it interprets thoughts or wishes as if they were deeds. As far as our subconscious mind is concerned, if you think it, it happened. This comes from way back on the human family tree, when instinct ruled behavior. For the earliest proto-humans, as it is for animals today, action immediately followed instinct. Random thoughts—"eat acorn," "kill stranger," "sex now"— became instant deeds. Without the presence of a rational mind, any thought was impulsively acted upon. Though evolution moved on, one corner of our minds didn't, leaving us with the thought-equals-action, guilt hangover. "We feel as guilty at the wish to break a sacrosanct rule as we do in committing the foulest of deeds," report Freeman and Strean.

This odd mechanism explains a lot of seemingly inexplicable behavior. Why, for instance, you feel guilty even thinking about taking a vacation. In your head you've already taken it, so you put off scheduling one until it's too late. It's why you get nervous about asking for a day off. Your mind has already registered that wish as a transgression. And it's why you play the after-hours guessing game. Your wish to leave work at closing time makes you feel guilty about doing it, which causes you to work longer to feel less guilty, in a needless spiral of self-inflicted punishment. You wind up sweating off inches worrying about something that never occurred. This is the kind of logic, or lack of, that operates with the guilt response. Most of the guilt you lug around with you is imaginary, based not on what you've done but on what you wish. You are simply being manipulated by an irrational and out-of-date mind that thinks the year is 100,000 B.C. Our task is to check the calendar and join the second millennium, reducing or eliminating the "unreal" guilt we create in ourselves by identifying what triggers the emotion and then sending it packing.

Guilt Triggers

Guilt ownership varies widely. Some people wake up guilty. They're tormented all day by imagined faux pas—they shouldn't have slept so long, shouldn't have had that Ding Dong, shouldn't have made that comment about the mismatched socks. But others don't seem to be bothered at all by slights thought or committed.

The variance between people tells us that unreal guilt is a highly relative affair, and that some people get along perfectly well without it. We all have a different guilt inventory based on our upbringing and personality. Those whose parents were hard to please, for instance, will be more prone to guilt, since they will be trying harder to please to avoid loss of love, a prime motivator in the guilt response. Certain religious backgrounds pump up the guilt in ways that feed the unconscious mind's mandate of thought as deed. You've sinned if you've thought it. Personality has a major influence on how much guilt you're packing. If you have difficulty expressing anger, you're too security-oriented, shy, have low self-esteem, are overly driven, or too judgmental, you're going to be more subject to guilt triggers like the following:

ANGER

Guilt is often a substitute for anger. From our earliest years we are taught to suppress and hide anger when we get upset. While that helps keep homicides down, it can also muzzle healthy expression of discontent. When anger over not being able to gratify desires is repressed, it turns into guilt. In fact, anger is the prime catalyst of guilt. When you're mad about what a friend or the boss said but don't dare communicate it, you repress or deny the feeling. Although you think it's out of mind, it's still simmering in the subconscious, where thought is deed, making you feel guilty about the denied wish to lash back. To ease the guilt you bring more punishment on yourself, by others or self-inflicted, through overwork.

Some societies, such as in Mediterranean countries, are comfortable blowing off steam all day long. Stabbing the air with your fingers and flashing the veins on your temples are routine methods of social intercourse. But not for us. There's too much of the old Puritan tribe in us. So a lot of us are walking, or driving, around in a slow burn, which turns the anger inward to unconscious wishes of vengeance, which may explode from time to time in conscious rages of the sort we are familiar with on highways and Little League fields. All of this means a constant drumbeat of guilt. The way out of the cycle is to use the anger to motivate communicating its cause in a thoughtful way. When you let your supervisor know that the vagaries of closing time aren't working for you, that you have responsibilities to your personal and family life as well, you go a long way toward ending the anger-guilt cycle and creating personal boundaries. You no longer have to waste needless time and emotional energy plotting your daily escape from the office.

UNREALISTIC EXPECTATIONS

We're bred on the dream that we can achieve anything we set out to do. It's the ideal that drives our opportunity society to incredible success, but it also saddles those who don't reach their goals with incredible guilt and anguish, which can lead to working yourself into an early grave to compensate. Excessive expectations are a major cause of runaway guilt—and work. When what you want or want for others can't possibly be accomplished, but you can't admit that, you set yourself up for the anger-guilt cycle. Millions of Americans are walking around at this very moment, seething with subconscious wishes for vengeance over their unfulfilled goals, while feeling inadequate because they haven't measured up to an impossible expectation. That leaves them vulnerable to work guilt and its corresponding need to prove themselves.

The obsession in our culture with being number one fuels a lot of goose chases. It blinds us to the reality of "number one-ness," the operative root being "one." Yet we're conditioned to think that we all should be there, or we are nobody. The number one game is potent enough to make even the most accomplished feel guilty when they're not, because someone always has a bigger house, newer wardrobe, or more exalted special ranking. The real number to focus on is the average American life span, 76.1 years, which is getting shorter everyday for those swept up in the scorecard mentality of the material race.

PERFECTIONISM

Like workaholism, perfectionism is another mistakenly admired trait. It's a relentless guilt trigger, bringing on the angst from all sides. Perfectionists are forced by intense low self-image to feel guilty about anything and everything—comments, sales reports, E-mails that are less than Hemingway productions. Anything that doesn't meet their unmeetable standard can topple their self-image in an instant. Perfectionists are driven by their affliction to be chronic overworkers. It takes a lot of time to make things flawless. In the process they wind up with only a perfect setup for the guilt of failure.

This is a futile road lined with grief over any number of inconsequential thoughts or deeds. It's a burden you can live without. Strive for quality, yes, but not for competence over unrealizable perfection, which is a drain on your health and efficiency. Leave the perfect scores for the bowling alley. The less pressure there is to be perfect, the less chance there is to set yourself up for failure and the anger-guilt response. As a wise man once said, "Liberation is the acceptance of non-perfection," which happens to be the-not-so-mortifying state of being the only thing we can be: human.

BUSYNESS

The compulsion to be constantly preoccupied triggers guilt whenever the action stops. With your worth and esteem tied to productivity and tasks, you become an instant deadbeat when a bout of leisure intrudes. To keep yourself from the guilt of being the thing you hate the most—lazy—you pile on the hours. The itch to incessant activity is largely driven by self-worth issues, a misplaced identity in the job that requires constant output to prop up the productivity ID.

The fidgetyness that comes over you in idle moments is the needling of chronic work guilt. It's telling you that you have no value unless you are embroiled in activity. Without a nonwork identity and the awareness to see through these unreal jabs, you will continue to plead guilty. In fact, the inability to enjoy life or feel energetic or valid when you're not working is one of the acid tests of workaholism, say researchers.

ENJOYMENT

This absurd guilt trigger is alive and well in more of us than we'd like to admit, and it shows just how far over the edge we're dangling. The adoration of busyness has made simple enjoyment a squirmy affair for a nation programmed for incessant output. We've been brainwashed to think that we have to jump into task formation at the hint of a restful moment. It's as if every time your dog or cat curled up on the floor to rest, you kicked them and told them they had to be up doing something useful. Go chase some mice! Practice your fetching! Kicking yourself with leisure guilt at the first sign of enjoyment is just as crazy. All the minutes of your waking life are not meant to be in the service of duty—as your nights in the sack attest.

As it is with all unreal guilt, low and no self-image is the real culprit here. You can't enjoy yourself because you're not worthy (successful) without a pile of work. This guilt is a complete delusion, an irrational response to false beliefs about where your esteem comes from. If you can't feel or even recognize happiness because it makes you uneasy, you have given the slavemaster the ultimate triumph, snatching the prize and point of your time here before your very eyes. If you feel guilty about enjoying yourself, it's a self-fulfilling prophecy: you won't.

Are You Not Worthy?

The irrational guilt that drives overwork has one basic premise: You are not worthy of having time for yourself. You must work and produce to have any value. Bosses and co-workers who play on this insecurity get you to do what they want, because you'd rather have a dentist's drill squealing in your mouth than feel guilty. But in the mere act of going along to avoid guilt, you plead guilty. You're admitting that you are beholden, that you have committed some infraction that you need to work off. Your admission comes by way of a nondecision, when you ignore what you want to do and agree to be herded by the guilt-inflictor. The way to break the cycle is to make the decision you want to make. You do it or not because you choose to do it.

As Dr. Sultanoff explains it, guilt is trumped by the exercise of your true feelings. "If you choose to do what you want in life, then you're healthier, and you don't feel guilty. You do what you believe is morally right, because you want to do it, not because you feel guilty about doing it."

This shift in thinking is the key to liberating yourself from irrational-guilt commands at work and in the rest of your life. It replaces the manipulator's decision with your own. You rephrase manipulated imperatives into decisions you *want* to make, not *have* to make. Sultanoff illustrates: "Say a close friend of yours is having a birthday party. It's a Saturday night, and you've worked hard all week, and while you really like your friend, you don't really want to go. But you believe you should. If you go, you feel resentful. If you stay home, you feel guilty. If you're able to say, 'I don't want to go, and I'm not going to because I don't want to'—with no 'should' here, because there's no right or wrong—then you don't go, and you feel okay. Or you say, 'I don't really want to go, but I'm going to go, because it's important to my friend,' you've changed the thought to 'I'm going to choose to go, I'm empowered to go, because it's important to my friend.' Then you go and don't feel resentful."

Choice destroys guilt. It says, "I'm valid," "I choose," instead of "I lose." And what you're choosing is to not deny the feelings of guilt. It's running away from guilt that keeps you bending your will to others to absolve yourself, having to constantly do more to prove yourself. You beat guilt by staring it in the face, by accepting the limitations of yourself and your colleagues, by telling yourself "It's the way it is, and there's nothing to feel inadequate or angry about." Acceptance wipes out the vengeful wishes that foment guilt.

You can trump guilt with a realistic appraisal of the facts, not the flight-or-fight anxiety of retreat. When we feel guilty, "we are responding emotionally as if the worst possible consequences are real and that they are in fact occurring," points out Dr. Ostrow. You need to focus on reality, what actually exists. If co-workers want to work three extra hours, that's their compulsion. It's not right or wrong or necessary. You can choose to not make that decision. You've done your job for the day and done it well. You are worthy.

Co-Worker Coercion

It's not enough that you have your own stockpile of guilt, there are always a few folks at the office who want to unload some of theirs on you. Misery loves company, particularly when it comes to guilt. A basic human strategy for coping with guilt is to try to get rid of it ASAP by dumping it on someone else or bringing others into complicity with you. Pass-along guilt is a staple of the workplace and contributes to many a late night or skipped vacation.

This type of co-worker coercion thrives in highly competitive workplaces where cooperation goes as far as the controller's name on paychecks. Where it's dog-eat-dog, the blame game rules. This is the turf of office martyrs. In an attempt to ease their own guilt about not being enough, they overindulge and then get resentful if you aren't flogging yourself, too. To feel less victimized, they recruit others into their lifeless existence, passing along their repressed anger and resentment in the form of guilt.

The guilt wars operate behind thinly veiled humor and averted eyes. When Los Angeles–based managed-care case-worker Troy Overfield took a day off to be with her ill mother in Las Vegas, she returned to jibes of "so how was Vegas? Did you win any money?" Victoria Criswell gets static from co-workers when she tries to leave the office on time. "I'm not one of those people who only works six hours out of the eight that I'm there," says the southern California designer. "I shouldn't have to get grief just because I want to leave on time."

Because the work ethic is so ingrained, so pivotal to how we feel about ourselves, we are easy prey for the accusations and aspersions of our peers:

- "Leaving already?"

- "Do I have to do everything myself?"

- "Where can I get a tan like yours?"

- "If you had gotten that stuff to me on time . . ."

- "I hope you enjoy yourself tonight—while I'm here slaving."

- "Some of us work for a living."

- "Another vacation?"

The subtext of these charges is victimhood. These woe-is-me refrains seek out pity wherever it can be found. Manipulators tweak your guilt buttons so that they can have some company in the victim ward. Soon enough you feel guilty if you don't go along with them, resentful if you do. Now you're a victim, too. You've abdicated freedom of choice, given up responsibility for your own decisions and feelings to someone else—a portrait of the classic victim—and overworker. As author and PBS host Dr. Wayne Dyer describes it, victims "find themselves doing things they really would rather not do, or being manipulated into activities loaded with unnecessary personal sacrifice that breeds hidden resentment."

Victims allow themselves to be manipulated because of a false belief that they have no control over their lives, that others know better or are stronger than they are. They are easily taken advantage of by conscience tweakers. They are forced to do things they don't want to do, because they can't tolerate the guilt, which is not really guilt but a feared disapproval by others. When you can't say No, others make the choices for you.

The marionette game ends with your choice. Refuse to take the guilty bait, and the rap can't stick. Psychologist Les White says the keys are trusting yourself and knowing the choices you have. "That's much more important than everybody watching the clock—'so and so is staying an extra five minutes, so I have to stay an extra five minutes.' That's a waste of time."

You may have to get along at work, but you don't have to go along with the chain gang when it's draining the life out of you. Letting others dictate your conscience is a lose-lose proposition. You lose self-respect, and you lose your way. You also enable the manipulators to stay mired in self-defeating morass.

Boss Follies

The folks who play the guilt card best are those ultimate arbiters of the right and wrong move: authority figures. They know that guilt is such an intolerable feeling that most of us would do just about anything to avoid the most damning word in the English language: "Guilty!" As keeper of the career rules and your paycheck, the boss is in an ideal position to wield the guilt stick, something many bosses are quite happy to do to extract additional hours or obligations. It's not always necessary that anything even be said. In fact, it usually isn't in the after-hours dance of discretionary overtime. Unspoken social pressures are enough to make days longer than they need to be. Guilt-wracked achievers, layoff anticipators and success-trackers set the late-night pace. Co-workers, unsure of what the protocol is, follow them. The mere presence of a boss staying late is interpreted as a signal that it would be a good idea if you did, too—do as I do.

"It's kind of a no-no to go home before your boss," concedes Mathew Beck, a Massachusetts computer technician. "I do it every day, but I think some people feel badly about that. My CEO really believes in what he's doing, developing educational software. He works every weekend, both days. It's a bit difficult to say, 'Goodbye, I'm going to have some fun while you're staying here all night.' But it's his company."

It's a crucial distinction. Bosses have different stakes and responsibilities. Some may find it easier to get their work done when everyone else has gone home. Paula Hughes, a consultant and business professor, liked to work late when she was president of the University of Dallas, because it was quiet and she could avoid the traffic by going home later. What she found out, though, was that her staff thought, " 'Well, she's working late, I better work late.' So what I would do is leave at five, giving them permission to leave, and then I would come back later."

As far as co-workers go, they may be modeling the boss's behavior and staying late to score points, because they have no life to go home to, or because they can't help themselves. So all may not be what it appears to be after closing time. It's not necessary to model supervisors' or colleagues' late shifts in discretionary overtime situations—and not healthy, either, because some of these specimens could cross the Sahara on foot without a water break. The Australian designer we met earlier, Cristina, found that out in her first week working for a popular New York fashion retailer and catalog company. Operating under the taboo against talking to your boss about real office closing time, Cristina did as she saw her boss do and found herself working daily until one o'clock in the morning, coming back at 9 A.M. "I was in shock!" she recalls. "I used to cry every day, because it was so different than what I was used to in Australia. I thought it must be normal for here. I couldn't do it, so it made me think I was a failure or there was something wrong with me."

She wound up talking to colleagues and an HR person about the extreme habits of her supervisor and concluded she had a lunatic for a boss, who spent most of her day chatting and could only really start functioning from 8 P.M. onward. Cristina decided to cut the midnight shift down on her own, and through her deeds reached an understanding with her boss. "I work hard during the day very solidly, and she can see that," she explains. "I don't stand around and chat. She's pleased with my work." Cristina is still putting in long hours, but 7 P.M. is a more typical departure time these days.

Managers who run their own lives badly will do the same for yours. Clearly there are plenty of this breed out there. If you've been sucked into a boss-modeling pattern that's ruining your life, you need to speak up or change your behavior. If you do a quality job, no boss worth working for is going to want you resentful and burned out. It's just too hard to find good staff. If the boss is unreceptive or belligerent about the issue, and the hours are ridiculous, you may have to question whether it's in your interest to remain at that job. No job is worth abusive conditions that keep you from having a life. As one correspondent to Work to Live wrote "It was made clear at our company that leaving at 5 P.M. was not to be expected. The president of the firm told me that the company was similar to a cult and that if I did not want to be a cult member, we should part ways." This was not a sign of health and happiness to come, which this employee was smart enough to realize, deciding to become a contract employee off-site, where "I am happier and have much more control over my life."

You shouldn't have to chronically loiter after hours simply because nobody knows what the hell to do and is afraid to talk about it. Would your employer like it if you provided free work after-hours every day? Of course. They'd be happy to see you come to work with a sleeping bag and a Coleman stove. But do you have to? No. The way to get out of this rut is to make it clear in words or deed, that you are a civilian, with civilian responsibilities.

Early in her career, publishing editor Julie Barbato didn't have the nerve to speak up, and she wound up working countless hours needlessly. Now it's different. "People who are less outspoken than me truly get taken advantage of, because they won't stand up to the boss," she states. "By five or six I was out of the office at this book packaging house I worked for. I would stand up to the boss, and she loved me for it. It was a hoot! Hugged me, kissed me, when I left. Meanwhile, this poor woman who worked for five years, slaving away, gets her paychecks withheld, doesn't even get a goodbye."

When it comes to interpreting the unspoken rules of discretionary overtime, the translation is really up to you. You can crack the code by eliminating the grip of unreal guilt. Or you can always bring your sleeping bag.

One-Minute Guilt-Shop

It's one thing to know that the vast chunk of work guilt is irrational, but it's quite another to cut these habitual waves of angst off at the pass, before they come threatening you with damnation. You'll need to re-program yourself to react differently to a response mode deeply entrenched in your work ethic, both consciously and unconsciously. It won't be easy at first, but with practice, you'll begin to see that there are a lot fewer "rights" and "wrongs" than you think. They're just choices.

There are a number of steps you can take to retrain your brain to get out of the reflex of self-inflicted, guilt-inspired overwork. Here are some practical guidelines:

- **Spot the Storms.** The place to start is to spot unreal guilt storms as they begin forming and before they dump on you. In a daily log, keep track of the number of times guilt crops up. Write down what touched off the guilt—a comment to a coworker, a thought to leave the office "early" soon after closing time, unanswered E-mails. What thoughts and feelings accompany the guilt? Note any recurring triggers. Also note how baseless the guilt events are.

- **Find the Pattern.** What physical and emotional signs accompany the guilt when it crops up? Does your face flush? Do you get a nervous stomach? What is your mental state like? Do you have obsessive thoughts over the guilt event? Write down the steps your body and mind follow down the guilt trail. The more you can be aware of the process as it unfolds, the easier time you'll have of catching the process in its tracks.

- **Submit It to the Unreality Test.** Are you actually causing harm, or is it just the anticipated anxiety of unreal guilt? Write down why you feel guilty or resentful. If it's based on unreal guilt, examine the false belief behind it. Do you feel you have to be productive to exist? Is the angst coming from feared disapproval?

Give the situation a realistic appraisal. Chances are it's projected anxiety, much ado about nothing.

- **Trace the Inflictor.** Note alongside each trigger event where the guilt's coming from. Is it really your fault, or is it due to a co-worker, company policy, understaffing, or unrealistic deadlines? Who's manipulating you to do something you don't want to do? What's their motivation? To spread the blame? To find a misery partner? Why should you buy their guilt? As you focus on the source, you begin to see the illogic, the motive, and the manipulation. If the guilt is self-inflicted, move on to the next step.

- **Oust the Thought Police.** If the guilt is your creation, the cause may not be anything you've done, but something you've thought about. What wish is the culprit causing you to overcompensate with excess work? A desire to quit your job? A wish to take a vacation? You can't be prosecuted for thoughts, except by yourself. Learn to spot the thought police as they squelch your desires and turn them into fantasy guilt.

- **Avoid Denial.** As you feel a bout of guilt coming on, don't deny it or push it aside. Acknowledge the feeling. Get it out of the subconscious, where it forces you into compensating behavior. Flush it into the open, where you can submit it to the unreality test and leave irrational anxiety behind.

- **Choose or Lose.** Guilt is optional. You eliminate the cycle of guilt-resentment when you, not the manipulator, make the decision to reject the guilt or accept it. Choice gives you the power over how you want to feel. If it's not possible to opt for your desire, you can take the bite out of duty or obligation anyway with the knowledge that you choose to do it on your own terms.

- **Practice Imperfection.** Life is perfectly imperfect, and since you're a part of it, you're going to make mistakes. Science call mistakes "trials," and you should think of them that way, too. They're steps on the way to finding what works. Perfectionism and fear of failure keep you locked in guilt-driven inadequacy, which forces overwork. You need to get comfortable with the way of the world, nonperfection. Try practicing little mistakes to get used to the fact they're not the end of the world. Other than you psychics out there, we're all flying blind.

- **Change the Terms of Guilt.** The way you speak can convict. Try to avoid judgmental terms like "should" and "should not." They are the voice of the slave master, convicting and reprimanding you for uncommitted transgressions. The past is past, so the revisionism of "should" is history. Change the "shoulds" and "should nots" to "I wills" or "I won'ts," removing the judgmental factor of one decision being "right" and another "wrong." They're simply choices made with the best information you have at hand.

In the end, you have the power to eliminate or moderate the late show. Trust in yourself, in your work, and your choices, and there's no longer any reason to feel you didn't do enough or stay long enough at the office. Focus on results, not appearances, and make sure your boss knows about those results, and you should be able to get a lot more time working for you for a change—without a nightly guilty verdict.

5

Stop in the Name of Maalox

Take a Break, Get More Done

• • •

"Without being awake and remembering our values and identity—in other words, without stopping—our going can get us
into trouble."

—Dr. David Kundtz

I t's got to be in the Constitution somewhere, probably in the fine
print. Because the right to continuous motion is a right we all know
we have. Anything that impedes activity and forward progress is a clear
violation of the law. You can see people exercising their kinetic rights
every day, complaining loudly when they are forced to come to a complete stop at a bank line or checkstand queue. Or in city traffic, when
the car in the lane next to you spots a stopped vehicle turning up ahead.
That driver has the right to immediately barge into your lane to avoid
having rights of progress interrupted.

We don't want interruptions. Outta our way! The right to keep going is taken especially seriously in our working lives. We've got to keep
driving, pushing, wheezing to the finish line of retirement. Breaks are
pooh-poohed. One-third of Americans eat their lunch at their desks;
the same amount never leave the office all day. Not even biology can
stop us. "Taking a break is the hardest," admits managed-care worker
Troy Overfield. "I want to get things completed. I don't like things

hanging over my head. So even when I'm sitting there, and I need to go to the bathroom, I will try to complete a project I'm working on."

Nature may call, but work has our number. The compulsion to not break stride is something we take pride in, because to be in action is to be productive, moving forward forever to our next task. (How much better can it get?) But it's not much different than other compulsive behavior, from doorknob checking to hand washing. It's a repetitive ritual designed to counteract the anxiety of obsessive thoughts—you're not worthy unless you're in motion.

One of the downsides to being eternal action figures is that we never arrive anywhere. Life on the run is blurred, out of focus, seen but not registered. Working without letup also makes your days a lot more stressful and unhealthy than they need to be. It can trigger ulcers, back problems, vision disorders, and rob you of the energy outside the office to do things you need to be doing to relieve stress, from exercise to tasting the world around you. To snap out of the compulsion to keep going nonstop, you need to free yourself from the clutches of the second Office Commandment: *Thou shalt not take breaks or a lunch if there's too much to do.* As you are about to see, you can resist the urge of ceaseless activity, and turn every day, not just weekends, into one with personal possibilities.

Motion Sickness

Indy race cars do it. Tigers in Bangladesh do it. The fleetest and most ferocious beasts make pit stops. But us perpetual-motion machines have to keep moving. A pause in the action is an intrusion on our manifest destiny of momentum, on the mantra branded in our racetrack minds: "Get things done. Get things done. Get things done." We're so uncomfortable with stopping to refuel that the preferred synonym for loony is "out to lunch." As the pile of work has grown with downsizing and E-tools, it's created more pressure to work straight through to stay on top of everything. We figure if we just take care of a couple of things that are dangling, instead of taking a lunch, we'll catch up. We don't.

And it's the same tomorrow. "I'll sit here at 7 or 8 at night and say, 'Well, just one more thing to make tomorrow easier,'" says Steve Winston, a publicist at Comforce Corp. in Florida. "But we all know that doesn't make tomorrow any easier. The next night it's the same thing. One more thing winds up to be another two hours."

We fool ourselves into thinking we'll get ahead of the game by powering through, but it's a mirage, pure heat waves driven by work guilt and the hurry-worry mind. Continuous commotion isn't even more productive. Studies have repeatedly demonstrated that productivity increases when there are breaks in the action. One of the most famous, the Hawthorne Studies, was conducted over a five-year period from 1927 to 1932 at the Western Electric Hawthorne Works in Chicago. It found that when five-minute rest pauses were introduced, worker output increased. When the breaks increased to ten minutes, output increased again. When workers were given a shorter workday, output increased yet again. Two studies in the 1990s continued the theme: Rest breaks work. Researchers found that "fleeting respites," as they called them, improved performance by allowing workers to keep up the effort level consistently higher than when there are no breaks. One of the researchers involved in those tests, Ken Doerr, told me that "quality went up with microbreaks." Even "very small breaks give you a chance to catch your breath, try a new approach."

You may think you're getting more done as a nonstop desk jockey, because the blizzard of activity makes it appear that way. But when you're operating in rote hurry-worry mode, without thought or design, it takes you longer to do things, and you may have to redo them later. It's easy to get into a mechanical frenzy where you can convince yourself you can't let up for a second because there's too much to do. But what's really operating here most of the time is the false urgency of "performance momentum," as W. Timothy Gallwey calls it in *The Inner Game of Work,* activity done "without conscious intent or awareness of purpose." It's an autopilot of habitual motion in which all appears to be urgent because we haven't taken the time to step back to think about what it is we're doing or define what is truly urgent and what isn't. It's a familiar bind. We get locked on unconscious output, devoid of the input needed to tailor the right effort to the job. This "reactive momentum," says Gallwey, has "movement, often frantic movement, but not mobility. A lot of things may get done, but there is no guarantee that those things will take either the project or the person doing them to successful outcomes."

We need time to step back and think, to assess priorities, determine where things are going, to check attitude, assumptions, and needs, argues Gallwey. Stopping is critical to "help a person or team disengage from the tunnel vision of performance momentum, so that mobility and more conscious working can be restored."

And so you don't fall apart. Knee-jerk work sets the stage for more serious diminishing returns for your health. What happens, says Yale Medical School's Dr. Mark Cullen, who studies the causes and effects of job stress, is that "we get so far on task that there is little or no maintenance" going on. Cullen's research has also uncovered something very interesting about how overload affects your job satisfaction: Overly tasked people working without letup don't like what they've done at the end of the day. It turns out that uninterrupted, intense time on task strips all the accomplishment, and the fun, out of what you're doing. No wonder it's so hard to find joy even in professions we like—there's just too damn much of it.

But the office "break" has become almost anachronistic these days, part of a bygone blue-collar workplace. There's a perception that white-collar folks don't need breaks, because, unlike physical blue-collar work, all they do is sit on their butts. What do they need a break from? Hemorrhoids? We're back to the superworker myth again. It seems somehow weak to need to stop. We should be able to keep going till the paramedics arrive. In fact, knowledge workers and white-collar types need time-outs as much as anyone on an assembly line, maybe even more so.

The fact is our physiology prepared us for hunting and gathering, not for hours on end of mannequin duty at workstations. The ritual posture that most of the American workforce assumes everyday— sitting trancelike at a computer monitor for eight to ten hours—is loaded with reasons to take a breather. "You get a lot of repetitive motion injuries—carpal tunnel, back problems, neck problems, stress," a source at an orthopedic group told me. "People are working too long without taking a break, getting tired, and pushing themselves to get a job done."

Regular time-outs, which are part of the law in most states, should be demanded by employees and encouraged by management. A study by the National Institute of Occupational Safety and Health (NIOSH) found that brief but frequent breaks can reduce the risk of a host of injuries bred by nonstop vigils at workstations. Four five-minute breaks throughout the day for walking or stretching resulted in less discomfort in the neck, arms, shoulders, and back, for study participants. Workers also reported less eye strain. The kicker to the research: Productivity didn't fall off at all from the extra breaks.

Rest stops break up rigid postures and can help prevent an assortment of back injuries, from bulging discs to lumbar strain. Medical experts advise frequent breaks and exercise to prevent and treat carpal tunnel syndrome (CTS), the painful and sometimes disabling inflammatory disorder that affects wrist, hands, and fingers, now an epidemic among office workers. With over forty million people on computer keyboards every day, CTS cases have surged from 27,000 in the early '80s to several hundred thousand today.

Another injury triggered by unbroken sessions at the keyboard, is computer vision syndrome (CVS), a complex of eye and vision problems caused by staring for hours on end at computer screens. CVS affects 90 percent of the 70 million workers in the U.S. who use a computer for more than three hours a day, according to the Occupational Safety and Health Administration (OSHA). The problems include eyestrain, dizziness, blurred vision, headaches, change in color perception, excessive fatigue, and double vision. It can also aggravate existing conditions, such as farsightedness, nearsightedness, and astigmatism. Scientists have found that we blink less when we're zoning into the glow, which creates dry eye problems.

Since humans were designed to spot saber-tooth tigers off in the distance, not Internet fine print, the muscles of the eye are in their most relaxed state when looking at faraway objects. The eyes need to stretch, which is why excessive close-up duty can disrupt distance vision. People who have been in a submarine for a while have trouble with distance vision when they emerge from close quarters. Their eyes have adjusted to see only short distances. The same thing happens with chronic staring at a screen less than an arm's length from your nose.

To stay off the medical circuit, you have to make your breaks an automatic part of the day-to-day. Beyond the traditional fifteen-minute break, ergonomic experts are now recommending frequent brief stops for those with intensive computer usage—thirty seconds every ten minutes, or if you can't do that, five minutes every hour. During that time you should get up and move around, gaze out the window, do some stretches, walk down the hallway, or around the block. Once your body starts aching your concentration has already left, so you may as well join it.

Break for Brains

Like many of you, I was raised to be persistent, to keep on trying until I needed a stretcher. Whatever it was—if I was working on a story, and got stuck, I would try to will my way through. I would break my concentration if I stopped, went my warped thinking. Stepping back at the point of overload wasn't even something that occurred to me. That would be weak. We're supposed to soldier on and bust those blood vessels to the finish line. A rebellion by a few back muscles put an end to my delusion of mind over posture. I was forced to admit mortality and take breaks, and once I started doing it, I noticed right away: It works. Every time I take a break I get fresh ideas—every time. It always succeeds in jump-starting whatever I'm working on.

Mental strain is just as hazardous to productivity for a white-collar worker as a hand injury is to a blue-collar worker's output. The mind is not a brute-force instrument, although we act like it is. There's a limited amount of time it can stay focused without fatiguing or wandering. Dr. Jim Goodnight, founder and CEO of Cary, North Carolina-software giant SAS Institute believes that software "developers can do no more than two hours of great work a day," says SAS spokesperson Trent Smith. "In the first couple of hours you'll do pretty solid code and not many errors, but as you go on after that, the number of errors increases dramatically. So if you're putting in sixty hours a week, you're basically burning yourself out and not really helping the company that much more." This is one of the reasons SAS has a thirty-five-hour business week.

Researchers who measure brain activity say photographs of tired brains show so little activity, they look like brains that are sound asleep. Yet because we're uncomfortable dealing with the subtleties and brownouts of the mind (how many insurance plans cover psychiatric visits or depression?), we still treat people whose main tool is their head as if they were widgetmakers.

One of the best things you can do to change the pace is to literally step out. Walking not only gets the blood circulating and muscles loose, but it also gets the mind functioning again. The act of walking allows the mind free reign to wander past the blockages and stresses of the day, and should be a part of any regular break routine. German philosopher Friedrich Nietzsche said that he hardly ever had a good idea that didn't come while he was out strolling. Most of the time the creative part of the brain, the right side, is drowned out by the noise of the logical, ego-fixated left side, particularly when we're under stress. But a time-out on foot can change all that. The act of motion keeps the dominant left side of the brain busy, freeing the right brain to roam. That's why ideas seem to flow when you're doing rote physical things, such as driving, running, or taking a shower. When the left brain is preoccupied, the right can veer into the theta state, which is where ideas are born. "Those people who feel they have to power their way through all the time only tell me they don't understand creativity at all," declares Mark Gorkin, a psychologist who specializes in stress treatment and is a consultant to Fortune 500 companies. "You have to learn to let go, so your subconscious mind takes what I call an incubation vacation. Taking breaks and being creative are, in fact, not opposites, but go hand-in-hand."

This is what psychologists mean by the concept of balance. One side of life, rest and recreation, complements the other, creativity and work. A survey by the McKinsey consulting group asked managers where they had their most innovative ideas. What it found was that the ideas came in their free time, when they had stopped working. The lowly coffee break may just uncover that idea you've been grinding your teeth to find. Or even win you the advantage you need for a promotion. A Center for the Workplace study discovered that 70 percent of an employee's most useful information about the inner workings of the company came from chats with colleagues on breaks, where informality breeds candor.

As it is in sports, socializing, or speech-making, relaxation is the key to success. Forcing the action leads to tightness, tension, blockage, and overcooked gray matter. Though it's contrary to the gospel of persistence, maximum creativity and efficiency come indisputably from stepping away.

Snooze or Lose

The best evidence that stopping is good for you comes from the latest developments in sleep research. It appears that one of the best things you can do for the company's bottom line is take a nap. Dozens of studies report that a single fifteen-minute nap at midday can dramatically improve alertness, performance, and overall health. NASA is a believer in sleeping on the job, so is Apple Computer, which has an employee nap room. Other companies whose employees officially nod off in quiet rooms include Yarde Metals in Bristol, Connecticut; the Burlington Northern and Santa Fe Railway Company, in Fort Worth, Texas; and Great Dane Trailers, in Savannah, Georgia.

What these savvy companies have discovered is that coming to a full stop isn't so bad after all. The power nap, as it's known, restores energy and improves performance. Nap enthusiasts say it revitalizes their work in the afternoon and gives them more energy when they get home. The principle is the same as the one that tucks you into bed at night. The human body requires restorative maintenance, a full stop, to be able to operate at top capacity. A fifteen-minute nap does the trick, providing enough rest that you can even get by with less nighttime sleep. A much longer nap would make you sluggish, but the quick snooze is a revitalizer.

The restorative powers of the midday break are well-known in Spain or Italy, where the siesta tradition still holds sway for some workers. From one or two to around four every afternoon, the pushing and shoving of the working world stops for a stroll home, a leisurely home-cooked meal and a few z's. It's a time that allows hearth and homefront to share the stage during the workday. Workers in Seville, Spain or Florence, Italy can look forward to a demilitarized zone in the middle of the day, where enjoyment, great food and wine, and a catnap buffer the four hours of career chaos that lay on either side. This half-time diversion refreshes while providing daily participation in social and family life. Anna Escobedo, a work-life expert in Barcelona, says that "a siesta is very healthy after a good meal. I frequently sleep a half [an] hour after lunch during the summers."

As it turns out, we are what's known as "biphasic" creatures, requiring days broken up by two periods of sleep instead of one up-till-you-drop "monophasic" shift. Dr. Claudio Stampi, founder and director of the Chrono Biology Research Insitute in Newton, Massachusetts, explains: "All animals, including humans, have a biological rhythm. One is a twenty-four-hour rhythm—we get tired by the end of the day and go to sleep—and there is a secondary peak of sleepiness and a decrease in alertness in the early afternoon. Some people have difficulty remaining awake, doing any sort of task between the hours of 1 P.M. and 4 P.M. For others it's less difficult, but it's there. So there is a biological reason for siestas."

Power napping may have more going for it than we even know. Einstein took a twenty-minute nap faithfully every day. Thomas Edison, John F. Kennedy, and Winston Churchill were all enthusiastic afternoon dozers—and notorious nonslackers. Stopping for a snooze could be the most industrious thing you can do. Who knows what cosmic theories and political inspiration lay on the other side of a fifteen-minute afternoon slumber?

Taking Care of Busyness

The need for continuous motion is fueled by the looming bogeyman of idle time. As I will keep repeating, YOU DO NOT HAVE TO JUSTIFY TAKING TIME OUT. It is the wellspring of everything else you do. Health, creativity, and productivity flow from it. You can guarantee underachieving performance if you don't take breaks.

The time bugaboo is reinforced from all sides by cultural messages, personality traits, and good, old human nature. These things get translated into a variety of pressures and emotions that keep you going at all costs. Let's examine some reasons for this and how they work on your vulnerabilities—and then find out how to stop them in their tracks.

MOMENTUM

The law of continuous motion dictates that a body in motion must stay in motion, even if the only real motion is a pulse, because a body at rest will stay at rest, and we don't want that, no sir-ee. Aided and abetted by adrenaline and caffeine, the momentum factor can hold off breaks, bowels, and common sense. The allure is a fake but seductive sense of progress and a finish line that never arrives, because there's always another task ahead.

Block Buster: Consider the source of this obstacle, work-ethic guilt, and you know there's nothing real about it. You will still have value, and your task will still get finished, if you give it a rest. What physically compels you to not stop is the adrenaline. Your body wants more of it to keep the rush going, which is only hastening your physical decline.

FALSE URGENCY

A lot of skipped lunches and breaks are the result of the current epidemic of false urgency. Most of that we bring on ourselves, with self-assigned, arbitrary, and over-optimistic deadlines no one else is holding us to. We are also led to squelch time-outs by the temptation to try to work as fast as the machines that supposedly serve us, a futile affair. Just because the technology offers instant access, it doesn't mean you have to be its leashed dog and respond to E-mails or cell calls instantly.

Block Buster: Management experts tell us that there are very few calls and almost no E-mails that have to be returned immediately. You can recognize false urgency by who's driving it. If it's all in your head, it's time for a break.

LAZINESS

Employers knew what they were doing when they got us off our feet and into our seats. Hours on the posterior creates a bonding between human and chair that causes separation anxiety for many. When inertial forces set in, extrication may take extraordinary measures—snooze alarms, U-Hauls.

Block Buster: When it's just too cozy to budge out of the chair, you need to physically snap out of amoeba formation. Borrow a technique from overeaters and overdrinkers and wear a rubber band on your wrist. At break time snap it against your skin. This is your cue to get vertical. Once you're on your feet, you should be able to handle gravity from there.

FEAR OF FALLING BEHIND

Taking two ten- or fifteen-minute breaks and the lunchtime you have coming to you legally is not going to make or break your job. If it does, there's a labor attorney who would be happy to see you. The anxiety of keeping up drives us to squander personal time to catch up. But what is "keeping up"? Just another arbitrary standard we set for ourselves that boxes us in. Once again, we're enslaving ourselves to unreal guilt, a projected fear that we might not be able to make the grade. You can't fall behind the only place you can be at any given moment, where you are.

Block Buster: Ask yourself who or what you are falling behind. The answer is: the Joneses, and your expectations, which come from an exaggerated notion of what you think others are demanding of you. Keeping up is an imagined anxiety that can't be measured or defined. When this block crops up, turn the tables on it. You're falling behind in taking care of yourself whenever you choose busyness over breaks.

BOSS JITTERS

Some people remain glued to the chair because of an extreme desire to show the boss they are all-business. They wouldn't want to be caught dead letting up from their work or chit-chatting, because they have an extreme fear of bosses. Super-conscientious people and the socially insecure wind up in this trap, clinging to their workstation like a life raft. They may think they are the only ones getting things done, and pride themselves on continuous output, but it's a code of conduct that can become a straitjacket.

Block Buster: The bottom line for the boss is results, not outnesting the Vermillion Flycatcher. No manager you want to work for is going to stop you from taking breathers. Keep in mind that the fear that keeps you grounded is really about you, not the boss. It's coming from an insecurity that says you have to continuously perform to have value. It's unreal guilt, and you can scrap it.

HYPNOTIZED

You are getting very sleepy. The hypnotist is the computer screen, and it's easy to fall under its spell. Before you know it, several hours have gone by, you've surfed twenty Web sites and forgotten your middle name. You are a captive of the monitor. Repeat after me: I will pry myself away from the glow at regular intervals.

Block Buster: Break the spell of this block by setting regular break times, say, 10:30 and 3:30 every day. If your watch has an alarm, set it for the first few weeks to get you untranced.

TOO BUSY

This off-the-shelf alibi is more of a predictor of behavior than a statement of fact. When you think you're too busy, you will be. While there are certain times when deadline-intensive tasks have to get done, most of the time this is the result of unconscious momentum or martyr action. What it really says is you like the approval you think you get for being extremely busy and heroic, and simultaneously, that you don't think you're important enough to take time for yourself. There is almost always time to take care of yourself. Ask anyone who's had a heart attack from job stress.

Block Buster: The product of too much adrenaline and knee-jerk behavior, overbusyness can be countered by thought, by determining: 1) if you're really too busy, and 2) why you are afraid to stop. Habit is the usual answer to number one, and number two is our favorite shadow, work guilt. The next time you think you're too busy, complete the sentence: "I'm too busy—to live."

MIGHT NOT BE ABLE TO GET GOING AGAIN

Some perpetual motion cases fear that by stopping they might not be able to get going again, that they'll somehow lose their initiative or edge on a downward spiral to vagrancy. Putting on the brakes is scary for some people, because of a false implication that they are setting a precedent for letting themselves go, which work-ethic types don't have to worry about. It violates the perfectionist, all-or-nothing standard, and the code of conduct that you have arbitrarily locked yourself into.

Block Buster: This is a classic case of fictional projection. You are no more likely to lose the work knack by stopping occasionally than you are the ability to tie your shoes after wearing slippers. Get out of the future and back to the real action on planet earth, the here and now.

Rules of the Break

Everybody knows that the most important person in the office is not the boss or the bookkeeper or even the sandwich guy; it's the tech wizard who keeps the machinery we are helpless to fix, running. As you know, it often isn't. The day when the copy machine, computers, the server, and the Web site are all in working order is such a rare event that it behooves all to buy lottery tickets immediately to take advantage of the cosmic alignment. Office equipment gets plenty of what we don't give ourselves: upkeep and maintenance. Breaks. And we're supposed to be the mortal ones.

Rest breaks aren't required by the Fair Labor Standards Act, but they are by most state labor laws. The standard policy is one ten- or fifteen-minute rest break per four hours on the job, one before lunch and one after, usually to be taken at a time approved by a supervisor. Consult your company handbook to find out the policy where you work. If there's nothing there or you don't have a handbook, ask human resources or your supervisor what the policy is. If your company claims to not have a break policy or is not honoring the one they have, you might be covered by state law. The state of Iowa, for instance, mandates that, "An employer shall allow an employee . . . a paid fifteen-minute rest break during every consecutive four-hour period of work."

There are usually stated policies for hourly workers, while the rules are more mysterious for salaried employees. Since salaried workers are paid the same amount no matter how many hours they work, they are theoretically free to take a break whenever they want. But many don't, or at least nothing that goes by the term "break," which seems too un–gung ho for anyone who considers themselves future promotion material. Salaried workers "step out for a minute," "go for coffee," or "get some air."

Your fifteen-minute breaks are considered paid time, while the "meal period," or lunch break, is usually unpaid. What this means is that lunchtime is really your time. You're not getting paid for it, so working through it is a very kind thing to be doing for your employer.

The amount of time for the lunch period varies, from a thirty-minute break to an hour.

Whatever the length of your midday break, nobody can use your time but you. That goes for your other breaks, too. Management isn't going to send you off with a royal salute, and in most cases would be quite happy if you were Velcro'ed to the desk. It doesn't matter if co-workers are eating at their desks. They have their own agenda, which can include doing the grindstone thing to impress one and all. Let them be worker's-comp poster children. You can take the road of up-keep and maintenance, to keep your machinery humming.

Pulling Out the Stops

You don't have to write off Life for five days a week anymore. With just a fraction of the discipline you apply to your career, you can find opportunities for living time right in the middle of your workdays. As you do, you'll see that the practice of stopping to recharge can rub off on your nights, too. Refueling throughout the day lets you leave the office with something left in the tank for more than remote zapping duty.

Start breaking away from rote action with small pauses, say, four five-minute breaks over the course of the day, as in the NIOSH study, to walk or stretch. Build up to regular stints away from your desk or working environment on your official fifteen- or twenty-minute time-outs, and from there build up to a whole new midday concept: the participation lunch. The key here is planning. You have to put yourself on the calendar, and keep the appointment with that VIP character.

Thought breaks are also important. To establish priorities and make sure your action has intention and not just habit behind it, the *Inner Game of Work*'s Timothy Gallwey recommends stopping at the start and end of each day, when you finish any project, when you make adjustments in your work, or you need to take care of problems.

Here's a clock-watcher's list of respite options, with some specific tips for snatching the time you need throughout the workweek:

FIVE MINUTES AND UNDER

Take a Breather. Stress and rigid postures cause our muscles to tighten and our breathing to get shorter and more shallow. Shake up this holding pattern with a few minutes of deep breathing several times a day or whenever you can grab an opportunity. These quick hits can be done without cutting into your real break time and provide a surge of oxygen and calm to frayed nerves. You can do them standing at your desk (to bring your legs back to life) or in a quiet area of the office. Breathe in deeply through the nose and then exhale back out again. Do this for three minutes. Throw in ten arm raises and ten pinwheels to bring your arms and hands back to life. Now lower your arms and shake them out.

Get on Up. If you're in a job that maroons you at your desk much of the day, set times to get up and stretch. You're not on a flight with turbulence, and standing in the aisles is allowed. Instead of E-mailing a co-worker, give yourself an excuse to move by delivering the message to the person. Take a couple of cross-office trips per day or whenever you get stuck on something and need to get unstuck. Travel can be fun!

FIFTEEN TO TWENTY MINUTES

Break Out. It's time to rediscover the lowly break, to refresh, to interrupt the stress spiral, to prevent repetitive injury and to keep the men in the white coats away. The first thing to do is physically remove yourself from your work area and leave the cell phone behind. Try to keep your breaks free of tasks, and that goes for personal ones, too, like paying bills. Make your time-outs sanctuaries of personal interest and rest, to calm the frazzled mind. Start reading that book you've been meaning to crack open. Listen to music on the Discman. Walk a few blocks and let your mind roam. Do some easy stretching exercises. Think about friends you want to get together with. Plan some outings with the kids. Figure out a new hobby or a skill you'd like to know. Or uncover one that got lost by the career wayside. Find a quiet place and meditate. Close your eyes and let the hurry-worry dissolve into stillness.

THIRTY MINUTES TO ONE HOUR

Start a Half-time Tradition. The goal here is to make the midday break what it is, your time, a nonwork zone reserved for personal time and a clear break from the circular work mind. Half-time is supposed to be a festive affair, so the accent should be on enjoyment. That means relishing whatever's on tap for its own intrinsic sake and not worrying about what's due at the office tomorrow.

Try to make your half-time events participant ones—a lunch with an old friend, a bike ride, things that get you out of order-taking mode and into directing your script. Use the time to discover a new magazine, or to study up on vintage wines, Rollerblade, buy a guidebook to a place you've been meaning to travel, plan a hike, practice your photography, or have lunch with all those people you can never get together with at night because of conflicting schedules. For relief on particularly stressful days, try a session at the local gym. If you're in an area with a park, river, lake, or countryside, spend some time with nature and let the tension fade to puniness in the grand scheme.

Sleep It Off. Late nights, early mornings, and insane stress stop at the nap room. Try to squeeze in a snooze on the job once or twice a week. When should you nod out? It depends on what time you went to bed the night before. If you're an early-to-bed, early-to-rise type, your biphasic swoon will hit in the 12 to 1 time range, making you a lunchtime napper. Night owls will find three o'clock in the afternoon more to their biorhythm. Nappers should find a quiet, dark room—one with a "do not disturb" sign would help. Then remove your shoes, slacken the jaw, and assume the shut-eye position on furniture or the floor. Talk your company into investing in Spent Tents (as in being "spent"), the brainchild of an architectural firm in Kansas City, Missouri. Spent Tents can be set up in a quiet corner of the office and be outfitted with sleeping bags, eyeshades, alarm clocks, and headphones that play relaxing music.

You Will Return

The most important thing about breaks is that they are not the end. You are not finished as a productive member of society, nor is whatever it is you were working on when you stopped. A break is merely "an interruption in continuity," according to Webster's. Don't panic. You are coming back, only in better shape than when you left.

As you begin to stake out personal territory in your workday breaks, you will start to feel more comfortable carving time out for yourself. This will make it easier to get off the task treadmill in your off-hours as well. You'll begin to see instrinsic enjoyment as a worthwhile goal in and of itself, and the demon of productivity guilt will drop away. You may even begin to treat each personal event or experience the way work tasks always are, as an accomplishment, one sweet victory over the forces of the grindstone.

6

Negotiate Your Boundaries

Say No to Overtime

• • •

> "To venture causes anxiety, but not to venture is to lose one's self."
>
> —Søren Kirkegaard

Marketing exec Karen Walker was proud to be working at a Silicon Valley tech company known for its innovation and employee orientation. It had been her only place of employment, in fact, for more than two decades. She was as loyal as Lassie to the firm, whose initials might as well have been her very own. "I will work something until I feel it's worthy of the company name," the self-admitted perfectionist tells me. In recent years, she hadn't taken more than three days off in a row, even though she had five weeks coming to her by virtue of her long service. She feared that something might slip through the cracks while she was gone. Her typical day was twelve to fifteen hours long, and 90-hour weeks were not unusual. Walker would leave the office so late some nights that she would have to turn the lights back on after the cleaning crew left. The day didn't end even when she went to bed. She couldn't sleep more than two or three hours without waking up worried about what needed to be done the next day. Once up, she would jot down ideas and leave messages on colleagues' voice mail at 2 A.M.

All of this had earned her a much-sought-after 5, the top performance review number at the computer products company that meant she "exceeded expectations." The punishing pace had also won her some other badges—hives, eyelashes and hair that were falling out, and increased dosages of thyroid medication. Oh, and there was one more reward: She was laid off after twenty-five years with the company. "I thought I was successful, because I was doing so well on the job and was ranked high," relates Walker. "What did all my hard work get me? So much for loyalty, so much for giving my life. It was a really hard lesson. I let so much of my personal life go for so long that I won't be able to recapture."

It's cold but true. Business is just business. We tend to lose sight of that fact, because business is personal for a lot of us. It's the source of our grocery money, social status, rent, health insurance, the kids' education, pizza delivery. We want to believe we matter to these organizations, because they certainly matter to us. But at pink-slip time we get a clarity that is obscured by the mad scramble to move up and keep up: All those extra hours don't mean squat. All that subordinating of family and personal interests doesn't mean a thing to the company, though it would have meant a lot to you and your family and friends to have the time you sacrificed for the job. It's an agonizing way to get clear on priorities. What if you could have had some boundaries on overwork going in to the company? What kind of an impact could that have made on personal and family life?

The career siren is a powerful seducer. It's hard to resist the allure of more money, titles, prestige, and even, our boss's requests to take on more work. But if we want to be all that we need to be in our bones and heart, we have to start saying No to unchecked hours, and break one of the most destructive commandments: *Thou shalt not turn down overtime or extra responsibilities.* This unspoken dictate works on the assumptions that: 1) you have no other life than work, and 2) you only appear to be mortal and have no physical limits on the amount of work that can be heaped on you. To counter these fictions, you need to let your private world and mortality out of the bag, or face eternal overload.

The good news is that it's quite possible to get those messages out to bosses and colleagues—as well as to let them sink in with yourself.

You *can* set legitimate boundaries on assignments that you don't need to take on. Learning how to say No is a big part of that process. Communication is the way out of open-ended work commitments that squeeze the life out of you. Not only is it possible to say No without having to get out of town by sunset; in most cases you're actually respected more for it. Such is the magic of candor and being true to your needs. Boundaries give everybody a clear idea of where things stand, which is what you want to be doing at the end of the day.

Can't Help Myself

Raised on the notion that all flows from hard work, we have come to assume in recent years that extreme hours are just part of the competitive battle—normal. Susan, the former World Bank editor who wound up on the floor of her cubicle from eighty-hour weeks and the back pain they unleashed, assumed that punishment came with the gig. "I never realized you could actually have a job and not be killing yourself," she told me.

It's a belief that makes it easy to turn hard work into hard labor, with only the prison stripes missing. We're afraid we'll lose our jobs if we don't overdo it, afraid we won't be as successful as we think we have to be to be esteemed by our fellows unless we stagger home late, afraid we'd be a quitter if we don't follow the insidious mantra of management that plays so well on our fears—"do whatever it takes." When we operate from fear, we play with a weak hand and wind up giving ourselves away, self-inflicting extra hours with hardly a word from the brass needed.

We would never put up with a boss like us. Except we do, because we are stunningly oblivious to the sweatshop of our own invention. We are convinced, in fact, that working late and coming in on weekends is the heroic, productive thing to do, and that our extra ethic will be the thing to whisk us past the laggards of the world to the prize of success, an undefined item that as a consequence always manages to stay out of reach, keeping us forever working more and more to chase it.

Type As, perfectionists and anyone trying to prove themselves till it hurts are prime warhorses in this behavior. I know the profile well, since

I have had many personal dealings with this particular character. I ran myself ragged for years. I had absolutely no mercy and like a battered NFL lineman, took pride in how much I was able to withstand. I completely bought assumption #2 of the Overtime Commandment, the immortality part—or at least the adrenaline made it seem that way.

There *is* a kind of transcendent feeling when you're overcoming stacks of work, vanquishing the anarchic forces of nonproductivity. The triumph over tasks is the veritable victory of good over evil. You can almost hear the angels sing when you leave the office at 9 P.M. They celebrate your industriousness, your intestinal fortitude, and remind you to stop at the pharmacy on the way home for your medications. This, after all, is what we're raised to do, rewarded from childhood for going the extra mile and showing initiative—gumption—until for some of us it becomes the prime directive of the universe. Overdoing it becomes who we are, validation of our productive mission, which makes it hard to fathom we might be invalidating our personal lives in the process, which have quite a different mission. When you're in this obsessive mind-set, personal life isn't even on the radar. We don't put any value there. It's all in the striving and achieving that we think is for ourselves but is usually for the approval of others.

Most self-inflicted overtime comes from automatic-pilot action, so half the battle in countering it is recognizing what it is we're doing to ourselves and why. Below is a list of some of the basic instincts that can drive you overboard and some suggestions on how to curb them:

JUST ONE MORE THING

This habit affects well-adjusted, but overly optimistic and badly organized, salaried souls. Productivity fever has a good grip here as well. The basic problem is a knack for underestimating how long it will take to get things done, and for scattershot work flow. The overoptimist takes on way more than can get done in the time frame allotted. The key here is to set realistic deadlines and employ a device that's useful for all overworkers: a *stop time,* a point beyond which you will not work each day. Set an alarm, if you have to. A good rule of thumb for more realistic deadline setting is to take your usual estimate of how long something will take and double it. If that doesn't work, add more time until you can consistently estimate project times within a few light-years.

HYPERDRIVE

Some people have an extra dose of what the academics call "achievement need," and it can drive you—and those around you—up the wall, because it's very hard to shut off. This raging desire fuels ridiculous hours and the belief that nothing else in life exists but career notches. It can take over your body as surely as a "Body-snatcher" pod until you are a self-obsessed, intolerant robot devoid of human properties such as social function, spontaneity, laughter, and love. It is, indeed, lonely at the top. And withering.

However, if the signs are clear that you need to gear down, there are some things you can do. Set up a stop-time program, and stick to it. Turn your energy loose on a fitness campaign. Learn to view the stoppages and the exercise as essential for the best results—which is what your achievement need is all about. Cut out all caffeine—coffee, soft drinks, and chocolate gorging. Try a meditation program. Your energy level will remain high but less obsessive and one-tracked.

PROVING IT

This is a powerful overwork motivator. Though it can be highly motivating, the need to prove yourself is ultimately futile, because it proves the opposite, the insecurity that drives it. It's a holdover from childhood, the wage-earner version of having to get Mom watch you do a cannonball off the diving board. When we're kids, we rely on outside input from the significant people in our life for much of our self-concept. But you shouldn't have to prove yourself to everybody you meet as an adult. It's a habit that keeps you forever controlled by the need to get the approval of others. Work alone can never offer the proof you need. Only one person's validation counts: your own. When you believe, everyone else does.

HERD INSTINCT

Peer pressure is a big part of all the Commandments' grip. As we have learned, we often adopt behavior to reflect what we perceive as the majority view. The trouble is that that view gets distorted by workaholics at the company, who have a habit of influencing the office behavior in their extremist direction. You can opt out of this destruction derby by becoming very clear about your priorities and about what you're willing to trade off for them. How important is that promotion? Are the extra dollars worth the personal life you're giving up? The herd can't play ball with your kid. It can't spend time with your significant other. It can't wander through the tidal pool of a South Pacific lagoon. It's your choice.

"I'M NOT A QUITTER"

What makes some of us tyrannical self-bosses is the little-reported habit of absolutism. We wind up taking personal codes of conduct to extremes in the false belief that we can never bend or stray from the party line known only to us. Any infraction buckles self-worth, because esteem depends on unrealistic performance of the arbitrary rule book you concocted for yourself. A helpful aphorism like "Don't be a quitter," turns into a dictate that must be followed to the death, and anything less is treason. Don't get boxed into extra work by your own doctrinaire dictums. You can finish that memo tomorrow and still have your persevering instincts intact. Yes, it's nice to be persistent, but some situations are impossible, and you do more harm by sticking with them. There are many other opportunities out there. The best way forward is not through the wall but around it in a new direction.

CENTER OF THE UNIVERSE

Keep track of the number of times you mentally judge others in a given day, and you know your ego is working very hard to make you the number one player in town. The ego is constantly trying to puff itself up, and it can convince you that you are doing a job no one else can, that you are irreplaceable. It makes you feel good that you are so important, but it also makes you rack up lots of extra hours to maintain your esteemed role as pivot point of the universe. When you think no one else can do the job, you don't share or delegate work, you take on loads you don't think anyone else can do, and you work through your vacation, because who else could possibly do what you do? Being the center of the universe is a demanding job you wouldn't apply for if you saw it on paper.

THE TO-NOT-OVERDO LIST

Ritual overwork will continue to plague your life unless you put in place some strategies to deal with it. You'll need drop-dead stop deadlines, a description that tells you why you need them, and you need to get organized. Here are a few steps you can take to keep yourself at bay:

- **Set Stop Times.** These are absolutely key to prevent the unchecked drift into the late shift. Set a time to leave work and stick to it unless it's an emergency.

- **Ban Weekend Work.** Make this a cornerstone of your new life policy. If you can't get done what you need to during the week, it waits till Monday.

- **Get Organized.** Prioritize, prioritize, prioritize. If you can't do it yourself, sign on with Franklin or one of the other planning systems.

- **Turn It Down.** Tell them you couldn't possibly do your work justice with the load you've got, and that it would be unproductive to take it on. What work would they like you to drop to take on more projects?

- **Share the Load.** Learn to ask for help and delegate. Don't let territoriality or perfectionism drown you in overwork.

- **Make Time an Achievement.** Turn the tables on the productivity mind-set. Start considering free time as an achievement, which it certainly is these days. This will help you value the time you need for yourself and target it. Pump your fist when you grab some time back for your life.

- **Take Personal Appointments Seriously.** Hold yourself to your personal appointments as if they were business ones. Don't cancel out your life.

Why More Hours Are Less

To help you cut back on endless hours, it's important that you know that the whole marathon at the office runs on a fiction: that more hours must be better. All the research says they're not. Fatigue studies show that concentration starts to fade after six–eight hours of time on task. The research has also proven that accidents and reports of depression go up in overtime. Tony Miller, owner of the cleaning-firm Jancoa Inc., knows exactly how little gets done after eight hours on the job—"not even 50 percent of the productivity of regular hours," he says. A study by the Business Roundtable found that excess overtime can substantially reduce productivity not just during the extra hours but also during the rest of the workweek. One report found that overtime work produces such shoddy results that, over a period of seven fifty-hour weeks, "the total work accomplished will be no greater, or possibly less than, the work accomplished if the regular schedule had been used."

Economist Juliet Schor explains how this works, or doesn't: "When hours get too long, hourly productivity suffers and eventually total productivity suffers. If people work really long hours, you see leisure showing up in the middle of the day, because it has to. People have to get their personal business done and have to get a certain amount of time off."

Long hours do produce more stress, though, along with increased health risk. Research has documented a higher incidence of coronary heart disease in men working more than forty-eight hours a week. A study by Northwestern National Life found that employees who worked overtime reported their jobs were highly stressful twice as often as those with regular schedules (62 percent compared to 34 percent). Chronic overtime can lead to what the Japanese call *karoshi,* "death from over-work." The term was invented after a spate of late-night salarymen were found to be dying in the prime of life. Japanese researchers looking into the karoshi phenomenon found a link between long hours, high blood pressure, heart disease, and an unhealthy lifestyle—smoking, alcohol abuse, sleeplessness, poor eating habits, fewer medical visits, and increased anxiety and strain. Another recent Japanese study showed that overwork (more than 61 hours a week) combined with sleeping five hours or less twice a week can double or triple the risk of heart attack. The Japanese take this research and subject very seriously, since there have been 30,000 deaths attributed to karoshi since the 1980s. As a result, the Japanese have steadily reduced working hours and created a national pension system for members of karoshi victims' families left behind. Since U.S. workers surpass their Japanese couter-parts by more than 100 hours each year. I'd hate to think what our karoshi numbers must look like.

So whether your overtime is self-inflicted, explicitly demanded, or implied by the behavior of managers and colleagues, the indisputable evidence is that chronic long hours don't produce much except shoddy work, physical decline and higher medical bills.

Saying No to Bosses

We often think there is no choice when it comes to overtime hours or accepting extra projects, but there always is. You can either go along with the demands, or you can decline in a diplomatic but firm way. One person who believes you should speak up is a boss herself. Barbara Hemphill, a time-management expert, author, and founder of the Hemphill Productivity Institute, puts it this way: "If all employees suddenly said to their employers, 'I'm not working 24-7 anymore,' what would they do? But because we all say we have to do it, we all have to do it. So if you can't speak up for yourself, do it for the rest of the world."

Ross Crespy paid a high price for not setting boundaries. After twenty-one years in the navy, he joined a management-trainee program with Rite Aid in Chula Vista, California. When he took the job he was told to expect to work more than forty hours: fifty to fifty-five hours a week. Crespy wasn't afraid of hard work and needed the money, so he took the job. Within a month he was doing seventy-hour, six-day weeks, and would go on to put in more than 100-hour weeks during the holidays, for a salary of $28,000 a year. "There was no life at Rite Aid," says Crespy. "You went to work, went home to sleep, then went back to work."

Crespy's extra hours weren't self-inflicted. Management was aggressive in working its salaried employees "as much as humanly possible," to make up for hourly positions they had cut. Store managers had become freight haulers. Crespy felt he was not in a position to go elsewhere, so he dealt with it. It was a fateful decision. In ten months on the job he not only suffered three back injuries, but he was also severely beaten and bloodied in a robbery at the store. The third back injury took him out.

"I showed up at five in the morning to get merchandise on the floor," he recalls. "I had moved hundreds of pounds of freight, when I literally collapsed, couldn't move my legs, couldn't get to a phone to call 9-1-1. I thought maybe I had a stroke." He wound up in the ER with a couple of blown discs, plus a pinched sciatic nerve. When he returned later in the day to the store, he found his supervisor in a rage, and even though he told him he was at the ER, he was fired on the spot.

It's no surprise that a company that treats its employees as callously as Rite Aid has more than just heartlessness going on. It would turn out that their abusive practices also broke the law. A court case with Crespy as the lead plaintiff determined that Rite Aid had systematically misclassified its salaried workers. Crespy and dozens of other managers weren't salaried employees at all, because they were spending more time doing the work that hourly employees do than managing. The multimillion-dollar class-action settlement awarded back pay for overtime hours to Crespy and his colleagues, and Rite Aid agreed to an overtime cap for managers at fifty hours a week.

The court victory helped, but Crespy bears the scars of overtime without limits. He has had numerous surgeries on his back, and today he still can't sit for more than an hour without pain. His case shows how critical it is to curb excessive hours, even if the boss is demanding them. Or leave immediately. Out-of-control work demands are a red flag that a company or a boss has an underlying problem that you could wind up paying dearly for. You could literally be risking your life by staying.

As Crespy knows, there are worse things to fear than saying No to abusive work. There are lost years, lost pride, and inevitably, lost health. What you think you're expected to do is not always what you are, or should be, expected to do. Just because the company demands unhealthy commitment, it doesn't mean you have to be its victim. Don't let the fear of No manipulate you into blindly following the Overtime Commandment. You can and should turn down extreme work demands, whether they are self-inflicted or ordered from above. No job is worth destroying your health, or a life unlived. You are the CEO of your life, no one else.

It's one of the shortest words we have, but it's so hard to say it— NO! Yet without this unpleasant term, we would be a slave to everyone and everything. Over the years we use it to map out our perimeter, to lay down the markers of what our ego and moral code accepts or rejects. We establish who we are as much by what we won't do—by saying No—as by what we will. The word that shuts us down when we're on the receiving end has the power of choice, decisiveness, and control when it's coming from us. It has the ability to free us from dangerous and risky behavior, and the impositions of those who would try to take advantage of us.

Along the way, though, we may have some experiences that give us a false impression of this critical term. Dr. Les White, who specializes in workplace issues at the Adler School of Professional Psychology in Chicago, says we have to get past the past. "Thirty years later people are telling themselves, if I state more of who I am or what my interests are, if I take a risk, I'm going to be shut down," he notes. "You have a choice. You have to speak out. What other instances in your life have you been able to speak out where you weren't shut down? Usually people are able to come up with something."

Surprisingly, what lies behind No is Yes. When you decide to exercise your perimeter defense to turn down excessive work demands, whether spoken or unspoken, you are really saying Yes to yourself. Yes to your family. Yes to friends you haven't seen this millennium. Yes to that trip to Paris you always wanted to take. Yes to getting back to your tennis or golf game. Yes to community work and making a difference. Yes to balance. Yes to all those branches of your tree that need to reach for the sky, instead of the Tylenol.

What usually happens, though, is that the need for approval or security is stronger than self-esteem and overwhelms weak defenses. You wind up unable to turn down extreme hours and extra projects, because you fear the disapproval of the boss or colleagues that may come with it—even if it is just workaholic grousing or guilt-mongering.

"People who can't say No, take more things on so that people will really like them," adds stress-psychologist Mark Gorkin. "They don't want to burden others, or they play the rescuer role. But when they don't get back what they think they deserve after all the sacrifice, they can become depressed or hostile. How could they be treated this way? I encourage my clients to stop being so nice and get more real. Say what you want, ask for what you need, and learn to deal with whatever comes back at you." When the No you want to say isn't said, it's often to avoid potential conflict—disappointment, anger, debate, bulging jugular veins. Approval is so much easier on the pulse rate. It seems like the better deal. But run the numbers. You trade a few minutes of unpleasantness and dripping pits for hours upon hours, week upon week, year after year, of unnecessary overtime, exhaustion, and lost living time. Is it worth it?

Julie Masser, a computer support technician in Texas, decided it wasn't. After being run ragged by a former employer, who kept her on the road for six months once, with only three days off, she speaks up now. "There's the misconception that if management doesn't have a personal life, then you don't have a right to a personal life," she says. "I tell them that's wrong. I don't *enlist,* when I sign on with a company. I *agree.* I feel that there ought to be a reasonable amount of choice after your designated forty hours in the week."

"To set boundaries you have to be willing to deal with some conflict and even some anger," Gorkin adds. "People who tend to be too nice and too accommodating are often the folks who are uncomfortable with anger and conflict. The ability to say No and negotiate is critical for survival in this anytime, anywhere working world, where there are no boundaries."

If you are being given last-minute assignments and put under the gun to finish them in times that aren't possible within the laws of physics, you need to communicate the problem to your supervisor. It's called "push-back." Many managers will push and probe your limits as far as they can, until they get push-back from you, when they'll back off. If your boss is one of them, you need to switch on the stoplights, or brace yourself for a burnout crash ahead.

Making the commitment that you're going to have a more balanced life is not without real risks. You might not get promoted as quickly. Quantity over quality of hours remains a factor in advancement at many companies still operating in dinosaur command and control mode— the last person standing wins. If you're in sales, you might make less money. With some irrational bosses, you could become more expendable. It's all a trade-off for what you know you need: balance, a real life. Do you want to be stampeded by the workaholics in the office, or do you want to play your own game, and wind up with a few extra years on your life span to play it?

If you're brave enough to endure exhaustive hours, you've got the courage to state your case for a life. You can start down that path with a three-step process that will help you get clear on the need to reduce workload and shape your case for fewer hours.

STEP 1: EVALUATE THE DEMANDS

As long as we run from confrontation on the overtime issue, we're keeping alive the fear of changing what we know must be changed. The way out is getting behind the abstract fear to measure the real impact of unchecked job hours. You need to carefully examine work demands and their impact on your personal responsibilities and goals in life. What are your priorities? Family? Growth? Contribution? What's the cost of overload to these priorities? What's missing in your life, and how will saner job hours help out? What is your motivation for staying on the overwork path? Future promotion? Rut? Time already invested?

Prioritize your list of the most important things in your life—parenting, relationships, health and fitness, growth, travel—and determine how much time you want to allot to doing them. What percentage of those areas is being addressed now? Ten percent? Forty percent? What emerges from this analysis will be a clear record of your values and priorities and the directions you need to go in for more balance. In essence it's creating a new definition of success, one that doesn't depend on unlimited job hours to gauge worth. When you are finished evaluating, you will be armed with an understanding of what you need to get the life you want, as well as the logic and facts to support your case, so you can approach the boss without guilt. Internal conviction makes your choice felt externally, increasing your odds of support.

STEP 2: CROSS THE RISK THRESHOLD

Next you need to convert the information from your evaluation phase into an anxiety-proof decision to break the silence. This is the risk assessment phase. Risk-taking is the process of managing uncertainty, of gathering enough information and skill to reduce unwanted outcomes. You have to risk to thrive and grow. To take the plunge, you'll need to first clear out some limiting anxieties—security, embarassment, failure. Push through security fears in the knowledge that there is no such thing as security. The essence of existence is movement and change—and we're part of it. Craving security causes us to stifle the universal essence of change in ourselves. Instead, focus on why you need to cut excess hours (for family, health, personal life). Psychologists tell us that motivation can beat projected fears any day. Where there's too much prophet, there's usually a loss.

There's nothing embarassing about wanting to set boundaries. The opposite usually occurs when you state your case—admiration for staking your ground. There is nothing weak about taking a risk to get more control over your life, as some of your colleagues too afraid to take action could tell you. What if your request doesn't work? The nature of risk is that there's a chance it may not. If it doesn't, what have you got to lose? Would you really be fired for stating how you could work more productively? I doubt it. Even if you don't get what you want immediately, you've made it clear that you have limits. You may have to take on more work than you want this time, but next time they might think twice before heaping projects on you.

STEP 3: MEASURE RISK FALLOUT

The act of speaking up is going to get a reaction, hopefully the one you want. But whatever it is, you need to be able to deal with it, counter it, and stay committed to your goal: work-life balance. The scenarios could include disappointment, understanding, sarcasm, acceptance, anger, empathy, or extremely loud bellowing. A few irrational bosses might even threaten you. Prepare yourself for the possibilities by once again revisiting the importance of reducing your overload—the personal and family time it's going to free up, the time for fitness and health, and to realize your balance mandate. This will give you the conviction to move ahead whatever comes your way.

Using Boss Psychology

Now this is where the blood really starts pumping. You've gone backwards and forwards over the pros and cons and have made your decision—you must have a life as well as a job. So why is your stomach in knots? Fear. It's natural. You're stepping away from the comfort zone and into the unknown. There is always some fear when you are growing, moving away from the familiar. Don't let the anxiety stop you. You can stop it, in fact, with your action. Doing kills fear and the powerlessness that stokes it.

Knowing it can be done helps. Time-management specialist Barbara Hemphill has seen boundary-setting work in corporations she's consulted. "You can train your boss and colleagues. You say, 'I leave work at 6 P.M., so don't bring me something at 5:55. It's not going to get done.' When you say No, it frees other people to do the same thing."

For your effort to succeed, you can't take an adversarial or negative approach. You want to strike a collaborative tone and invite the boss into a process to help you find a solution that could help the company as well as you work more effectively. As in any negotiation, success is going to depend as much on your knowledge of your negotiating partner as on your diplomatic skills. That means you'll need to understand a little boss psychology. So let's take a quick trip inside the world of boss-think.

1. **Bosses want results.** They want focus and quality production, which slip when you're overwhelmed with too much work or anxious about the obligations you're not meeting on the home front. Think about the ways that you can phrase your needs to suggest that accommodating them will help you do a more efficient job. They might include working from home one day a week, or a flex schedule that allows you to put commute time toward work and family time.

2. **Bosses have a lot of things going on.** So part of your task is informational. He or she may know you worked late this day or that one, but may not realize the full extent of your schedule squeeze. Bosses appreciate facts. All of this should be presented dispassionately, no whining.

3. **Bosses want honesty.** At least the good ones do. Their posterior depends on yours. Bob Senator, executive vice president of $500 million human-resource firm Comforce Corp., says that's what he wants from his employees. "One of the things that would bother me is if I thought people were keeping things from me," he says. "I would want honesty, and, if they're un-

happy, I expect them to come to me and tell me. If we're honest, we can face what challenges come along, and we'll know where everybody stands." Good bosses don't want good employees to be miserable. They want them to be around for a while and performing without distractions.

4. **Bosses don't want to figure it out.** There is a vortex of tasks swirling around your addled supervisor's brain. You don't want to add to that pile and presume to take his or her time away from other pressing matters. Think your proposal through, so that you bring a suggested solution, not just the problem, as a part of your pitch. For instance, if you need to delegate some of your work, find out who could take some of your overflow. Maybe there's some cross-training that needs to take place to get colleagues who are less-burdened trained to share the load.

5. **Bosses have bosses.** As you dread approaching your manager, he or she is going to be fearful of the next level up. Your proposal needs to take into account that your boss's output is covered and that his or her position isn't compromised with the higher-ups. How is the boss going to be able to look better or no worse as a result of your modification of hours? Mention how the morale boost and downtime will improve your production.

Besides understanding how the boss thinks, it's also helpful to gauge the style of your supervisor. How can you catch him or her at the best moment in the best way? Mondays and Tuesdays are usually the most stressful days of the week. Friday would be the best bet in most cases. Psychologist Les White suggests noting who and what the boss responds to, his or her style, and "acclimating yourself to that. You can work on changing your style, perhaps acting as if you're a movie star in a scene. If you look at it that way, you can step out of yourself and perform a little bit differently."

Another strategy to reach the boss is to bring him or her into the family. Let it be known that there are real people in your other life who are not insignificant obligations. To get the connection across, find opportunities where you can physically introduce members of your family to the boss. The supervisor will know there's a living, breathing face behind your proposal. The exposure policy can also work with your hobbies and interests. Enthusiasms give point and purpose to your work-life request and can be contagious. Your personal life has a much better chance of happening once its existence is known. When you're all work, the boss treats you accordingly.

Making Your Case

Start your presentation by reminding the boss what you have accomplished to date. As in any negotiation, you need to go into it with an idea of what you'd like to get out of it, and, if that doesn't work out, what you could live with. The currency in this case is time, not money. Calculate how much time you need to address the core values and interests you itemized in your evaluation phase. When would you need to leave work to bring those values into regular circulation? Suggest an ideal stop time that could make that a reality. Start at 6 P.M., for example, to be home for family meals, and only move later if you have to. But set a boundary beyond which you don't want to go. This is one of your untouchables, a limit you need to hold to as long as you can.

Of course, you also need a proposal, an offer of what you're looking for, and what the boss can expect in return. What solution would work for you? A flex time schedule with open start and finish times? Maybe it's a set number of hours. Pick your number, forty, forty-five, or, if you're now at sixty, try cutting it to fifty hours a week, and state your case for why anything beyond that is counterproductive. Maybe your plan calls for a four-day schedule, ten hours for four days a week, which frees up your Fridays for more weekend activities. Or maybe it's a telecommuting strategy that allows you to work from home a couple days a week.

It would be nice if there was a magic phrase you could spout, and your boss would suddenly agree with everything you said—"A three-day week? Brilliant idea!" In lieu of that, you'll have to prepare your words carefully, taking into account your specific overload situation, and your own nonwork goals. To get an idea of what bosses would say if they were in your shoes, and some more negotiating tips see Chapter 11, "Ask and You May Receive" (page 206). By all means, stay positive, don't complain, and show conviction for more balance.

Paula Ann Hughes, a management professor at Texas Women's University, suggests putting the focus of the conversation on priorities. "You don't want to give the idea that you're unwilling to do something, but it could be something like, 'I know I'm most productive during the first fifty hours of the week, and I really need to make sure we're in alignment here on what's important,'" advises Hughes, a former boss herself, when she was president of the University of Dallas. "And then say, 'Could I get some help on some of this stuff? Where would you suggest I get some help?'"

Enlisting the boss in problem-solving helps vest him or her in the new policy. "You kind of massage their narcissism," says Dr. Scott Stacy, a clinical psychologist who heads the Professional Renewal Center in Kansas City. "You say, 'How do *you* set priorities in your life?' What it does is force the supervisor to reflect and make judgments about how they want to do things."

The consensus is that you have to make it clear you are willing to work, but in a different way, one that allows you to take care of core values outside the office. You are setting limits but doing it with a plan for improved time management that will benefit the company. You will actually be helping the firm by not taking on more than you can handle. Make the point that it's better to do two things well than five badly. Let the boss know how many projects you're currently juggling, and what happens to your productivity, efficiency and medical tab when you get more piled on top of that. Cite examples and their diminishing returns.

In return, the major benefit for the boss is a more productive and healthy employee—in fact, you'll prove it in a trial run. Offer to demonstrate with a test of the new schedule that it won't reduce your production. If there is any drop-off in performance, you'll go back to the old system. You could also offer to come in earlier in the day if any gaps in performance occur. The overall win-win for any sane employer is a happy and productive employee, and that's what you're offering.

Santa Clara, California-based Pam Ammondson, who helps workers recover from burnout at her Clarity Quest workshops, says setting limits can be done. Workshop participants of hers "have gone back and been able to sit down with their bosses," she says. "They've set boundaries on a time to leave the office each day and stopped working on weekends. And you know something? It hasn't made them lose their jobs."

Of course, there are no guarantees. Workaholic managers will be clueless. Their one-track minds can't envision why anyone would not want to work every waking moment. Expect some incoming rounds of guilt. You're challenging the local culture. If so-and-so can follow the rules, why not you? There may be comments about your not being a team member. Don't get rattled. If you're committed to your new values, the guilt can't stick.

When the boss is completely inflexible, you could try the HR department, if your company has one. Larger firms may have wellness programs that might incorporate your work-life goals. If there's no willingness anywhere to change overwork behavior, and 50-plus hour weeks of stress are ruining your health, you need to think seriously about going somewhere else. As we saw earlier, failure to heed warning signs can open the door to problems that could forever change your quality of life, and even threaten it. You need a life outside of work to stay sane and fulfilled.

If you're ready to rein in runaway hours, don't wait until it's too late. Vanquish fear with action. A Native American elder once gave this piece of advice to a boy on his initiation into adulthood, as told by Joseph Campbell: "As you go the way of life, you will see a great chasm. Jump. It is not as wide as you think."

7

Exit Rush Hour

End Hurry-Worry and Busyness

• • •

"We are merely bolting our lives—gulping down undigested experiences as fast as we can stuff them in—because awareness of our own existence is so superficial and so narrow that nothing seems to us more boring than simply being."

—Alan Watts

They don't call it a rat "race" for nothing. We hit the ground running in our early twenties and don't stop until we're on the bingo circuit five decades later—if we don't flame out first. Even if you don't know you're in The Race, you're in it. You feel the urgency of your fellow runners all day, every day, breathing down your neck, pushing you to keep up with the stampede, a tide charging like wildebeests in pants across the urban Serengetis of America. You've got to keep moving, driving toward the water hole of success, a murky destination that has to do with getting enough material stuff to win enough approval to signal your arrival at the finish line of productive value.

Today The Race is bumping against the outer limits of the human pace, forcing us to compete on multiple levels at the same time, known and loved as the art of multitasking, or simultaneous inattention. The explosion of high-speed communications technology—pagers, E-mail, the Internet, cell phones, Palm Pilots, Personal Digital Assistants (PDAs), instant messaging—has us hurtling through The Race at warp speed, working the phones while checking E-mail while reading faxes.

The signs along the Information Superhighway read "Run, Don't Walk"; "G-Forces Up Ahead"; and "Hurry Up, Sea Slug."

Not surprisingly, some of us are going into oxygen debt to keep up, because what we're trying to keep up with are machines, devices that we both love and hate at the same time. They're indispensable, but they've pumped up the volume of work and tethered us to 24-7 access. However, you can live in the technological world without having to function as a hard drive with hair. There's a lot of hype and false urgency built into The Race and the seeming demands of the gadgetry and services that have us on their leash. FedEx may have to get it done overnight; most of the time you don't.

The pressures of The Race make us feel like we have to do it all right now. Or what? We'll explode? Apocalypse now? Is there a real business value behind the rush, or is it just the only pace we know? Those are questions that seldom occur, because we're too busy being busy to ask. We're swept up in the core commandment of the time crunch: *Thou shalt not work less than full blast all the time.* The false assumption behind it is that you can never go less than full tilt, or you'll have violated the work ethic, fallen behind, descended into hobo land. The hyper commandment has a lot of fun with us, whipping up frenzies where there are none and keeping us in a state of cringing anxiety about all that stuff we have to do. But there's not much more behind this commandment most of the time than chronic hurry-worry. You don't have to sprint all day, scheduling yourself back-to-back without a break in the action. You can exit rush hour and the forced march of The Race and find your own pace. To your own race.

And you don't have to turn the clock back to do it, either. The surge of technology and the realities of the global marketplace are here to stay. What you *can* do is recalibrate your relationship to The Race and the burden of time pressures. It's not the stressor that causes stress. It's your reaction to it. Read on and learn how to retune your inner rhythm and response to time stress, how to set realistic timetables, and turn off squealing devices without a trace of remorse. You'll discover how speed kills—productivity, innovation, creativity, health, and the whole point of the journey—and how you can get just as much done, and more, by relaxing in the heat of the contest. Moderating your pace goes against every unwritten cue in the workplace, but, as every real runner knows, no marathoner gets to the finish line by sprinting the entire distance.

The Creed of Speed

Speed is the creed of the information age, as much a belief system as it is a measurement of velocity. We believe, because we have become hooked on instant gratification. And we believe, because we have an almost religious faith in the productive value of time, which makes us want to boost the investment from our efforts by cramming as many tasks as possible into the day. Busyness has become the one true way to secular salvation—productive validation.

We get a lot of approval for operating in full-blast mode. It's behavior rewarded by social norms, bosses, and by our own sense that this is what we're supposed to be doing to fulfill our productive purpose—achieving, doing, making things happen. Action is nothing less than identity for many of us, to the point of a very bad habit, says author and workaholism-expert Diane Fassell. "There's this terrible addiction to incessant activity," points out Fassell, "supported by the underlying belief that if you were not constantly busy, you would not have the right to be or exist."

The faster we go, the faster we seem to need to go. All the high-speed tech tools and instant products and services aggravate the hurry impulse, creating an ever more colossal impatience with anything that doesn't get done in a nanosecond. It sets up the habit of false urgency, a distortion in time perception that raises tensions even when there doesn't have to be any. You wind up stressing over calls that don't have to be returned immediately or going into false urgency mode when the automatic teller machine springs a surprise five-second video on you before processing your order. These are not emergencies, but a time-crunched world can make you and your racing stomach think they are.

That's because we have been led to believe that there is only one speed—fifth gear. "We assume it's all-or-nothing," says Gil Gordon, business consultant and author of *Turn It Off,* a guide to gaining control over the digital deluge. "The '90s made everything faster. Faster time to market, faster turnaround, faster, faster, faster. The technology enabled that, and we became addicted to that kind of speed. We've become very simple-minded with these issues of how fast, how much, how soon, and we've kind of assumed that just because we can, we're compelled to."

Instant gratification used to be a specialty of toddlers, drug addicts, and antisocial types, but the accelerating Race pace, and advertisers smarter than we are have made it a household affair, from the thirty-second order or your money back at McDonald's, to high-speed DSL lines, to FedEx's same-day delivery. (It won't be long before they can ship it before you even know you want to send it.)

Flying on adrenaline, we've become so used to satisfying our needs instantaneously that anything that slows or stops us—voice-mail loops, express lanes that aren't—are interpreted as emergencies, if not galling outrages, needlessly quickening the pulse rate and launching the stress response. But they are false alarms, danger signals of quite another sort, of hurry-worry, our epidemic habit of rushing to go faster than we can, even if we're going nowhere most of the time. It all conspires to create in our minds and churning guts a constant urge to bolt—from conversations, projects, meals, free time, ourselves. We wind up living with one foot out the door, unable to be present for our lives, which requires the nearly extinct element of lingering.

The reality is you can't outrun yourself, and, unlike silicon chips, you can't double your processor capacity every other week. Humans have serious "bandwidth" limits. There is only so much data you can take in before you overload and crash. That's how many find out that although there are no posted signs, there are definitely speed limits. Needless time pressure turns up the heat by creating a sense that things are out of control, the chief trigger of the stress response. But why burn out, when you can simply select another gear? There is more than one speed of life.

Relax, When You Want to Go to It

Mount Kilimanjaro is Africa's tallest peak, a perfectly shaped, snow-topped volcanic cone that reigns over East African savannas. From the plains of steaming equatorial Tanzania it rises 19,341 feet to the ice-covered summit of Kibo, forming the classic backdrop of many a safari photo. Kilimanjaro attracts a host of adventure travelers every year who hope to climb this everyman's Everest and stand atop Africa. You don't need technical skills to climb Kili, but you do need stamina and conditioning. And something else: You can't be in a hurry. You need to build in time to acclimatize to the altitude. If you go up too fast, without allowing your blood the time to produce the additional blood cells needed to keep you functioning in the thin air, you wind up with altitude sickness, or high-altitude pulmonary edema [syndrome]. At that point, you've got one choice, get down the mountain or die. Scores of gung-ho jocks are bounced off the mountain every year this way, because they insist on racing to the top.

The local guides caution the climbers, *"pole, pole,"* Swahili for "slowly, slowly," but the speedway mentality can't process that concept. It needs the result, the pat on the back of achievement ASAP. The lesson here is that the fastest don't always finish, and if they do, they miss the whole trip. It takes four or five days to climb Kilimanjaro safely; you only spend thirty minutes on the top. Obsession with objective obscures the adventure, that vast chunk of your existence when you're not standing on mountaintops or podiums. Life is what happens between summits.

Those Tanzanian guides know what experts do in all realms of performance, that a relaxed approach is the key to success. The tense, uptight bodies and racing minds of the perpetual rush hour restrict peak performance—in sports, on the job, and in social life. Optimal experience requires effortless focus, not the forced straining and mental panic of speed mode. The hurry mind-set creates a rigid defensive posture, as you race against the clock and everyone in your way. It's a reactive mode that throws up a shield. You might be hustling, but you are in a constricted state, bracing for interruptions and threats to your schedule, wasting energy trying to control what you can't. This controlling pose undermines quality performance—which comes from noncritical focus and natural spontaneity—with anxiety and fear. When we are caught up in hurry-worry, we wind up forcing things to try to make them fit our timetable and standards. Guilt, stress, and anger run wild as we find we can't do everything the way we would like—without breaking stride. Speed winds up killing the productivity it's supposed to foster. The decisions you make at full speed are also often under the influence of adrenaline, which has been shown in research to lead to a loss of intellectual capacity, which hijacks good judgment.

So how can you get out of warp-factor seven and improve your creativity and health with a more reasonable pace? By changing ingrained beliefs that have got you chasing your tail, and by confronting and ending the fears that promote nonstop busyness. Let's take a look first at the false beliefs you'll need to toss:

SPEED TRAPS

- **"I must be busy all day, or I'm not being productive."** If you believe this, you believe that you aren't worthy of stopping, relaxing, or reflecting; busyness at all times is required to feel good about yourself in this telltale sign of workaholism. Let's all agree that this is absurd. In fact, the opposite of this belief is true. If you're busy every minute of the day, you can't possibly do work that's worth much, because you've had no time to plan, organize, think about, or enjoy what you've done. You can't be productive, either, when you're undermining your health. Try to see nonstop busyness for what it is, an excess need for validation and an inability to say No. First lesson: When someone asks you how you are, never say you're busy. Stop telling the story, and you stop reinforcing the behavior.

- **"If I slow down or stop, I'm wasting time."** This is absolutist, illogical thinking. What's a waste is your life, when you push your body without letup. We need a new definition of wasting time. I vote for this: Rote, mechanical busyness, without thought as to where that busyness is going or why. Stopping and moderating the pace is essential to arrival in one piece. As Dr. David Kundtz explains in *Stopping,* "The ultimate purpose of stopping is to ensure that when we do go, we go in the direction that we want and that we are not just reacting to the pace of our lives, but choosing, moment by moment, what's best. The ultimate reason for stopping is going."

- **"I'm too busy to stop."** This is a favorite alibi we've all used, a by-product of mechanical momentum combined with inbox panic. Fear of the to-do stack convinces you that you have to keep at it without letup, or you're not getting the job done, you'll fall behind, you're not worthy. What it's saying is that you aren't important enough to take time out for yourself. Most of the time it's a crutch, a martyr stroke for the pseudo self-esteem. There's a macho pose of immortality here as well—only lightweights have to stop. Try to see through all that to the excuse of busyness. No matter how busy you are, there's always time for a five-minute breather here, a call to a friend there. And stopping will let you get the job done better and more clear-headed. Your lesson: Stop in the middle of a really busy day for a brief personal time-out. Think about your plans for the weekend, find a movie to see, do a short meditation, or whatever you like, but make it nonbusiness. You'll be refreshed, and you'll see that the to-do stack doesn't grow a millimeter higher on your time-out. Don't let the unconscious momentum of busyness foreclose conscious living.

- **"I must get there faster than I'm going."** The stampede of The Race is driven by this belief. Whether you have to make the next green light or vice president of your company, the fixation to get there faster than you're able to go fuels hurry-worry. You can still get where you're going without having to be wracked that you're not there yet. The anxiety to be *there* reinforces all day the inadequacy of being *here,* which is a setup for continual unhappiness. In baseball some pitchers throw ninety miles per hour and have losing records, while others throw seventy-five miles per hour and post winning seasons. It's not speed but savvy that wins the game. Your lesson: When you catch yourself rushing, ask why. Chances are good there's no legit reason, that it's just habitual impatience or somebody else's pressure to hurry. Take a deep breath and let the accelerator up from the floor.

Fear Factors

The false assumptions that keep us running are held in place by fears that lurk just outside our awareness. They wind us up, and we get busy, not realizing the manipulation under way. Most are fears around the issue of nonactivity. Sometimes we keep buzzing with tasks or distractions to avoid the fear of something action figures don't have a lot of practice at: going inside. "One of the fears that keeps people moving constantly is that if they were not constantly working, they would probably have to deal with the deeper issues of life," workaholism expert Diane Fassel notes. "I think of the great 'why' questions—Why am I here? Why am I doing what I'm doing."

Busyness crowds out soul-searching because of a fear of self-criticism. But you can counter that with objective reflection, points out the Professional Renewal Center's Dr. Stacy. "When you look inside, and you're critical of yourself, then you're going to get busy to avoid the anxiety of dealing with whatever you've found. But if you can take an observing stance toward yourself that doesn't judge what you find or see but merely observes and takes a curious approach to what that is, then the door doesn't slam, and there may be the opportunity to find out whatever meaning is there. Then you're going to reduce the chances of getting busy again."

The inside passage is key to getting off the rodent treadmill. You have to take time to think, question, and assess, to find out what you want, not what peers or marketers pressure you to want. Reflection isn't a diversion from the action, it plots the course. The director of the out-side action is inside. So take a peek. It's not so bad in there. You'll find the answers to the questions you need to keep asking for growth and fulfillment: Where am I going? Why? Am I on track? What do I want? How do I savor being here? Ignore the battering rams and confront the shadows, because that's what is going to enable you to work to live. As Dr. Mihaly Czikzentmihalyi points out in *Flow,* "People who learn to control inner experience will be able to determine the quality of their lives, which is as close as any of us can come to being happy."

Let's tackle the chief fear factors that keep us running in place:

FEAR OF BEING ALONE

This is a biggie and naturally so for the social animal. The French philospher Pascal wrote that man's biggest fear is to be alone in a room with himself. We fear the silence of time not filled, the questions and self-judgment that may come up when we're not completely consumed with work or other distractions. Yet it's precisely the ability to stop and still your mind long enough to figure out what you need in life and whether your current course is getting you there that allows you to reach your goals. It frees you from the external noise to find out what a meaningful life is for you. Otherwise, you're running blind on some-body else's track, where busyness and productivity substitute for what's missing inside, peace of mind, which can only be generated within that same mind.

Don't let the fear of self-assessment keep you separated from your-self. Remember, you're on your side. But you can't hear yourself, if you're not listening. Solitude can be a powerful means to access your inner strength and true aspirations. "The capacity to be alone," writes Anthony Storr in *Solitude,* is "linked with self-discovery and self-realization: with becoming aware of one's deepest needs, feelings, and impulses." It's how you hear what's on your mind. Getting out in na-ture is a great stimulus for these solo conversations. Meditation is an excellent vehicle for getting comfortable with quiet time on your own. Fifteen minutes one or two times a day can go a long way toward reining in the racing mind that's chasing you breathless. Once you start, you'll feel the payoff of stopping and know that the antidote to The Race has your address.

FEAR OF BEING

In a culture where the value is on doing, getting, and having, the idea of simply being is about as welcome as a lobotomy. Strange, since what makes us crazy seems to be all the action, the striving and grasping from that bottomless pit of desire that only triggers more wants. We fear the state of being, because it appears to be not doing, which triggers massive guilt, which keeps us endlessly chasing the objects of our desire. Fishing on a glassy lake, having a long meal with friends, or watching the clouds blow by have zero *extrinsic* value. We're not going to get any outside strokes for them. Instead, we get inside strokes, which are much better. It's in these moments that serve no useful purpose whatsoever that we can find what we can't from the constant sprint to somewhere we're not: satisfaction with what is. The rush-hour mindset keeps contentment conditional upon future events. Yet the only place where happiness can possibly exist is where you are, the here and now. When you can let go of the rush and just be, you're free to indulge in the reward for all your strivings—to relax, socialize, create, and enjoy for the sake of itself, which turns out to be your sake. You are a human "being," after all. Time to live up to the billing.

FEAR OF BEING PASSED

The central premise of The Race is that you're not running alone. There are legions of others, seen and unseen, trying to leave you in the dust. That specter is not to be taken lightly in a hypercompetitive land, but at the same time it can lead to an irrational paranoia that whips us into a panic that we can never stop, never let up, or somebody's going to get ahead of us—which means that we'll fall behind. Hurry-worry over competition in the abstract is especially pointless. It hands over your life to a faceless horde, over which you have zero control in a comparison contest that can never be won. When you can get your eye off everyone else, you can see where it is you're going.

FEAR OF INADEQUACY

When identity is attached to action, and the activity slows or stops, it can touch off an impending sense of inadequacy. You may equate the change with laziness or not giving your all. That loads up the guilt, which makes you want to get busy right away again. There is no connection between being scheduled to your eyeballs and self-worth. You are no more a slacker to want speed limits and stoplights than the doctors, psychologists, and ER staffs who say you need them.

Change the Story

In the revved world of the modern speedway your body gets very adept at triggering the stress cycle. You can't blame it. It's just following orders that were handed out tens of thousands of years before supervisors or budget overruns were invented. The good news is that you don't have to sit there and be a chemistry lab. You can go into a different mode at crunch time, heading off adrenaline charges before they get started by recognizing stress triggers, reframing them so they don't push your buttons, and by getting tough with yourself—setting realistic deadlines, turning away excess demands, and getting organized.

Researchers are finding that the key to stress is something identified by the farsighted Morris Albert in the title of his 1975 hit: "Feelings." "It's not the event, or the traffic, or the boss or co-worker, it's your emotional reaction to it," says Bruce Cryer, President of Heart-Math LLC®, a company on the frontier of stress reduction in the workplace. "We know now that emotion drives the stress physiology cycle. You need to recognize the things that drain your energy on an emotional level. Most people don't see the stress building up, they don't listen to their internal voice or guidance. Five minutes of anger can lead to a six-hour depression of immune-system function."

Reframe the story and the stress can't bite. Choice gives you control over what you *can* influence in a stressful situation—your reaction to it. It's about emotional management, knowing when to press the case and when to step back, when not to react and move beyond ego, and it's as critical as time management to relieving stress at the office. Emotions are on a hair trigger when you and everyone around you are running at full tilt. The workplace becomes an emotional powder keg, lit by a gauntlet of slights, criticism, arguments, jealousies, resentments, anger, rivalry, favoritism, cynicism, payback—the list is long and juicy. Being able to prevent this army of emotional "viruses," as Cryer calls them, from infecting you, sapping your motivation and dictating your moods is a critical component of a healthy workstyle. "If you're in a negative loop, burnout is the ultimate outcome," notes Cryer. "You will drain all emotional reserves eventually."

HeartMath attacks the stress virus within companies by going to the place where it's generated and held on to, inside the minds of individual workers. "We say: Here's what's going on physiologically, moment by moment inside your body," explains Cryer. "Here's how what's going on emotionally affects that, and how that in turn affects how you think."

The goal of the program is to get workers out of the reactive mind, so they can recognize and manage stressful thoughts and emotions, then change the negative drains to positive action. HeartMath has developed several techniques to break the stress cycle, including some software that helps participants monitor how their physiology is responding to the pressures of the day. One of their key stress-reducing techniques, Attitude Breathing, is a three-step process that allows you to reframe your emotional reactions to stressful events instead of letting them stampede you into knee-jerk steaming and stewing. HeartMath describes the process below:

ATTITUDE BREATHING

Attitude Breathing is useful for calming yourself when feeling anxious. It helps to soothe and disperse anxious feelings, bringing you back into balance.

Step 1. Shift your attention to your heart and solar plexus/stomach area.

Step 2. Ask yourself, "What would be a better attitude for me to maintain in this situation?" Then set up an inner attitude, such as "stay calm," "stay neutral in this situation," "don't judge before you know the facts," "make peace with this," or simply decide what attitude is appropriate for your situation.

Step 3. Next, gently and sincerely pretend to breathe the new attitude you want in through the heart. Then breathe it out through the solar plexus and stomach to anchor it. Do this for a while until you feel the new attitude has set in.

Use Attitude Breathing to help release tension in any part of the body. As you do this, ask yourself, "What would be a more balanced feeling or approach to what I'm doing?" Once you feel more emotionally balanced, then pretend to breathe the feeling of balance through the area of tension. You'll start to feel the tension release as more of your balanced heart energy moves through that area. Attitude Breathing is especially useful when you feel anxiety or before entering a situation that usually makes you feel anxious (before a test, performance, or social encounter, for example).

Even for crusty engineers at high-tech companies, the results of dealing with emotion, instead of ignoring it, have been dramatic, according to Cryer. At Motorola, 26 percent of the HeartMath participants were hypertensive at the start of the program. After six months, all had regained normal blood pressure. There was a 56 percent reduction in sleeplessness and 38 percent reduction in indigestion. Ninety percent of participants said teamwork had improved and 93 percent said productivity improved.

Taking time out lets you change the stress story, which is all in the script that you write.

Keep It Real

When you suffer from hurry-worry, one of the afflictions that comes along for the thrill ride is a knack for underestimation. Since speed is the driving force, it jacks up all estimates with forecasts that reflect when you would like to finish in an ideal world. The result is hopelessly unrealistic deadlines that can't be met but can be stressed over. If you are continually misjudging task time and the hours in the day, you have to get real.

Realistic time estimation is critical to putting the brakes on schedules careening out of control. The faster you estimate turnaround times, the more work that's going to be given to you—that you won't be able to deliver on time. Build in more time to complete tasks than you think to allow for interruptions, mistakes, Murphy's Law, and the inevitable "scope creep": "Every project takes longer, costs more, and gets bigger," says management professor Paula Ann Hughes. She recommends making allowances for scope creep, either up front or as a safety valve down the line when it looks like you're not going to make the target. When estimating how long a project will take, determine a time estimate, then double it, then add in 20 percent more for scope creep.

There's another kind of deadline that causes racetrack problems outside the office. That is the arbitrary self-deadline. Every day we concoct things we have to do or places we have to be by certain times randomly selected, and then wind up stressing over these completely arbitrary objectives if we don't get them handled as planned. Try to avoid setting yourself up for to-do list anxiety by turning self-deadlines into more approximate targets, and by seeing the human comedy at work here in the mad rush to get to the dry cleaners, the market—to the grave.

Here are some keys to help you keep it more real and less hectic.

RUSH REDUCTION

- Don't take work home to complete someone else's unrealistic deadline. It encourages more of the same.

- To cut down on habitual rushing roulette, always leave 15 or 20 minutes earlier for appointments than you think you need to.

- Don't hold yourself to the false crises of self-deadlines that are habit, not need.

- Do speed checks to catch yourself racing unnecessarily. When you feel rushed, STOP, LOOK, and LINGER. What's the rush?

- When you are late, looking at your watch isn't going to get you there any faster. DON'T check any clocks until you arrive. You'll be amazed at how effective this refusal to play the time-stress game can be.

- Try to cut down on the number of times you check the time each day, since it usually only aggravates the compulsion to hurry.

- Ask yourself, what is the worst that could happen if you don't make your goal on time? For the vast majority of rushes, the answer is not much.

- Instead of fuming at unexpected waits in lines or at elevators, use these times to notice where you are. Look around. Take in the scenery. It may be the only time all day you can really be where you are.

- NEVER worry about anyone else's hurry-worry. They can wait until you're done. Right turns and checkout counters just don't matter. Worrying about whether you're holding up others allows them to dictate your pace, your life. It doesn't need any freelance directors. You're it.

- The desk does not have to be cleared at the end of each day. Don't give yourself impossible agendas.

- Missed deadlines are survivable. Some may seem like life and death, but they're not.

Over and Out

There is no better illustration of the addictive powers of busyness than the drug-like attraction that E-mail, cell phones, and various tech gizmos have for communication junkies. No question, they are handy tools. It's nice to have them. But when the E-mail dinger is going off every five minutes along with your cell's underwater version of the "William Tell Overture," it may be time for a trip to E-Devices Anonymous.

It's not that these gadgets are intrinsically habit-forming, it's that it's all so new, we haven't learned how to use them properly yet, so we've been seduced by the immediacy and apparent importance that seems to emanate from them, which rachets up the rush hour to new heights. "As much as people complain about E-mail, it's almost a masochistic thing—'I hate this E-mail, and why am I not getting more?'" notes Gil Gordon, author of *Turn It Off*. "There's an old saying: Give a 5-year-old a hammer, and everything looks like a nail. Give a businessperson in today's world a device that gives them instant access and makes them ubiquitously available, and everything looks like a crisis."

Pulse rates are being driven unnecessarily by the false crisis atmosphere of E-tools. Just because they chime for our attention, we think it's urgent. But the fact that you can get messages and cell calls instantaneously does not mean they demand an instant response. That's been the assumption, because there are no rules or boundaries on access. Now is the time to make some, or remain at the whim of anyone with an itchy finger or a stream-of-consciousness thought, day or night. As much as you're able to within the demands of your job, you'll need to set clear boundaries between work and home as well as within the office, so you can work without continual interruptions.

In fact, the interruption factor is a good place to start formulating boundaries, since it's an area that most people can exert control over. There is no reason that you should have to have a computer ringing like an ice-cream truck from incoming E-flak all day long. Turning off the E-mail dinger, for example, can keep mail intrusiveness to a minimum. You can do that usually by shutting off the sound device on the control panels of your computer. Also, keep your E-mail software closed until you need to check it, so you're not tempted to go into it every time a mail announcement comes up visually on the screen.

The main component you need to keep in mind in drawing boundaries, says Gordon, is "value questioning, to not always respond with equal urgency before determining the value." There are two questions, he maintains, you should put to every item rattling your cage:

1. **What's the value of doing it now?**

2. **What's the consequence of waiting?**

Instead of getting caught up in rote commotion, stop and qualify the business value of the communication. It's what we used to call prioritizing, before the immediacy of tech tools gave us the mistaken sense that instant delivery demanded an equally instant response. The fact is, most of this stuff is not urgent, just intrusions with special effects. Allowing them to chop up your workday is like having the U.S. Postal Service barge into your office everytime they find a piece of mail for you.

Besides immediacy, the other assumption that needs to be tossed is availability. Just because your E-communications offer 24-7 access, that doesn't mean you have to be in receiving mode the whole time. Limit access, and you've begun to rein in some of the anarchy. You can put a fence around E-mail and cell phone activity, for instance, by restricting it to a couple of organized retrieval times each day. By regulating access and immediacy, you can begin to clear time for what you really need to do each day. Here are some further guidelines for corraling E-tool anarchy:

RULES FOR E-TOOLS

1. Retrieve E-mail at designated times, say, morning, midday and late afternoon. Resist the urge to check mail every ten minutes, which can border on compulsive hand washing.

2. All E-mails do not have to be responded to by the end of the day.

3. Prioritize all E-mail, responding quickly only to those that are truly urgent. The rest can be tackled as time permits.

4. Quit out of E-mail software unless you're using it.

5. Switch off all E-mail dingers and noisemakers.

6. If you have a stationary phone at the office, leave your cell off as much as possible during business hours. That means cutting down on the private calls you would never have wanted to go through the switchboard in the old days. Take messages on the cell and respond in the way you would to calls on your regular phone.

7. You don't have to return calls immediately. Prioritize them. Debra Dinnocenzo, president of ALLearnatives and co-author of *Dot Calm,* says she's "learned that in business hardly anyone has to talk to me right now. It can always wait till the end of the day or the next day."

8. Never wear a pager unless your firm or the type of work you do makes it mandatory. Don't even think about wearing one on vacation.

9. Turn off cell phones when you're under time pressure. Try restricting cell access to certain periods of the day. If you're worried about important calls, check the messages on a regular basis. Don't let callers cow you with false guilt into an immediate callback.

10. Set up focus time zones, where all devices are shut off to concentrate on the task at hand.

Trim the Fat

Getting organized is the answer to many a time-crunch woe, and should be a key feature of your work-to-live program. It cuts back on anxiety throughout the day, by creating order and control where there was chaos and loose ends. There are a number of good time-management systems on the market, from the ones you probably know about, like the Franklin planner, to the quantum leap of the time redesign offered by Strategic Coach. The Toronto-based consulting company aims to reinvent the way we think about free time, transforming it from something we feel guilty about into the linchpin of a system that focuses abilities and cuts out distractions.

The central concept of the program is the notion that everyone has certain abilities, "things you're uniquely good at, that you get an enormous amount of energy from," says Strategic Coach co-founder and president Dan Sullivan. The goal of the system is to get you more focused on what it is you do best and what you love doing, so you can do it more quickly, make more money at it, and take more time off. The result is unprecedented amounts of time off and vacations for entrepreneurs, who the program is mostly geared to, and their employees.

The key to getting organized—and to work-life balance—is planning and "letting go of things," says Barbara Hemphill, CEO of Hemphill Productivity Institute. Author of Kiplinger's "Taming the Paper Tiger" series, Hemphill recommends that you target five priority items each day and stay on them. She also points the finger squarely at "clutter," which she calls "postponed decisions." "The reason the paper is piled up on the desk is that we haven't made decisions like, Do we really need to keep this? Who needs to keep this? What form does it need to be kept in? How long does it have to be kept? And can we find it when we need it?" Her solution is a system called FAT—an acronym that stands for File, Act, or Toss, the three moves that whittle down the junk. At one company she advised, the FAT amounted to twenty-three Dumpsters full in one day, for a forty-five-person firm.

Before you get under way with a personal reorganization, do a time inventory of your life for a couple of weeks. Keep a log of how you spend your time every day, and in the process patterns will emerge—where time is being wasted, where you're overcommittted. Dr. Steve Sommer, who teaches management at the University of California, Riverside, says that time logs show "that there are enormous areas of wasted time, where we could be more efficient. A lot of people don't re-alize how much time is being eaten up by commutes." Use the discoveries from your time log to plot bold new directions, removing time drags and adding in their place more quality time for yourself off the speedway.

Time can be on your side, but not by default. You have to make a concerted effort to run your own pace and challenge speedup, with comprehensive time management, realistic deadlines, not falling for the full-blast hoax, and by something quite exotic. I'm talking about indulging in a rare quality that may be the best way to temper a run-away life: patience.

8

Banish Bravado

Don't Work Yourself Sick

• • •

"The heroic life is leading the individual adventure."

—Joseph Campbell

R eal achievers don't take sick days. That's the message in your supervisor's abrupt voice when you announce you've got the flu and won't be coming in. You know the tone. Like you just stood him up. It barely hides the repressed rage on the other end of the phone. Why doesn't the boss just come out and say it? "You're a wimp!" The gist of the call: If you can breathe, you can work. The unspoken feeling comes through loud and clear. You can't take it. You're weak to have come down with whatever you've got. Or to have allowed it to prevent you from soldiering on into the office.

The cuts don't get much worse than that for the all-American ego. In the most competitive culture on the planet, taking yourself out of the game is to not compete, which is soft, tantamount to malingering. It's the equivalent of forfeiting—and you know how that counts on the scorecard, in the loser column. Barring a full-body cast, most of us will find a way to drag ourselves to work rather than go through this humiliation. The overwork culture doesn't suffer human frailties well. Most bosses don't want to hear about it unless you're on life support. You should transcend that bag of skin you're in, so something can get done around here. And workers don't want to be seen as less than gladiator-like, afraid they'll fall behind or be outflanked by a healthy rival.

We prize the ironman image and the myth that comes with it—that we, too, can overcome the liabilities of our own anatomy. In recent years the pursuit of invincibility in the workplace has become a competitive arena all its own. Warrior-workers vie for bragging rights on sick leave not taken, overtime hours worked, bags under the eyes, and any and all wounds sustained in the line of fire. These are the Purple Hearts of achievers, we are led to believe, through tales of round-the-clock entrepreneurial heroes and the twisted beliefs spawned by downsizing. With more work being done by fewer people, all trying to outwork the next guy in a futile bid to impress the boss, a kind of bravado arms race has set in, with the macho bar being set higher and higher.

The pressure's on to cave to an Office Commandment that makes you work when you're sick, feel guilty if you take care of yourself, and overcompete to prove your toughness: *Thou shalt not be a work wimp and take your sick leave or personal days.* However, you can learn to counter the bravado pose, along with its health hazards and life squelching, once you find out what's behind the phobias that drive macho work behavior. The reality is you don't have to work yourself sick to prove your toughness. When you see how competitive manipulation and territoriality keep you controlled by others, you can leave the ironman act behind and replace it with the human alternative: balance.

The Illusion of Invincibility

Seattle private investigator Tom Lewiston could feel it coming. His workaholic buddy Richard, who once worked a year and a half straight without a day off, already had had a heart attack and a case of pneumonia to show for his exploits. Now his friend was back on the job at Boeing, overdoing it again with a schedule that could put down a Clydesdale—up at 2:00 A.M., out the door by 3:15, at work by 5:00. He worked until 4 P.M., went home, ate, and went to bed. So Lewiston wasn't surprised when his friend came down with yet another bout of pneumonia. "I told him, 'Your resistance is down, your body's tired,'" Lewiston says. "'It's telling you there's something wrong. You need some rest.' They wound up hauling him out of there in an ambulance. He was one of nine people in a few days span who were taken out by ambulance, several of them with heart attacks."

Richard was lucky. He survived. When Muppets creator Jim Henson contracted streptococcus pneumonia, he also ignored his body and tried to work through it. The famed puppeteer could certainly afford to take a day off, and as the boss, had no one but himself to say No to. But the intensely driven Henson kept up his grueling schedule. By the time he was admitted to the hospital, it was too late. He was dead at the age of 55.

What causes otherwise sane people to work so relentlessly that it borders on a death wish? Ambition, money, workaholism, and fear all play a role, but the ultimate engine is the macho ethic that rules American work culture. It's an attitude taken to its worst extremes by men, but you don't need a jock strap to play this game. There are plenty of women caught up in the self-flagellation, better known as superwomen. In a 24-7 marketplace there's a premium on presenting yourself as equally unstoppable, impervious to mortal frailty. The bravado culture is marked by idiotic martyr displays, chest-thumping bluster, and denial of physical reality. But that reality, particularly in the form of arteries, can't be denied for long. Bryant Stamford, a health reporter for the *Louisville Courier-Journal,* called the pose "Macho Ostrich Syndrome" in one of his columns, citing it as the true source of heart disease, an epidemic that would be largely preventable if not for all those heads in the sand.

The metaphor captures the denial of both employees and employers in a world where everyone complains about health-care costs. Only 56 percent of companies in a recent Hewitt Associates survey offered sick leave, while employees at those companies used an average of only four sick days a year. Typical sick leave benefits range from twelve days a year for federal employees, to ten days in private industry. Few parents, particularly fathers, use the benefits of the Family Medical Leave Act (FMLA), which guarantees workers twelve weeks' unpaid leave for the birth of a child, caring for sick relatives, or for a personal illness. If management signaled that it was okay to get healthy and employees could get past their bionic delusions, perhaps American business wouldn't be looking at double-digit increases in health-care expenses for the next five years.

The heads are buried, of course, because the macho routine is only a front. Behind it is something quite unstudly: low self-esteem. Continual need to prove your toughness—which is equated to worth in the competitive arena—comes from an internal belief that you aren't tough at all where it counts: in the esteem department. A critical part of our psychological moorings, esteem is not the product of artificial confidence boosting or positive pep talks. It's a complex intersection of experience that makes us feel we are competent to cope with life's challenges and worthy of happiness. Most experts agree that it's the foundation of motivation and psychological development. Dr. Nathaniel Branden, a pioneer in the field and author of *The Psychology of Self-Esteem*, has called it the single most decisive value judgment you can make. It's what you really think of yourself, and that self-estimate determines all your other decisions.

The crucial thing about self-esteem is that it can't be shaken by external events. It's not beholden to outside approval—the mother's milk of overwork and the macho sweepstakes. When you have a healthy sense of self-esteem, your belief in your own worth remains resilient no matter what setbacks or pressures may rock your world. However, when your esteem depends on what you produced today, your image is going to hang on the daily output, which can make you work sick and champion extreme work displays. People who get caught up in this mentality tend to "believe that the sole criterion of virtue is productive performance, that nothing else matters, that no other sphere has moral significance," points out Branden. They fill up their lives with work "in order to evade feelings of shame and guilt stemming from other areas . . . so that productive work becomes, not a healthy passion, but a neurotic escape, a refuge from reality."

Self-esteem is so critical to a positive view of ourselves that when we don't have it, or have enough of it, we have to invent it. We concoct what's known as a pseudo-self-esteem. Unlike true self-esteem, which is felt and validated internally, the pseudo-esteem comes from external approval, from things that provide us with a ready stream of praise—

such as financial success or workhorse behavior. By focusing worth on an area of positive feedback we can disguise the lack of esteem felt either consciously or unconsciously. On the work front, this triggers bravado behavior to attract approval to pad the pseudo-esteem. You wind up letting your self-image be dictated by everyone but the only person who can create it: you. So it shouldn't be surprising that one of the hallmarks of the poor self-esteem that fuels bravado conduct is that it erodes the ability to feel satisfied. You don't really believe it, because external approval isn't felt internally. It's a patch of pseudo-esteem, which makes you need to work more to get more approval.

Working through serious illness or pulling seventy-hour weeks you don't have to is not rational behavior. It's motivated by fear. Fear that you might not be anybody special if you only worked forty hours. Fear that a rival might eclipse you while you're recovering from a bug. Fear of not getting your daily dose of approval. In other words, insecurity, the bottom line that drives even the most macho among us to put their bodies on the line to relieve insecurity. Former pro-football player Dave Meggyesy, quoted in Alfie Kohn's study of competition, *No Contest,* conceded that, "Although I played time and again with injuries, and told myself I was doing this because it was in the best tradition of the game, it was really to get approval of the coaches . . . The more approval they gave me, the more fanatical I played."

While it's fabulous to win an Academy Award, the Super Bowl, or a Pulitzer Prize, and bask in the recognition of your efforts, the essential drive behind it is approval. "To be number one is, above all, to be noticed," writes Kohn. "To be noticed is to be someone; to be someone soothes a trembling self-esteem."

It's the same in the workplace, where bravado masks a fear that you're not worth much. As psychologist and author Rollo May explained it, "When one acts to gain someone else's praise, the act itself is a living reminder of the feeling of weakness and worthlessness. . . . The person who feels weak becomes a bully, the inferior person a braggart; a flexing of muscles, much talk, cockiness, an endeavor to brazen it out, are the symptoms of covert anxiety in a person or group."

Because feelings of weakness and worthlessness are intolerable to the human psyche, we're driven to deny them by engaging in the opposite behavior, jacking up the pseudo-esteem by working sick and racking up extreme hours. Health is no object. Personal life is no object. Family is no object. We delude ourselves that we are warriors, that our bionic efforts put us on the offensive to achievement, but it's all just a defensive maneuver. We are supermen and superwomen only in the fantasyland of our pseudo-identity.

"It's a myth, misinformation," declares Dr. Lillian Glass, author of *Toxic People.* For many women, the invincible crusade also involves being a supermom. "We've been sold a bill of goods, because this is just ridiculous," says Glass. "You cannot be a stay-at-home, full-time mom and be a superstar executive. Something has to be balanced out."

But balance doesn't generate the approval that flying around in capes can. No one comes up to you and says, "Hey, way to balance!" (unless you're at the tire store). Or "You really did a great job making time for your kids last night!" You will get praise, though, for leaping tall stacks of memos in a single bound, or for toughing out a bout of Kryptonite flu. If being the superhero of the office is where you get the approval needed to feel good about yourself, you're going to remain a captive of the bravado contest, leaving it to others to define you. It's a role that can require more and more extreme feats to win applause. The pseudo-esteem can never get enough strokes, because it's a fragile construct that is easily threatened. We fear being a wimp because at some level we have the belief that we *are* a wimp, and any little insinuation jabs that wound. Workplace heroics attempt to paper over the guilt for a core insecurity.

Yet all the effort to convey strength succeeds only in creating weakness. The body runs down, as does the spirit. If you go back to the office too soon after an illness or injury, you risk prolonging the ailment. Push the limits, and you can wind up with post-viral syndrome, a lengthy bout of fatigue and/or depression, or, as we have seen in the case of Jim Henson, much worse scenarios. Antibiotics may be able to knock out the germ that causes the bug, but your body needs time to heal from the ordeal. A case of tonsillitis and swollen glands can require three weeks to completely cure. Come back earlier than that, and you could have a serious recurrence of the problem. It doesn't make any sense for the company to have you around in your contagious or weakened state, either, as the bug can get passed around to others.

You can save yourself a lot of abuse when you stop running from the bogeyman of appearing weak. The next time you feel the dreaded specter of wimpdom, try substituting another word for weakness: "human." Vulnerability is not a character flaw or a disease, it's your lot. Accept this reality, and you can start to work from a place of strength—the inner recognition that worth is self-generated. That creates a real confidence that others can feel, and they'll be less likely to question sick days or pile the work on you.

Fear of looking weak doesn't just make your workweeks longer, it also makes them more cautious. When you're worried about keeping up a front, it makes you reluctant to take the risks you need to grow, which is what you have to do to maintain strong self-esteem, which is not a static affair. It must constantly evolve and expand to maintain its strength or it sags. People with a strong esteem base have "an eagerness for the new and the challenging," according to Branden. "A fondness for the familiar, the routine, and a fear of the new is a virtually unmistakable indication of a self-esteem deficiency."

Real supermen and women aren't afraid to fly.

Courage Is Your Path

The macho masquerade obscures the fact that courage comes not from going along with an admired mania but from a conviction to follow your own path in the face of fear. Webster's tells us that "courage" is the "mental or moral strength to venture, persevere, and withstand fear, danger or difficulty." You'll note the definition does not include bench-press requirements. Bravery is in the mind and will, not in the false heroics of bravado. It's in the fortitude you display to yourself and family to find a path to balance when others around you are in death-wish formation. It's in the recognition that the real wimp on the block is the one who caves to no-life work schedules that wreck personal health, marriages, and childhoods. And it's in the realization that the esteemed virtue of being able to take it like a yak is a fraud.

There's also something else about courage. It contains a vision that lets you see beyond the fear to the benefit on the other side. As Rollo May put it, "Courage is the capacity to meet the anxiety which arises as one achieves freedom."

BRAVADO DETOX

If you've got tendencies in this direction, or know someone who does, the way out begins with a downgrade of external approval and a recognition that getting the job well done and not overdone is enough. It will require a reframing of identity away from the exclusively work and material definition to a broader base of attributes, activities, and experiences. Here are a few guidelines to help you change the martyr mind-set.

- **Ignore Office Quacks.** Instead of being manipulated by a generalized fear of taking a day off for your health, break that anxiety down. What is the real issue? What others will think? Dismiss co-worker and boss diagnoses. Your health doesn't need to be ratified by anyone other than a real doctor.

- **Don't Add Relapse to Injury.** There's nothing to be proud of when you work sick. You run the risk of making the ailment worse and possibly spreading it around to others. Get in the habit of seeing behavior like this for what it is, unhealthy. And wimpy if you're doing it to avoid being seen as a wimp.

- **Don't Support Martyrs.** When people tell you how sick they are, inform them they should have stayed home and that they're jeopardizing the work and health of the team. When martyrs brag about the hours they worked over the weekend, ask why they couldn't have done it on Monday. Refuse to let anyone get away with celebrating self-destruction.

- **See Sick Days as Opportunities.** Instead of viewing colds, flus, or other maladies as impertinent interruptions, see them as opportunities to recover strength needed for a long year of work. View them, too, as reminders of the incapacity that can come if you don't take care of yourself.

- **Take a Mental-Health Day.** Many companies today have mental-health days, reflecting the brain strain wreaked by modern jobs. Yet more than a few of you don't take brain breaks, because of the fear of being a head case. It's not 1957 anymore. You need any break you and your migraines can get in the land of the world's shortest vacations. If your company doesn't have this policy, see if you can get one started.

- **Use Your Head.** Use brains, not brawn, to guide your work habits.

- **Don't Be a Hero.** No matter how much of an action hero that pop culture may lead you to believe you are by being so indestructible, the reality is you're in a job, not a multiplex blockbuster. Denial of this fact will get you more than a few days off and may close your act down permanently. There are no Purple Hearts. Until you get to the operating table.

Overcompete and You Self-Defeat

It is colorless, odorless, and scientists have yet to detect it in the atmosphere, but you and I know it's in every molecule we breathe: competition. From the time we're barely out of teething every cell in our bodies is caught up in the race to beat others and avoid having them beat us. Popularity and approval, we learn, come with gold stars, the best handwriting, or the top performance on the kickball court. It's not long before the daily scorecard is emblazoned within—tracking our place in the standings—who we beat, who we lost to, how much praise we got today, how much criticism, if we are ahead, if we are behind, if we are a winner, or if we are a hopeless loser. And the final score is: your self-image.

With so much at stake, the frenzy to win and the terror of losing can easily overwhelm rational thought, particularly for the driven, Type A personality. Winning really is everything for these relentlessly over-competitive people. The entirety of self-image can be on the line over something as meaningless as a game of racquetball. But how can you be too competitive? That's like a heavy metal band playing too loud, or a Formula One racer going too fast. Clearly we all like to win—in business, love, sports, or Scrabble—and prefer it to the alternative. It's like so much of what we've been discussing in these pages. Overdo it, and you lose it—your health, your hearing, your control of the wheel. Just as you can drown in a lake from water that's harmless in a glass, excessive competing can deep-six you in an ocean of needless work and paranoia.

For those who can't shut off the competitive drive, the idea of stopping, for illness, vacation, or relaxation is fraught with guilt and terror. You'd appear weak by being so feeble as to let yourself be struck down. What if a rival got a leg up on you while you were gone? Maybe the boss will find out he or she could get along without you. In the frantic mind of the overcompetitor irrational fears seem perfectly logical. They're products of the defensive mind, a bunker state that saddles you with anxiety and paranoia and causes you to drive your body like a crash-test dummy to feel like a worthy member of the human race. You can never let up, because everyone is a potential rival, a threat to your self-worth if you don't beat them before they beat you. Obsessive competing keeps you in a perpetual state of siege, always looking over your shoulder for danger, always working more than you have to to protect your place in the standings. Your life ceases to be anything defined on your own terms. It's all based on comparisons, how you're doing in relation to others, what that causes others to think about you, where you think other people expect you to be.

But, even success brings no relief, because the social-comparison process "imposes a naturally escalating standard of acceptability on achievement," writes psychologist Steven Berglas in *Reclaiming the Fire*. To maintain self-worth derived from winning, you have to keep comparing yourself to those above you, and with wealth being the primary gauge of success in American society, someone else is always going to have more. Winning by stockpiling the spoils of success doesn't do much for esteem anyway. Basing your worth on material possessions "leads to extraordinarily fragile self-worth," social psychologist William B. Swann, Jr. points out in *Self-Traps*.

No amount of competition, comparatives, or vanquishing of rivals can boost your core esteem or make you fulfilled. Outpointing others can make you feel good temporarily, but the euphoria is short-lived. The thrill of victory doesn't last long because you can no more hold on to it than to a sublime Hawaiian sunset or a concert you wished could go on all night. It's here and then gone, because life is movement, a ceaseless parade of moments that can only be experienced at a single place in time. You can't bottle your victory and pull it out tomorrow for an encore.

Winning is very ephemeral, yet we are led to believe that it is a lasting place that we must continually attain to feel good about ourselves. The problem is that esteem doesn't come from any one event or goal. It comes from all spheres of life in an ongoing process of challenges and satisfactions. A preoccupation with being number one is a sure setup for *not* being number one most of the time (P.S.: the vacancies are limited) and for the post-victory blahs. Because what comes up must come down. Even Neil Armstrong had to load up the dishwasher when he got back from the moon.

I hope you're sitting down for this next clause, because it turns out winning and succeeding are not the same thing. This heresy brings us to yet another installment of the Ass-Backwards Principle, where what we thought was gospel is turned on its head by the research. Proving your superiority over somebody else does not prove competency. Which is why it can't do the thing we're convinced that it does exclusively: bolster self-esteem. "Instead of contributing to our self-esteem, beating people contributes only to the need to continue trying to beat other people," writes Alfie Kohn in *No Contest*. "The more we compete, the more we need to compete."

Kohn cites voluminous studies to back up his claim that competition isn't the only way to achieve goals and is less effective than more intrinsically motivated approaches such as cooperation and independent effort. A report on 122 studies that measured the impact of competitive versus non-competitive approaches on performance found the vast majority gave the nod to cooperation over competition. Some sixty-five studies determined that cooperation fosters higher achievement, while only eight found competition more effective (thirty-six showed no statistical difference). "Superior performance not only does not require competition; it usually seems to require its absence," Kohn states. "Competition need never enter the picture in order for skills to be mastered and displayed, goals set and met."

This is not to say that competition is without its rewards. There's the thrill of victory, financial gain, and all that attention. But you can be an expert rock climber, engineer, or guitarist without having to constantly beat someone else to do it. Contrary to the apparent law of the land, intrinsic motivation—wanting to master, grow, learn, and pursue accomplishment for its own sake—beats outside motivation—grades, raises, status—as a promoter of excellence. The critical difference, according to Kohn, is that we *choose* to be good at things we enjoy; defeating others is something we *have* to do to keep egos from being deflated. Quality or excellence isn't the objective, winning is. Competitive pressures force talented people out of the game, award contracts to the lowest bidder, not the best, produce TV programming geared to the lowest common denominator, and sap productive energies in pointless scheming and jockeying that places the ego of the individual over the collective goal of the company. The point I'm making is not that competition should be junked. It's clearly the way of the economic world. But you can't let the competitive yardstick dictate your worth, because it's not capable of it, just as a business card can't reveal your real ID. In fact, when you're forever having to work sick and rack up insane hours to prove you're better than anyone else, you aren't a winner at all. Because you've lost yourself in the chase for others' approval.

A more healthy approach to competition is to get the focus off beating everybody and onto the specific areas of excellence that others bring to the table. It's an approach that frees you from the self-defeating stance of me-against-the-world and lets you do what your esteem need demands—advance your abilities. What does a colleague or rival do well that you could role model? Not so you can top them, but so you can be as good as you can be.

Ultimately overcompeting is about giving up control of your life to others, which is why it can never do what we're led to believe it's supposed to—put you in charge. As Wayne Dyer put it: "If you can't be happy without someone else out there whom you must defeat, then you are being controlled by that person, which makes you the ultimate loser, since people who are controlled by others are psychological slaves."

Control Your Basic Instinct

There's another thing that makes us afraid to take sick days or vacations. It goes deeper still, to a behavior as old as humans and beyond that—protecting your turf. It makes you stew about other people getting into your business while you're home ailing. It makes you reluctant to take vacations or cross-train colleagues who could help you out while you're on holiday for fear of encroachment. It makes you roost at your desk like an oriole baby-sitting a perpetual brood of eggs. We are territorial creatures, no different in that department than gibbons or schnauzers, and that fact makes for a double commandment against your absence from the workplace—the Office and the biological.

Robert Ardrey described our urge for guard duty in *The Territorial Imperative:* "The territorial nature of man is genetic and ineradicable. The dog barking at you from behind his master's fence acts from a motivation indistinguishable from that of his master when the fence was built."

This powerful but little-considered influence on our modern lives dates back to the days before humans were capable of rational thought and had to be guided by their genetic programming to find meals and produce offspring. Like other remaining innate drives, such as the survival instinct and the sex drive, the directive to establish and hold territory is an automatic behavior designed to perpetuate the species. Staking out and defending territory ensures food sources and a safe environment for the family, tribe, or nation. Today social controls keep us from staking our claim to whatever showroom vehicle or parcel of land we fancy, but territoriality still has a fierce hold on the ancient limbic section of our brains. You can feel it in the surge of adrenaline when a car cuts in front of you, setting off a road rage that seems to come from nowhere, making you want to vaporize the transgressor. Or in a host of other invasions of your space—queue jumping, telemarketing, cars parked too close to yours, people who want to work on the machine you're defending at the gym, and, of course, interlopers in your work domain.

As the main provider of sustenance, the job easily fills the territorial bill. The instinct is to guard that cubicle and its domain to perpetuate yourself and your family. When threats appear—a new supervisor, downsizing, nosy colleagues—you react the way the species always has, by digging in and flashing jugular veins. Territoriality is essentially a defensive device to protect what you have won. While it's smart to have this radar up in a realm where moving up can mean onto or over someone else's turf, this prehistoric drive can also get the best of you. That's what happens when you feel you can't miss a day at the office for illness or vacation.

Excess territoriality is often masked by the belief that no one can do the job as well as you, or that you have to be there to keep everything running smoothly. But underneath is the telltale grip of the limbic brain. Once you recognize that, you can fight back with the weapon that keeps you from acting out other harmful impulses: reason. Catch yourself in the territorial act. Is someone really going to plant their flag on your chair while you're out sick? Is your job really in jeopardy if you take the vacation that's already on the company's books? Is the office really going to fall apart if you're out sick? Remind yourself what's at work here, a dinosaur urge that is depriving you of your health and life.

You are not a Doberman pinscher and your desk isn't Fort Knox. Let go of reflexive territoriality, and you'll find that both you and the company can survive perfectly well without this bit of undue diligence.

Nonstop guarding of turf robs you of focus and energy, of the resources when you really need them. Like the rest of bravado behavior, it drains you—for nothing. Whether you overwork to keep what you've got away from others, to stay ahead of others, or for the approval of others, by coming into the office sick or not taking your vacation, you are saying you don't count. That isn't doing much for your esteem or your ultimate life satisfaction. Don't get painted into a corner of self-destruction. End the comparisons and the need for others' validations and you realize you don't have to overdo it anymore. Because the real audience is you.

9

Lay Down the Law

Know Your Work Rights

• • •

"I think they cheat for a couple reasons. The first is that everybody's doing it. The other reason is that there's very little incentive to comply. They save money by not complying with the law."

—Matt Righetti, labor attorney

(on why companies create phony salary positions)

"No matter how many hours I would be there, I could never get finished," recalls Jill Hess, of her days as area manager for discount retailer Mervyn's in Irvine, California. In a tale of the times, the single mother of two was stretched as far as even her iron will could go, by an employer who would go to any length to wring extra work for nothing from her. Mervyn's had been on a downsizing kick, and the slack would be picked up by salaried people like Hess, who could be—and would be—worked unlimited hours because salary status made them exempt from overtime pay.

When she was hired, Hess was told that her job would be forty hours a week, but it turned out to be an onslaught of twelve-hour days, six days a week. She worked as many as twenty-four days in a row. Hess would sometimes have to come in at two in the morning to get merchandise onto the floor. "I'd work an overnighter, then the store would open, and I wouldn't have enough people to run the store, so I'd be running all over the floor ringing up each department. Lunch was nonexistent. Then freight would come in, and I'd have to unload the truck. When I would have a day off, they'd call me at home and want me to come in."

It would get worse, much worse for Hess, who found herself in the middle of a Kafkaesque drama shared by tens of thousands of other American workers, asked, no, commanded to do the work that used to take several people to do, then ripped into because they can't get it all done. "My whole body hurt. I'd have migraine headaches, back spasms," she recalls. But it wasn't physically possible, even with fourteen-hour days and six-day weeks, for Hess to complete the incompletable.

She was beginning to think she was crazy, because she couldn't do everything asked of her, no matter how long she worked. Hess was about to realize, though, where the real insanity was, as she became the central character in a potboiler straight out of *Erin Brockovich*. Mervyn's had misclassified her and thousands of other workers to be able to work them hours on end for free. She wasn't salaried at all, and legally had a right to six years of overtime pay. The company was also forcing hourly employees to come back to work after their eight hours and work off-the-clock for free. All to make up for slash-and-burn cutbacks that had pared staff to the bone. As you will see shortly, Hess made a fateful decision that would change her life. She decided not to take it anymore. Soon she would find herself tailed by shadowy characters, ostracized at work, and getting a crash course in employee rights.

The corporate race to the bottom touched off by the downsizing frenzy and executive greed sweepstakes has made labor but an afterthought in the frenzy to meet or beat next quarter's estimates. Many of you are being asked to do the jobs of several people and are being held accountable for what can't be done by one. The risks to your health and sanity are very real in this never-enough climate, so it's more important than ever to know where you stand legally. Contrary to a widely held commandment—*Thou shalt not have any legal rights as an employee*—you do have workplace rights, and have redress when they're abused. Find out what they are in this chapter. For instance, How many hours can you be forced to work? What makes someone salaried and exempted from overtime pay? How rampant is the practice of misclassification? Very. There could be hundreds of thousands of you who are owed overtime pay for salaried jobs that aren't salaried. What's the law on vacations? How does the FMLA (Family Medical Leave Act) work? You'll also get the scoop on the foundation of employment law, the Fair Labor Standards Act, passed over sixty years ago and definitely in need of an update. It's where your alleged forty-hour week came from.

Let's power up with a little spin through the fine print of your working life.

Workplace Rights

One law towers above all the rest. It's the Fair Labor Standards Act (FLSA), passed in 1938, which set the forty-hour week and established the minimum wage. The law was designed originally to get more people working in the Depression years, and to protect against the abuses of the day—low wages, hiring children, and working people long hours without premium overtime pay. The FLSA established the two-tier system of the workplace that continues today. Hourly employees are eligible for overtime pay—time and a half after forty hours in a week, double-time after twelve hours in a day—while salaried employees have no limits on hours and are "exempt" from overtime pay. This is the law that determines most of your workweek. It has several gaping deficiencies, including the lack of any paid-leave provision, as is provided in other industrialized nations. We'll take a closer look at it in a minute.

Considering how much time is spent on the job, most people know next to nothing about their legal rights, and most employers don't know much more than that. A lot of confusion arises from this void. Let's take a look at some of the bigger misconceptions of workplace law:

- You're salaried if you are paid by the month. Wrong. You must also have management and/or administrative responsibilities or be a "professional"—doctor, lawyer—and meet a certain income standard.

- **You're salaried if you're a nonclerical worker.** No again. You have to qualify on management and salary grounds.

- **You are entitled to severance pay.** There is no law guaranteeing a payout after a termination, but it's smart to ask for one.

- **Your vacation benefits can be reduced.** It's against the law to change paid leave after the fact.

- **You can't be fired without cause.** You can be, unless you have a "just cause" provision in your contract. But even without it, the reason must be a legal one. You are still covered under the anti-discrimination, whistle-blower, and other federal statutes. Employers also can't fire you for engaging in protected activities, including jury duty, using your medical or family leave rights, or refusing to do something that's illegal.

- **You have no right to a vacation.** Under current federal law, this is stupefyingly true. But an employer has to give you any vacation that is specified by a policy, either verbally or by a policy handbook. If you have a "use it or lose it" policy, you have to take the vacation by the end of the year or you forfeit it. But an employer can't black out the whole year as "too busy" for you to take a holiday.

- **You are entitled to ask for more vacation time.** This is true if your company has a vacation policy, or even if it doesn't, though it's probably wasted breath in the latter case.

- **You can't be harassed on the job.** Unless it's a case of discrimination, by sex, race, disability or other protected category, your boss can be a complete tyrant, a bully. There are laws against this in Europe. The National Employee Rights Institute (NERI) in Cincinnati, Ohio, is currently trying to develop an anti-bullying law in the United States to make abusive behavior in the workplace illegal.

- You have to be given three warnings before being terminated. You don't have to be given warnings, though a case is harder to prove if there isn't a trail.

The best way to take advantage of your rights in the workplace is to know what they are. Familiarize yourself with your company's policy handbook, do research on workplace law on the Internet or at the library, check with state agencies, or pick up books on employee rights at your local bookstore. You have to do your homework before you rush off with any accusations. Here are a few tips on things you should and shouldn't do to protect your job as well as your rights:

1. Try to get an employment contract when you're hired, spelling out duties and what the expected workweek will be. If you know up-front that it's going to be 60 hours, you can decide whether you want the job or not, or whether you want to negotiate.

2. Don't put your foot in your mouth. You don't want to complain about something that turns out not to be illegal. Research it first.

3. Think first, then act. "You have to think of the consequences of your actions," says Don Sessions, an employee-rights attorney in Mission Viejo, California. "Sometimes someone will get a negative review and they make a federal case out of it. Is it worth it?"

4. Get expert advice. Seek out legal advice from people who know the arcane details of employment law—an attorney specializing in employee rights.

If you think your workplace rights might have been violated, you can find information at no charge from the Department of Fair Employment and Housing, the local office of the Department of Labor or its Web site (www.dol.gov). If you're a union member, try the National Labor Relations Board. All employees can find legal help through the National Employment Lawyer's Association, which has 3,000 members, and the nonprofit workers rights group affiliated with it, NERI (www.nerinet.org), whose Web site offers advice and discussion groups.

Vacation Protection

There is no paid leave statute in the United States, as there is in all of Europe, Australia, Japan, and Canada. Your company can give you zero time off if it wants, and there are some that do exactly that. Your vacation time will be determined by the policy of the firm you work for, or one that you negotiate with them. Whatever that policy is—typically a week to two weeks after the first year—you are entitled by law to take it.

"If it's in the policy, they can't take it away," asserts Rene Barge, an employment-law attorney in Fountain Valley, California. "What is legal is to put caps on the amount of vacation that may be accrued. If I work for a year, and I've accrued two weeks of vacation, under a use-it-or-lose-it policy, I would lose my two weeks if I don't take it before January 1. I'd get two new weeks to use, but the other time that had accrued would be gone."

You also have to have the opportunity to take the time allowed under your policy. Some companies will black out large chunks of time that are off-limits for your vacation. If you repeatedly have your vacation requests turned down to the point where you can't get the time off, that is the same as yanking away the benefit you are entitled to. "If it's arbitrary, and you already have your reservation to some place, and then they jerk you around and say, 'You can't go,' that's wrong," declares attorney Sessions. "If people have a right to take the vacation and they're not able to and complain about it, and they're retaliated against, the employer is risking a suit on retaliation."

Be sure to check your company manual or any contract you have to determine the details of your vacation policy. If you have negotiated a vacation with your employer that goes beyond the policy, get it in writing.

The Family Medical Leave Act

This relatively recent law, passed in 1993, is the leading work-life balance law on the books, but it has operated well under the radar for most workers. Few take advantage of its benefits. The FMLA is designed to let employees tend to family and health responsibilities in times of need. It provides up to twelve weeks of unpaid leave in any twelve-month period for the birth, adoption, or foster care of a child; for the care of an immediate family member; or for your own health needs.

The law allows for both parents to spend some time at home with a newborn, though few fathers so far have taken advantage of the opportunity. If you have a serious health problem, and you can't work though it, the FMLA offers the chance to recover. You have to provide medical documentation if your employer wants it, as well as periodic health reports on your condition. In all cases, employers must maintain health benefits for workers who use the FMLA, and all employees must get their jobs back on their return to the office. The FMLA applies to any company with fifty or more employees and all public agencies regardless of size.

The Salary Sweatshop

The ultimate staff for corporate management these days would be an all-android team. They could be run seven days a week, be called in at any time of the day or night, and flown across the country on sales trips for weeks on end. Except the 'droids are already here. They're called salaried employees. These working machines have become the answer to downsized companies' dreams, providing two people, and more, for the price of one.

Unlike hourly workers, salaried employees are exempted by the FLSA from overtime pay. They can be worked an unlimited amount of hours, something business has eagerly capitalized on in the service economy. Out-of-date regulations and widespread abuse of the salary exemption have ballooned the ranks of these white-collar workers, who now make up a third of all U.S. workers.

The salary has always been a trade-off of more duty for more money and responsibility, and most achievers gladly take it on for the chance to advance. But the extra time required has gotten so extreme that the cost in net dollars for time put in and in lost time for family and personal life are making some people think twice about promotion. One woman told me she considered all the years and money she spent on her education to be a fraud, because it led to a 24-7 salary gig where she wasn't making much more than the hourly workers at her company, once all her unpaid overtime was factored in—and they got to leave at 5 PM.

"I can't tell you how many important sounding supervisors are working sixty-hour weeks," notes attorney Sessions, who has seen people time and again caught in the salary trap. "If they just figure out how many hours they're working a week and divide it by their salary, they can figure out their hourly wage. Seven times out of ten they're making less than the people they're supervising, who are entitled to overtime compensation."

How do you know if you are a bona fide salaryperson? This is one of the biggest questions in employment law, and certainly the one with the most potential impact on your quality of life and paycheck. The common assumption is that you are salaried if you are paid on a salary basis, a set amount each month, instead of hourly. But that's just one of several tests that must be met. The Fair Labor Standards Act requires that, to be "exempt" from overtime pay, or salaried, you have to make a benchmark wage. The salary test was originally created to protect lower-income workers from the nonpaying overtime demands of a salary. But the base level of the test hasn't been adjusted for inflation since 1975. The current minimum, a wage between $155 and $250 a week, has made this provision meaningless, making 99 percent of workers today eligible for exemption on the income test.

The second test for a salaried worker is the exemption for managers, administrators, or "professionals." It requires that you be paid a base salary level that indicates managerial or professional status. Levels are set for each category of those workers—executive, administrative, or professional. Certain professionals with advanced education—doctors, lawyers and beginning recently, some computer technicians—are also automatically exempt. Finally, you must perform the duties and responsibilities of a manager or administrator, such as independent judgment and discretion, called the administrative exemption. State laws can be more specific than the federal law. In California, whose law has the toughest language, you have to manage at least two people and spend at least 50 percent of your time on management duties to be salaried.

The salary exemption is the most misunderstood rule in the workplace. With so many believing that all you need is a nonhourly wage and a college degree, phony salaries have multiplied. The Economic Policy Institute's Labor Economist Jeff Wenger, who has studied the problem, thinks that the number of workers falsely tagged as salaried "is not in the tens of thousands. I think it's perhaps in the hundreds of thousands."

Most of the pseudosalaries come from violations of the management and administrative discretion tests. The administrative exemption applies to "a high-ranking person who supports the infrastructure of the organization but is not actually delivering the product or the service," explains Seattle labor attorney Steve Winterbauer. "The classic example is the director of human resources. That person is exercising discretion, judgment, and policy-making on the administrative side of the equation. Some employers figure, 'Well, administrative means my entire administrative staff.' Then a lot of folks who are in clerical positions are paid a salary in the mistaken belief that they are exempt when they're not. They're entitled to overtime."

Clerical and white-collar workers are routinely misclassified in this way. But the biggest offender on the salary issue is the phony management exemption. There are droves of workers in the service economy who are called supervisors and managers but who are doing little of each, working the cash register and flipping burgers just like the people they're supervising. This is rampant in the retail world, where companies have discovered that they can cut staff and make it up on the backs of salaried managers, because they don't have to pay them overtime. But managers have to be managing to meet the test. Many are not.

The misclassification uprising in California since 1996 offers a glimpse of the stunning dimensions of the problem nationwide, as well as a lesson in the importance of understanding your workplace rights. Each state can have its own interpretation of the FLSA. California's law has the toughest language, because it quantifies management duties, which are left vague in the FLSA. The Golden State requires you to manage at least two people and spend at least 50 percent of your time on management duties to be salaried. Sounds reasonable. But not for retail chain after retail chain, found to be blatantly violating the management rule.

Through the first six months of 2001 workers won misclassification settlements from Rite Aid Corp. ($25 million), Taco Bell ($13 million), and U-Haul ($7.5 million). Farmers Insurance Group came out on the losing end of a landmark $90 million judgment. Farmers had claimed an administrative exemption for its adjusters, but the court didn't buy that, ruling that the adjusters, some of whom were working more than twelve hours a day plus Saturday, for only $30,000 a year, exercised no executive discretion and were, in effect, performing clerical duties. The verdict was the first big class-action victory for administrative workers and was a sonic boom heard by employers across the nation. Other companies who settled out of court in misclassification suits include Starbuck's Coffee ($18 million for current and former managers and assistant managers), Bank of America ($22 million for 6,000 personal assistants), and Pacific Bell ($35 million to engineers).

Employees on their own had little chance of taking a large national company to court for overtime pay lost to misclassification, but the dynamic changed when labor-attorney Matt Righetti helped pioneer the use of class-action suits to pool the damages of hundreds and thousands of misclassified employees together in one case. Righetti, who has won suits for workers against Rite-Aid and U-Haul, confirms that the reason there are so many phony salaried managers these days is due to downsizing. "The amount of hours that the company can schedule hourly people is inflexible [because they would have to be paid overtime], but the amount of hours they can work salaried people is completely flexible. There's no limit. The hourly work has to get done, and they can't hire enough hourly people to do it and stay within their labor budget. If the manager doesn't stay within the labor budget, that manager gets fired. So they wind up doing all the work themselves."

There are class-action suits filed under the federal FLSA, but they are harder to win than in California, because the test of management duties is broadly defined as "primary duty," rather than as a percentage of time spent managing. Righetti thinks "it's a crime that the rest of the nation ignores reality. What's wrong with making the job description match with what's going on in the workplace? What is fair, what's reasonable about having a bunch of corporate attorneys and HR people sit in the back room and cook up a fallacious job description in order to fit into an FLSA exemption, when the person's flipping burgers or stocking shelves?"

If the California interpretation were extended to the rest of the country, there could well be millions of misclassified employees who should be paid overtime. Rare spot checks by the Labor Department show rampant abuse. An investigation of 136 nursing and personal-care facilites in 2000 found that some 84 percent of employers had violated FLSA overtime regulations, while 15 percent had broken child-labor provisions. The poultry processing industry was worse. Of fifty-one randomly selected facilities, a perfectly miserable 100 percent were in violation of unpaid hours of work, while 65 percent had misclassified employees.

There's a lot of rot in the system. You have to self-protect. If your position is called salaried, but it doesn't meet the test, you could be owed back pay for all the overtime you have worked. If you have any doubt, it's a good idea to keep a log of the hours you work. It's a good idea to do that anyway, even if you are definitely salaried, to get an idea of what you're putting into the job. If you are a legitimate salaried employee struggling with endless hours the bad news is that you do face unlimited hours—unless you negotiate limits (see Chapter 11, "Ask and You May Receive," for negotiating tips). You do have one interesting legal card available to you, though:

THE DOCKED-PAY PLAY

If you are told you can't be paid for your overtime work because you're salaried, but you are then docked for coming in late or for a doctor's appointment, you instantly become covered under the FLSA hourly requirements. Any time days away from the office are registered as unpaid or you're told to make up the time later, you are being treated as an hourly worker and are eligible for overtime pay.

Get Up, Stand Up

Working hard goes with the territory, but you don't have to be a whipping post. That's what happens when labor laws are not enforced and employees don't feel empowered enough to defend themselves. Jill Hess had hung in for six years, because Mervyn's management was playing the gambit that traps so many workers. The carrot of promotion was being dangled in one hand while the abuse was being heaped with the other.

"I was up for a promotion to be a store manager. Store managers make upwards of $70,000, and that's what I really needed to support my children," remembers Hess. "You're thinking, all those years of working, you're almost there. Maybe if I work a little bit harder. That's what we were being told."

But as the harassment intensified, Hess came to a depressing realization. The situation was out of control. She was spending more and more hours at work, and terrified of being let go. "I would come home late after my kids had gone to bed and leave sometimes four hours later, before they were up," she recalls.

So she gave up her long-fought dream of being a store manager and paid a visit to a lawyer. Between the interminable hours and constant badgering from supervisors, she thought she might have a case of harassment, but, instead, she learned that she had quite a different one. The attorney, Rene Barge, knew little about the exempt laws herself when Hess walked in her door that fateful day. But Barge investigated and found out that she was onto something big: Hess and all the other area managers at Mervyn's were misclassified. These purported "managers" weren't salaried workers at all, and should be paid time and a half for all their overtime.

As Barge dug into the case, she uncovered the roots of the overwork era and overstrapped workers like Hess coast to coast. "One of the main forces driving the work was cuts in labor hours, dramatic cuts," says Barge. "They were cutting labor to the bone. People were working insane hours. Dayton Hudson, the owner of Mervyn's, bragged it had cut 110 labor hours per store per month for a savings of $118 million." Management was replacing those hours with the free overtime of their misclassfied area managers, and that wasn't all. Barge found a second level of hourly paid coordinators who were working off the clock. They were pressured to clock out after eight hours, then come back and keep on working for free.

Barge filed a class-action suit against Dayton Hudson. It would turn out to be a harrowing experience for Hess, as the lead plaintiff, who compares the experience to that of the lead character in the movie *Silkwood*. "I was scared to death," recalls Hess. "I had to go to work the next day. I was up against this huge corporation." She had the consolation, though, that when the word leaked out, calls from other Mervyn's managers at the breaking point "flooded in. We were all in similar situations. There were stories of people passing kidney stones because they couldn't get a doctor's note, people falling asleep at the wheel of their car, horror stories."

One day she came out to the employee parking lot to find that the windows of her car had been smashed. After coming home late from closing the store another night, she found a carful of men watching her house. "I pulled in the driveway, and all I could see was their heads looking at me. I thought somebody was going to shoot me or kill me or beat me up, so I started honking my horn. As soon as my ex-husband ran out of the house, they took off."

She weathered a year and a half of being ostracized by other employees and of harassment by managers trying to get her to quit, but she and Barge prevailed, winning a settlement of $7.2 million. In all 1,500 people joined Hess in the exempt manager case, and there were 3,000 in the coordinator case, where Barge won $3 million for the coordinators. Some 4,500 people won back pay for their overtime, because one brave woman decided she wasn't going to be victimized any longer.

"People need to stand up," declares Hess, "or it's not going to change. You can make a difference in the lives of everybody else and for yourself. You need to be able to stand up to have a life."

Forced Overtime

It's not only salaried people who face the overtime gauntlet. Hourly workers are being driven late into the night by mandatory, or forced, overtime. It doesn't seem at first to make any sense, since overtime for hourly employees means pay at time and a half or double-time. But companies in high-skill industries have found that it's cheaper to pay hourly employees overtime than to hire more people and pay them benefits. Two industries, in particular, have been hammered by this scheme, health care, and telecommunications.

The downsizing wreaked by managed care on the health industry has pared staffs at hospitals and clinics to barely functional levels in some cases. This has ratcheted up the pressure on everyone left on staff to work harder and longer, with less help and less margin for error. We're not talking about widgets or software. There are lives on the line here, in the hands of nurses who may be at the end of a twenty-hour day. One survey revealed that nurses in acute-care hospitals are doing about two-and-a-half months of overtime each year.

"Nurses don't have time to do the proper monitoring and assessment of patients," says Jamie Cohen, of the Service Employees International union (SEIU), the largest health-care union in the U.S. "They are being asked to make a choice no nurse should ever have to make, between the financial demands of the hospital or putting their patient at harm and losing their license."

Understaffed, overstressed personnel are making mistakes, sometimes fatal ones. A report in 1999 by the Institute of Medicine found that errors in the nation's hospitals cause between 44,000 and 98,000 deaths per year. One-third of nurses say that patients on their units missed or got delayed medication because of understaffing, while 8 percent report that at least once a week patients are given the wrong medication or dosage.

"The story I hear from nurses all over the country is: 'I leave work at the end of the day and I put my head on the steering wheel, and I wonder, did I do something, because of the fast pace and being tired, where I left somebody at harm?" says Cohen, whose union represents 715,000 nurses, medical residents, and long-term care aides.

To fight forced overtime, more nurses have been unionizing— about 15 percent to 19 percent of nurses are union members. The SEIU has been able to ban mandatory overtime in some contracts, or restrict it through disincentives, such as double-time for any overtime, in others. Health-care workers and their unions have also launched legislative intiatives in a number of states and in the U.S. Congress. Draft legislation that would establish staff-to-patient ratios and limit mandatory overtime for nurses, residents, and doctors has been introduced in the U.S. Senate and House. The California state assembly passed a law prohibiting mandatory overtime beyond eight hours in a workday, while bills prohibiting or restricting mandatory overtime for nurses have been passed in Maine and Oregon.

The substitution of overtime for hiring has also been a blight in telecommunications, which you can vividly hear anytime you try to get a human on the line from your phone or cable company. Slash-and-burn cost-cutting and consolidation is again the culprit, and has set off overtime-triggered strikes at a number of companies, including Verizon and U.S. West. A 14 percent cut in staff in 1998 at Bell Atlantic, just as many new technologies were coming on line, such as cellular and Internet, forced technicians into seventy-hour weeks, fifty-two weeks a year, while customer-service representatives were working ten-hour days, five days a week.

The overtime demands set up the classic dilemma faced by parents today: Your job or your kids. Joseph Bryant, a technician at Bell Atlantic, couldn't pick up his kids from school at 6 P.M. on the nights he had to work overtime. He asked if he could be assigned a regular overtime night, so he could schedule child care, or do weekend overtime, instead. His co-workers even volunteered to work his overtime hours, and still company policy wouldn't budge. Bryant wound up having to leave his overtime assignment six times to pick up his kids, and for that he was fired. His union, the Communication Workers of America (CWA), which has been at the forefront of the forced overtime issue, took up his case and won full back pay and reinstatement. In the judgment, the arbitrator gave voice to the frustrations of millions of parents. "As Congress recognized under the Family and Medical Leave Act of 1993, an appropriate balance must be struck between workplace needs and family demands in an environment wherein both parents often are responsible for work and child-care duties."

The family-busting hours spurred workers at CWA-represented companies to demand changes in the system when contract talks came up. Employees at Bell Atlantic South can now use child-care issues as a "reasonable excuse" to decline mandatory overtime. There was a cap placed on overtime hours—no more than ten hours a week during seven months of the year and fifteen hours a week the rest of the year. A strike against Verizon by CWA in 2000 resulted in mandatory overtime limits, in some cases cutting them from fifteen hours to 7.5 per week.

The forced overtime battles in the medical and telecom fields point out the need for more organized involvement to curb the abuses of a system out of control. With only 13 percent of Americans unionized to-

day and the market imposing its overtime will, that leaves only one recourse—federal or state legislation. The Work to Live campaign believes
it's time to move forward on national protections (detailed in Chapter
15) to restore quality of life and a working environment that doesn't
borrow its game plan from the Industrial Revolution.

10

Live Now or Never

Don't Squander Your Vacation Time

• • •

"Because we don't know when we will die we get to think of life as an inexhaustible well. Yet everything happens only a certain number of times, and a very small number, really. How many more times will you remember a certain afternoon of your childhood, some afternoon that's so deeply a part of your being that you can't even conceive of your life without it? Perhaps four or five times more. Perhaps not even that. How many more times will you watch the full moon rise? Perhaps twenty. And yet it all seems so limitless."

—Paul Bowles, *A Sheltering Sky*

Kevin was the kind of employee bosses would clone if they could. His entire existence revolved around his sales job at a hard-driving seminar company. He would work weekends, go the extra 200,000 frequent-flyer miles, whatever it took. Known as a traveling machine, he racked up business trips of five and six weeks in a row for years on end, even though he had a family and kids he seldom saw. Nobody gave it much thought, including Kevin, because that was the way of the world at this company—job was life. For Kevin and his colleagues, the field of vision had narrowed from the wide planet they lived on to a tiny tunnel of focus, the company. Like a patient with advanced glaucoma, they could see only what appeared in the pinprick of that hole, which was locked on what seemed to contain all that was worthwhile under the sun: the doings of one company on one block in one city in one country on one continent. Then, while only in his forties, Kevin became seriously ill with cancer. He died a short while later.

Debra Dinnocenzo worked with Kevin. "I remember the day that I walked into the building, and we had a flag at half staff, because we were going to Kevin's funeral," recalls Dinnocenzo, co-author of *Dot Calm*. "The next day the flag was flying high again. Kevin lived and breathed his job, and died, and it didn't really matter for the organization. We never lost a client, never had a workshop not delivered, and something hit me about the inordinate commitment he had made, and the sacrifices he had made, the time he had missed with his family. It didn't really matter."

Had Kevin known it didn't matter, my bet is that he would have taken a very different course, spending more time with his family and doing things he liked to do for no other reason than that he liked to do them—five-week business trips not being among them. But like so many of us, he was convinced that it mattered, and that it mattered so much that surrendering his private life, family, and, ultimately, his health, was worth it. What was the calculation that told him that? Or that tells millions of American Dreamers like him that company allegiance at any price is worth it? That a life without life is worth it? Is it the financial equation? Moving up? Ambition? Achievement? Or is there even a calculation at all?

Few of us weigh a deal that's just assumed to be worth it. Who knows going in that it doesn't matter, that giving up everything for a future security that doesn't exist is a lopsided deal? Not many of us, primed to "make it" to the exclusion of all else. How different would our lives be if we could accept that fact now? The only equation that's usually made is that the job is number one. Everything else is a distant second. But as Kevin's family and friends discovered, there *is* a calculation to be made: that as important as the job is, there are things that are more important, things that really do matter—family, relationships, and the joy of living. And they matter now, because tomorrow is too late.

But that sentiment has yet to alter the prevailing message in the workplace, which continues to be life postponement. You can get to it later, like in the next lifetime. That comes across loud and clear in the area that more than any other defines the postponement mentality: vacations. The vacation is your one chance each year to get your life off hold, recharge and connect with what really matters, the people and passions that fuel you. It doesn't take a Vulcan to know that anyone who would pass up this all-too-brief opportunity to get in some living and avoid being a gibbering stress case would be highly illogical. Yet one in four Americans don't take the vacation time they're entitled to, many of them year after year, and both employees and employers are at fault.

Some people are hopelessly wrapped up, consumed by the illusion that all of consequence in the galaxy is the job, and they can't miss a second of it. Others are paranoid. Defensive overworking has spilled over from the late nights and weekends now to vacations. In the downsized, cutback world, employers stall, black out, cancel, and sow doubt about the wisdom of a vacation when there's so much going on, which is always. The result is that increasing numbers of you are falling prey to the postponement commandment, *Thou shalt not take your entire vacation, or any vacation when there's too much work at the office.*

If you're one of them, you'll find out ahead how to break through that illogic by extracting yourself from the work-is-everything mindset that makes you put your life on hold. Irrational fear and guilt give this commandment its power. You can take back your time by dropping these albatrosses. You'll also learn how to defeat employer-driven vacation static, such as stall tactics and intimidation, and how not to settle for less than all the time coming to you, which is like handing back part of your paycheck. You wouldn't do that, would you? I thought not. That would be dumb, like living for a time that hasn't begun. Now is the future you've been waiting for.

Skip Rehearsal

Film director Roman Polanski once said that aspiration was the best time of life. Life was more exciting, and he felt more alive, before he made it big with films such as *Chinatown, Rosemary's Baby,* and *Frantic.* His point was that the adventure is in getting there, that the road to achievement brings out the best and most vital elements in us. While that's easy for a rich, successful director to say, it's also true.

The real movie is a cinema-verité shoot happening now. We're so focused on the objective, that we see everything else as warm-up, rehearsal for the living we're going to do when we get where we think we have to to really live. We are neither there nor here, on hold in life limbo for the final cut. When we operate from this state of perpetual nonarrival, always directing our lives into the future, it becomes easy to fall into the postponement syndrome—"I'll take that trip to Europe some day when I . . . [fill in the blank—"find someone to go with," "save up the money," "get the time"} "I'll join that dance class when I lose weight;" "I'll take my vacation next year, when the work lightens up." When today is conditioned on tomorrow, the present becomes irrelevant, a way station to somewhere else, and, therefore, impossible to be here enough to enjoy.

Postponement implies you'll get to it later, but it's a self-deception, about as sincere as the busynessperson's anthem, "Let's do lunch." Because behind the postponement curtain is a familiar nemesis, fear, supported by guilt and insecurity. In the case of skipped vacations, or abbreviated ones, the anxiety can include fear of leisure (nonproductivity), fear of enjoyment, fear of co-worker static, fear of job loss, or all the above. Let's take these life killers one at a time:

- **Leisure Fear.** If you suffer from having to constantly produce to feel worthy of existence, not working brings on the terror of worthlessness. The only way out of the box is to gradually develop some leisure skills and outside interests. Treat it as a productive challenge. Your objective: enjoyment. Take a photography course, try a dive lesson, something to break the logjam and get you comfortable with the world outside.

- **Enjoyment Fear.** This ultimate absurdity of the overwork ethic is an aversion to feeling good. Enjoyment triggers guilt, because you're not being productive. You don't deserve to enjoy yourself, because you are here to work. Course of action: Lighten up. Lose the twenty-first-century Pilgrim routine. If you are being conned out of the good times of life by this fear, you are being screwed.

- **Job Fear.** The overwork bravado of some corporate cultures may leave the impression that you should skip or take only a few days of your vacation, but if there's a vacation policy on the books, either stated or in practice, you're entitled to take all of it by law. Don't forfeit your living time. Remember Kevin at the beginning of this chapter. He got one day at half-mast.

- **Co-worker Fear.** If you work with a bunch of no-lifers who snigger when you take your full vacation and make slacker cracks when you get back, you are entitled as a free adult to completely ignore these juveniles and have the time of your life with the vacation you've sweat to get. Consider the wisecrackers to be what they, in fact, are—part of a cult, the cult of the living dead.

The fears that support the rehearsal approach to life delude us into thinking we have all the time in the world. It seems that way for a while, until very quickly the mirror tells you differently, that you are the one who's up for postponement. It truly is now or never.

Turn Your To-Do List Into a To-Be List

My ticket out of productivity mania and obsessive focus on objective was a love of travel. There is almost nothing finer for me than to be somewhere I've never been before with a map in my hand and untold discovery up ahead. For a while I took my to-do list with me on vacation, as all busynesspeople do, until I realized that the juice of travel wasn't getting somewhere; it was simply BEING there, letting it all happen around me, experiencing the ride in lingering detail.

The best parts were all unplanned—bumping into a cast of colorful fellow travelers, being invited to local people's homes, winding up in amazing places that were not on my itinerary. It's the act of travel, not the destination, that unleashes the magic, drawing spontaneous encounters and serendipities your way like a giant magnet. You don't have to do anything except show up. When I showed up in Zimbabwe, I wound up in the middle of a village of stilted thatch huts that could have come out of the ninth century, where all the grandmothers smoked cannabis bongs. Nobody else. My new friend Lazarus lived there, and he told me that it was a custom for the grandmothers of the Tonga tribe, sanctioned by the government. He was surprised to learn that we didn't have a lot of grannies smoking cannabis back here. Then the whole village and a couple of nearby ones, for good measure, put on a twilight dance and music fest as wonderfully strange as everything else in this back of beyond, with folks blowing riffs on homemade whistles that shrieked with the dissonance of a vintage Ornette Coleman improv. The eccentric jazzman once told a band member puzzled by his atonal scale, "all notes are correct." They were here, and are, whenever you let it all rip without judgment.

When I showed up in the Sierras to climb Mount Whitney, I got the most sublime morning I've ever seen, a primeval dawnrise gilding conifer and granite—and later on the trail a lesson in courage. It came in the form of a skinny, hunched-over 13-year-old boy climbing with his parents and brother. His mother told me that he had a spinal defect that would have to be operated on, and there was no guarantee that he would have the ability to do anything rigorous again after the operation. The boy acted decisively to go for Whitney now while he still could. As I bouldered down the shale scree from the summit, I could see him moving well in the distance, pushing toward me up the last section, which had me wheezing the final steps. I caught up with him. "Hey, only a half hour to 14,497 feet," I encouraged him. He gave me a thumbs-up and grinned wide, on the verge of victory. At 13 he knew what people three times his age still didn't. Now is the time. I was sure he'd conquered the first of many mountains.

Travel and participant vacations drop us into the natural spontaneity of life, which we've forgotten about in our clinical work bunkers.

It's a realm that's exhilarating because we haven't predicted or re-hearsed it. As a result, we experience life in first run, without déjà vu, utterly brand new. When you're there to be there, instead of blazing to get somewhere else, you can truly relax and taste what's in front of you. You don't have the success syndrome barging into the picture, the pile of expectations, the need to do everything right, to have the ultimate vacation. You're relieved of command and the rest of the infernal steering committee.

These journeys have helped me to know that you can't quantify enjoyment, fun, play, passion, wonder, impulse, laughter, adventure, and the freedom of experiencing it all as it happens. All of these delicacies need you to be fully present to happen, unconcerned about payoff or where it's all leading. "To be or not to be" is the question, after all, not "to do or not to do." Productivity obsession keeps you in the "not to be" column, because your gaze is gone from here, fixed on the result. Continual chasing of goals and end-points, as Alan Watts wrote, "is like trying to abate one's hunger by eating merely the two precise ends of a banana. The concrete reality of the banana is all that lies between the two ends." That's where the nutrients are, which we lose sight of when we are swept up in end points.

Being gets you off the doing treadmill, off the exhausting cycle of needing to have results to validate yourself. You find you are qualified to enjoy yourself without the barest hint of a productive reason. You can be exactly who you are, not who you think others want you to be, and it's in these moments that, ironically, others like you the most, since we are all attracted to the authentic person, the "human" being, not the calculated one.

The same goes for pure enjoyment. It seems to find you more when you're not trying to achieve it as an objective. There's something about enforced enjoyment, that, like laugh tracks, fails to convince. The more we try to have a good time, the less successful we are. So the humble state of being is its own reward, dishing out the ultimate payoff—contentment—though none is sought, through the internal prizes of enjoyment and happiness. As Dr. Mihaly Czikzentmihalyi discovered in his study of what makes people happy, "When experience is intrinsically rewarding, life is justified in the present." It doesn't get better than that.

Joseph Campbell argued that it's not the meaning of life that we're in search of but rather the feeling of being alive. In other words, we've got the preposition wrong. It's not the meaning *of* life we seek, but meaning *in* life. It's the experience of living we're after, which we're sealed off from by career quarantine and too much social conditioning. The times when we feel most alive are those when we're in the unselfconscious moment. With the mind relieved of the burden of self-awareness, we're free to abandon ourselves to the experience—no matter who is looking. You're no longer plotting fate, you're dancing with it—even if you don't know how to dance. That's the harmony and aliveness you can tap when you can release yourself to the simple experience of life.

Those caught up only in work mode are "missing the other side of life, the life that they once imagined," says software engineer and frequent traveler Del Cornalio. "What's the big deal about working on someone else's agenda, making that the most important thing in your life? What happened to your own personal agendas? Why is it that making someone else rich is more important than taking off six months and going to the South Seas?"

As a first step toward bringing more of this into your life, try turning some of that to-do list of yours into a "to-be" list. What are some ways that could allow you to go for the experience and not the result? How could you spend more time in "being" mode? A tip: Look for things that make you feel at home, in awe, inspired, or impassioned. Those are great places to be. Here are a few suggestions on where you can be where you are:

- Get out of town.

- Get back in touch with friends lost in the work frenzy.

- Find a new hobby. Spend more time with an old one.

- Wander to places you haven't been before and see with new eyes.

- Linger over meals with company.

- Hear great music and transport your stir-crazy soul.

- Acquire wonder lust. Let your curiosity be your guide.

- Get out in nature.

The idea is to lose yourself, and the usual self-conscious straining, to the surroundings. Don't be in a hurry to go anywhere else. Don't watch the clock. Don't analyze. Just be there for whatever occurs. Practice the forgotten art of lingering, the essential ingredient in developing interests, passions, and friendships. In the process of opening yourself up to experience whatever takes place, you pop out of the controlled bubble to collide with new people and possibilities swirling just outside your rut. You grow. And it's not moss for once.

The Life You Save May Be Your Own

If a vacation did no more than get you out of your box to taste the world rumored to be out there somewhere, that would be a lot. But there's much more. As we learned earlier, vacations can reduce the risk of death from heart attack, hardening of the arteries, or high blood pressure. The University of Tel Aviv's Dr. Dov Eden has performed extensive "respite" studies, and has documented that respites from work ease the "effects of stress on well-being by punctuating the otherwise constant aggravation caused by incessant job demands." With job stressors removed, the body has a chance to recover from the battering of nonstop adrenaline and cortisol set off by the stress response. In a study by Dalia Etzion and Ornit Sapir vacations were shown to substantially reduce stress and burnout, as well as health-related absenteeism.

The physical restorative powers of the vacation are supplemented by the psychological and emotional boost you get from time off. Doctors Arie Shirom and S. E. Hobfoll found that a break from stress helps regroup lost emotional resources, which plays a key role in stemming burnout. Rest and reconnection with family and friends on a vacation resupplies lost emotional resources, such as social support and a sense of mastery. The study recommends at least a couple of weeks as the time required for this patch up to occur, which is why weekend trips can't restore you to health after a year in the cubicle trenches. Researchers have also found that leisure experiences have a critical buffering effect on the psyche, providing a "stress-sheltering effect" an ability to cushion the blows of life, as well as an ability to induce positive moods. That's a big item for burned-out souls locked in emotional exhaustion. A change of mood changes everything.

It's not just your health that is strengthened by vacations, so is your social life. This is one of the great spin-offs of the holiday experience. Time is the fastener of friendships and kinship, and without it our connections to those near us drift, and we have no time to make new ones. The shared experience of vacations can bring families and friends closer together and introduce you to a host of new people you actually have the time of day for. Without time pressure or the rigid social code of home, you can get to know people in a couple of hours better than folks you've known back home for years. Psychologists call it the stranger-on-the-train effect. It's a powerful experience that restores your faith in the human race; exhilarating, in fact, because it yanks you out of the separateness of the work fortress and pumps you up with another potent nonproductive reward: a sense of belonging. It *is* your planet. The first birthday greeting I get every year comes from Germany, from two people I met in Belize years ago, vacation fans you'll meet in Chapter 15.

And there's something else we get: the space to appreciate our most precious resource, time, an item we're normally too busy to enjoy. We think there's an inexhaustible supply of it, but the inventory is extremely finite. The reality was brought home to me in a bizarre little church in Evora, Portugal, whose walls, columns, and ceiling are plastered with the femurs, tibias, ribs and skulls of hundreds of sixteenth-century monks. The Chapel of Bones was designed by a creative sort to aid in the contemplation of mortality. It makes it pretty clear where things are headed. An exit sign reinforces the message with a bit of monk wit, "WE THE BONES ALREADY IN HERE ARE JUST WAITING FOR THE ARRIVAL OF YOURS."

Excuses, Excuses

The choice between being a punching bag for two weeks at the office and having a tropical drink in your hand somewhere where you don't know what day it is, is a tough choice, I realize. But there do seem to be things that are preventing some of you from making your God-given choice to leave the sparring ring. Some of those could be pressures coming from the management side, while others are in your head—inertia, guilt, and habitual preoccupation. Since no reason, boss-related or otherwise, is an acceptable alibi for giving up the time of your life, let's take a closer look at how to overcome some of the typical excuses that can deprive you of your vacation.

TOO BUSY (BOSS VERSION)

This is easily the most common alibi for skipped holidays, used by management to keep holidays on paper and by employees caught up in overwork fever. As one worker wrote to Work to Live, "when a vacation is requested, it's 'never a good time,' there's 'too much work to do,' 'a deadline to meet.'" Clearly there are periods of the year that are more hectic than others and not appropriate to take off. But no supervisor should be able to black out all your requests for vacation time because it's too busy. You're entitled to whatever the policy is by law. When repeated requests are turned down, it could be a case of bad management (evidence of issues such as understaffing or financial difficulties) or sheer intimidation. But one thing is clear about intimidators: They only respect people who push back. Demonstrate your resolve and take your vacation. The only way this unconscionable behavior is going to end is when we all stand up and say, No Way, as the employee above did, and quit for a saner workplace.

TOO BUSY (YOUR IDEA)

There is plenty to do at the office these days for everyone, but don't let it tempt you to try to clear it all away before you're able to make a getaway. If you're in hurry-worry mode, false urgency can convince you that you have to do what you don't. Unless the work is a true emergency, busyness is not a valid reason for shunting vacations aside year after year.

TOO GUILTY

When you start feeling guilty about leaving the hive, stop and notice the irrational thought and your manipulation by others. You'll soon recognize that the guilt isn't real. You have put in your fifty weeks for the year. This bogus guilt is coming from a runaway productivity belief—that output determines worth, and without it you are pond scum. Remind yourself of all the work you've done through the year, all those hellacious commutes, all that Mylanta you've ingested. Time to go, isn't it?

HAVE TO PLAY DEFENSE

Fear makes us do things that make absolutely zero sense. Defensive overworking through your vacation is at the top of that list. Giving up your vacation in the hope that this bravado display will protect you from future cutbacks is an irrational drop in the ocean of management decision-making and politics. If you can't make an impression in fifty weeks, it's highly unlikely that another two will make much of a difference. You need to trust your abilities and not live from fear—which is exactly that, not living.

SOMEBODY MIGHT PASS ME

While competition is a fact of life to be aware of in the workplace, too much focus on what others are doing or might do if you took a vacation can lock you into permanent guard duty at your workstation. It's like never wanting to leave your house in case a burglar hits it. You can't control the rest of the universe, only your own behavior. Let it go, so you can discover the freedom of not having to hold on to what can't be owned or possessed, the decisions of others.

TOO MUCH STATIC

Don't let bravado cracks from management and co-workers cramp your vacation plans. Refuse to shave a minute off your holiday because someone wished you "happy loafing." These lame, cornpone opinions should make you smile in the knowledge that these characters are so clueless as to what really counts in a life span that they are high comedy. The fact that some people choose to be miserable is not your problem.

CAN'T LOSE TOUCH

This is a growing excuse in the wired world, where contact addiction is rampant. If you have this compulsion, you need to understand its sources—habit, insecurity, and false urgency. You think you can't lose touch, or you'll miss something. But what you're missing is the actual experience of life. Clinging to E-mails and cell calls as human lifelines distracts you from the real thing. It allows your life to be dictated by the facsimile of human contact, which forecloses opportunities for the bona fide item.

NO PLANS

One of the biggest obstacles to quality vacations is the lack of thought that goes into them. We haven't been trained to think of holidays as valuable parts of our lives, so we don't think of them at all until it's time to take off. Great vacations don't happen at the last second. When you don't have any plans, you wind up working by default. Or you take a short nonvacation, squandering your time with odd jobs around the house. Don't let single-minded focus on work relegate your vacation to an afterthought.

WAIT TILL NEXT YEAR

The Postponement Commandment has a field day with people whose vacation policies let them carry over the time to the next year. About half of all big firms have this policy, according to Hewitt Associates. This is a common strategy with bravado types who like to boast about the six months they've stored up in accrued vacation. If you want to get out of the habit of accruing empty pages for your life scrapbook, you have to live now, or never.

NO MONEY

You don't need to spend a lot of money or have waiters dancing at your fingertips to have a great vacation. There are bargain rates galore on everything from flights to hotels. You just need to do a little detective work. I flew to Japan round-trip from Los Angeles for $488 recently and spent almost nothing while I was there, because I ate at local Japanese eateries, not obscenely priced tourist places, and stayed with a friend. You can spend a week in the South Pacific, in Fiji, for as little as $799, which includes flight and hotel. It takes as little as $15 a day plus food and gas for a vacation in one of our national parks. Check out flight consolidators, wholesalers who buy plane tickets in bulk, for rates sometimes half the going price, or hotel discounters on the Web. Too often the money excuse is really something else: procrastination. The key to quality time off is that you make it happen, with legwork and creativity.

PTO Stands for Pretty Ticked Off

If somebody told you that you could get fractionally more health-insurance coverage, but if you were sick from work more than five days out of the year, your coverage could be cut back or could disappear, would that be a good deal? Or what about the possibility of increased social-security benefits—but only if you missed no more than five workdays per year; otherwise, your payments would decrease or possibly vanish altogether. Would you want to risk losing social security? I don't think so. So why gamble your benefits on the vagaries of health?

Yet that is exactly the deal being foisted on an increasing number of you by the creeping rot of PTO, the paid time-off program, another factor in the vacation war. Hewitt Associates reports that 18 percent of large companies are using PTO programs in 2001, up from 6 percent the prior year, but my sense from talking with workers across the country is that the number is much higher for small business. Brought on the market by your friends in the managed-care world, the PTO bank lumps sick days in with vacation leave into a "bank" of time. The typical program gives workers fifteen days of leave for the first five years. It holds out the illusion of a three-week vacation—but only if you are in perfect health for the entire year. Every sick day comes straight out of the PTO pot. If you are in a car accident, get mono, contract a bronchial infection, or wind up with any injury or disease that puts you down for more than the sick-day average of five days, each additional day comes out of your vacation. "PTO is obscene," says Simon, a salesman in Southern California who came down with a serious stomach disorder that required a surgical procedure and numerous doctor visits. "I said to my boss, 'You think I caused this disease to happen? There's nothing I can do about it. I have to get the medical attention.' Since I've used up my sick days, my vacation time is now being eaten up. It's pathetic."

PTO is nothing more than sleight of hand, an attempt to cut back on sick leave by taking it out of the hide of vacation leave. While the standard amount of sick leave accrued in a year by non-PTO firms is 9.3 days, PTO shrinks that to five days. Supporters of PTO say it cuts down on absenteeism. About one-third of the companies using paid time-off banks claim a reduction in absenteeism, and 25 percent say it has reduced costs, but most say it has had no effect on their costs or don't have the faintest idea what it's done, according to Hewitt Associates.

Since the average sick leave used by workers each year is 4.7 days, you may pick up a big .3 of a day in extra vacation with PTO, or you may lose it all if you get sick or injured, not a remote possibility in the high-speed, high-stress workplace. What can you do about it? Raise a stink, if you can, or if you hear of it being considered by your HR department, see if you and fellow employees can head it off at the pass.

PTO turns you into a riverboat gambler with your own vacation. Why should you have to turn benefits that are a right of citizenship in the rest of the industrialized world into a crapshoot? We can do better. It's time for real vacations, not shell games.

Take It All Off

If the Postponement Commandment isn't canceling vacations, it's shrinking them, forcing you to take shorter holidays and not use all your time in one go. If your policy gives you two weeks, you might only take a week of that. Or you keep yourself from taking the full vacation your accrued benefits entitle you to. People with three and four weeks off actually use that time in one shot about as frequently as Congress makes a nonpolitical decision.

This is a classic case of how work guilt leads to self-sabotage. It's understandable. The overwork culture promotes gobs of guilt for anyone who would want to take off more than the bare minimum that their consciences should be able to live with, which is a few long weekends and a week at the outside. You would not be a valid productive member of society, otherwise. Besides the guilt, there's fear, fear that taking all of your time at once will mark you as someone who enjoys not working—imagine that!—which could undercut perception of commitment and work ethic. Summon the firing squad.

The system keeps you undercutting your own best interests as long as you act from the unspoken fears of the Office Commandments. If you can push past those fears, you will see that you can take longer vacations than you think. Walter Perkins, a senior vice president and manager at engineering firm Frederick R. Harris, told me that he would allow staffers to take three weeks at a time, if "your job is covered. But no one has ever asked me. Two weeks is the longest I've seen."

Three weeks was definitely doable for Anita Salustro, an account exec in Lansing, Michigan. A friend at another branch office of her company, AARP, told her that "she did it, and it was fine. Then I realized, hey, I can do it, too. It was all in my head, as it's in the head of so many people I know. I survived it, loved it. I realized that there's life outside of work. I came back and people didn't miss me that much. My company didn't fold." She wonders why she let the fear keep her from taking her full holiday for the many years she's been entitled to it.

Brooklyn attorney Chris Ronk took all four weeks coming to him. "I think most people in the office were jealous," he says. "One guy came in my office and said, 'You're going away for an entire month?'" Ronk went to Greece, where he climbed Mount Olympus, walked the Sumeria Gorge in Crete, lazed on the beach on three islands, and saw the ancient sites of Athens and the Peloponnesus. "It was exhilarating all around," he recalls. "There are tavernas all over the place where people are hanging out and drinking coffee or beer. They don't seem to feel the need to be busy all the time."

A non–bite-sized vacation is critical not just to make a complete break from the office and rally emotional resources crashed by burnout. It also allows you to live at another pace, off the race, where things can unfold as they will, and you don't have to sprint through your holiday. For all these reasons and common sense, the Work to Live campaign has proposed three weeks as the minimum vacation time for anyone who's worked at a job for a year, increasing to four weeks after three years. We need that time for our bodies and minds to fully recover and still have time left to discover. As Dr. Desiree Ladwig, a German work-life expert who has advised the European Union, puts it: "With three weeks you have the possibility to go beyond your own skin, how you organize your whole life. What are your priorities? You can be like a mouse in a cage, running, running, running, and never realize you're caught without this time to think about it."

Life Assurance

I've always liked the term "life insurance," because it does nothing of the sort, insuring only the opposite. You've shelled out enough for a fund you will not be around to tap. How about funneling some to a real-life program? We'll call it Life Assurance. Unlike life insurance, Life Assurance actually does something for your life.

Southern California adventure-legend John Goddard definitely had a Life Assurance program. Instead of focusing all his energies on a single job or profession that leads to the proverbial money, success, and the approval and envy of all someday, he concentrated on experiencing life now. What assured it for him was a list he put together at the age of 15 of all the things he wanted to do before he died, 127 items in all. They ranged from canoeing the Nile River, to climbing Mount Kilimanjaro, to learning how to fly a plane, studying tribes in the Congo, visiting the Leaning Tower of Pisa, diving the Great Barrier Reef, riding an elephant, playing flute and violin, writing a book, running a mile in five minutes, learning French, and seeing the Great Wall of China. He's done all those things and much more in a life that says idealism doesn't have to die with youth. To date Goddard has accomplished 100 of his 127 lifetime goals. The explorer-scientist was the first to explore the entire length of the Nile River and then the Congo River. He has climbed twelve of the world's highest mountains, and has visited 120 countries. Needless to say, Goddard, now age seventy-five, is not someone who feels unfulfilled.

Carl Jung once said that we are afraid of growing old to the extent that we are not really living now. How many of us have ever penciled out even five nonwork related things we'd like to do in our life span? How many of us even think in terms of what we'd *like* to do in the prime years of our lives, as opposed to what we think we're supposed to do? When I ask people about their goals or adventures outside the office, most usually draw a blank. Like some ancient language gone extinct from lack of use, our imaginations seem to have forgotten how to imagine anything off the obligatory circuit.

A Life Assurance plan brings your imagination back to life. What I have in mind is a mini-version of Goddard's master plan—your Personal Life List, a to-do page that puts you and balance on the agenda for once, for near-term and long-term life goals. You would actually dare to chart out some of the things you would like to do for no other reason than that they enrich your life. Productivity is not required!

Your Personal Life List gives you permission to dream again, and to set leisure goals. What an astonishing concept. You give your life new direction simply by forcing these unspoken desires onto the printed page. They are no longer out of sight and mind but part of a concerted effort to clear time and make them happen. Too many of us have been operating on somebody else's dream of success. It's time to make the dream yours.

THE PERSONAL LIFE LIST

Define the Mission. The first order of business in preparing your plan is to define what areas of life are important to you and which ones need more attention. Begin by writing a mission statement for yourself. What's most important in your life? What must you absolutely have more of for balance in your life? Do you need to be more social? Have more R&R? The main categories of your leisure plan would include: Family, Social Outlets, Relationship, Travel, Learning, Creative Time, Exercise, Community Service, Personal/Spiritual Growth, and Mastery/Challenge. Check off which would make the biggest difference in enriching and balancing your life.

Start Brainstorming. Next, take each of your selected categories and put your kid hat on. Start compiling a wish list for each. For example, under the Social category, you might list "Weekly Lunch Date with Friend," "One Concert per Month," "Join an Astronomy Club." Under Learning and Growth, you could list "Go on an Archeological Dig," "Take a Gourmet Cooking Class," or "Start Yoga." For the Travel category, you might pencil in "Cruise the Amazon," "Go to a Health Spa in Colorado," "Cycle the Wine Country in California," or "A Blue Lagoon Cruise in Fiji."

Determine the Means. Once you have sketched out your leisure dreams, then it's time to figure out how you can make them happen. How much time or training would you need for a particular leisure goal? How much money? List three things you need to do to start moving down the path toward your goal. When you've completed the third, add three more, and so on, until you've reached your target. Post a sheet of paper with your goals in plain view, so that you see them daily and they become a part of your mind-set.

Reinvent the Schedule. After you have pinpointed key leisure goals, work up a time line and daily schedules that can make them happen. How much time do you need to shave off the work schedule? Where can you cut? Do you need to enroll your kid in more day care? Examine your home schedule to see where you can find more time, such as reducing TV time. How much extra money could you add toward one of your goals if you cut back on spending for things you don't need?

Toss Assumptions. It may take an adjustment in limiting self-beliefs to contemplate or complete a life goal. You may think you're too old to learn a musical instrument. I know a guy who started guitar at age 55 and by 62 he was an excellent classical guitarist. An old dog *can* learn new tricks. You may think you can't take a bike trip in France or Italy because you don't have anyone to go with. There are dozens of adventure travel companies that package group trips full of singles. You may think you don't have the time to take a diving class. Sorry, that is not a valid excuse anymore. Proactive organizing of things you really want to do will create the time you can't find when you don't know what's on the other side of the office.

Extend Your Plan. It's best to start out tackling just a few of the main leisure categories. As you achieve leisure goals in those categories, you'll gain the confidence and skills to branch out to some of the others. Build a balance of ongoing leisure activities—a lunch with a friend each week, a regular exercise plan—with targeted, loftier goals, such as traveling in Spain or rafting the Salmon River in Idaho. A mix of nearer and farther goals will keep you fresh, enthused, and involved.

By shifting from the subconscious batting down of leisure activities that is our normal work-hyped mode to one of intention, we escape inertia. We catch ourselves when the lame excuses surface—no time, no money, etc. A prime lesson of behavioral science is that humans do what they *think* they can. The Office Commandments make you think you can't do much but toe the drone line the rest of your life. Do you really buy that? I didn't think so. Step right up to a life that's assured.

Ask and You May Receive

Negotiate Fewer Hours and More Time Off

• • •

"A life lived in fear is a life not lived."

—Catalonian proverb

There are few things more terrifying for the average American consumer than haggling with a car salesperson. Maybe death by army ants. Or anaconda. And when you step into the showroom, it can sort of feel like you're going to an execution—yours. Your nemesis knows all the tricks to pick you apart and squeeze you, the special features you have to have or you'll feel like a loser; how to act wounded if you start to walk away, and the price that can't be any lower or the boss will fire them on the spot, and it'll be your fault! We're like lambs to the slaughter, because negotiating is not one of our strengths as a people. We're spenders, not fighters.

We're also literalists. One nation under a bar code. We believe that a price tag should mean what it says, since all consumers should be treated equally. Pricing that depends on negotiating ability offends our democratic principles, since some of us—most of us—will end up on the short end of the deal, snookered by people more talented at the game than we are. What we forget to realize is that what goes on the price tag is the result of a series of negotiations, from the seller of the raw materials to the manufacturer to the wholesaler to the retailer. The apparent firmness of pricing really gets exploded when it's time to clear out product, and things are suddenly 50 percent off that once-fixed price.

Negotiation is actually more the rule than the exception. It's happening all around you all the time. You negotiate with friends about which movie you want to rent, with your significant other for attention and closet space, and with your workmates and boss every day, as you try to sell your professional skills. So it's not like you are inexperienced at the art of bargaining for what you want. Most of us can handle it as long as the negotiating doesn't seem like negotiating. It's the overt bargaining that is the stopper, particularly when it comes to going up against someone we perceive has us at a disadvantage—i.e., the wheeler-dealer car hawker—or an authority. Double the nerves when it comes to an authority in the workplace.

Quintuple it when the negotiation is with the ultimate authority figure and holder of your purse strings, the boss, and about something that appears to contradict the hard-working image you've been trying to create on the job, if not the fabric of the work-ethic itself. The idea of bargaining to work fewer hours or increase your vacation time seems as ludicrous as it gets, little short of advertising you have a suspect work ethic. That's because it's a violation of one of the most sacred Office Commandments: *Thou shalt not broach the subject of fewer work hours or more vacation time with the boss.*

But like the sticker price on the showroom floor, it's all subject to negotiation. Company policies are not the black-and-white world we're led to believe they are. There are various shades of gray, and alternative ways of getting a green light. Believe it or not, people do get more time for their lives by asking for it. And you may, too, when you ignore the Commandment that demands your silence. You'll find out in this chapter how to pull off the seemingly impossible feat of getting more vacation time and fewer hours. By asking. You'll learn how and when to make your best pitch to get your life back in balance. Sometimes the only thing standing between you and the time you need is the sound coming out of your vocal cords. Ask, and you just may receive.

Break the Silence

The experts tell us that in the exciting new workplace the average worker will have seven–ten jobs over a life span. What that means is: 1) boom times ahead for Kinko's and resume paper suppliers, and that 2) from here on out most of us will never be at a company long enough to see more than a two-week vacation. The standard vacation policy doesn't bump up to three weeks until you've been with a company for five years. So if you ever want to get a real vacation, you're going to have to push for it, negotiate for the time, and support efforts to get vacation-legislation passed, or you'll be stuck with year-one vacation status for life.

You'll also need to speak up if you want to stop the endless spiral of excessive hours. Downsizing isn't going away; it's here to stay. The hours are going to keep piling on, masquerading as norm until there's push-back. Just because vacation time or long hours are "company policy" doesn't mean those conventions can't be bent and modified to keep valuable employees in the fold. As sales-guru Herb Cohen points out in his book *You Can Negotiate Anything,* "It's all negotiable. You have the freedom to choose your attitude toward any given set of circumstances and the ability to affect the outcome."

Remember, we're rugged individualists in this land. Let's start acting the part. It begins by abandoning the assumptions that support the Silent Commandment. For instance: It's a black-and-white world. Company policy is company policy. No means No. Salespeople the world over smile when they hear these statements, because they know the reality—that policies are pliable, and, with the right approach and persistence, they can change to meet the reassessed needs of the policy-setter. They also know that a no is just a knee-jerk reaction from someone who hasn't been sufficiently persuaded yet.

When you take too much at face value, you're stuck working unlimited hours without any recourse. You are if you think you are. Career-coach Gail McMeekin, psychotherapist and owner of Creative Success.com, sees this defeatist attitude too often. "There's a sense that things are not negotiable, so people just play along. They don't take responsibility, and they'll whine and complain. There's a lot of passivity."

Passivity. It's such a glaring contradiction of the image we have of ourselves as opportunitymakers and self-determinists. Yet the mirror doesn't lie. Most of the time we feel helpless to do anything but demonstrate our world-record ability to take it. You can't rock the boat, after all. Another effective assumption that holds us in check. You have to be the good sailor and never question where the admiral is leading you. But as we have seen in recent years, from Enron to the dot-bomb fiasco, it pays to pipe up. You have to push for time for your life, or your years will be sucked up by a workplace without stoplights, or by your own unconscious workaholism.

Look at this way: We hear a lot these days about company valuation. What's yours? If you thought you were being underpaid, would you go to your boss and ask for a raise? My guess is you would. One thing we don't seem to have much trouble negotiating for is money. That's a valuation we understand. But there's just as much value in time, even more so because it's so finite. You have to see a negotiation for time in the same light as a raise. It's payment in time that you should consider as much a part of your take-home as cash, which it is— the hours with which you spend your living. Just as few people ever get raises they don't campaign for, you can't get more time with mental telepathy. You have to step up and speak up, or forever hold your lack of peace.

The Mortal Manager

The boss gets salad stuck in his or her teeth. Looks around for clean underwear, too. In short, your superior isn't particularly superior when it comes to the business of being just another befuddled human trying to keep it together. Sure, there are big bucks and titles, but the chief steps on gum just like you do. Don't be thrown by the throne-room.

Being the workaholic, guilt-wracked types that we are, we place a lot of stock in pleasing workplace authority. It's a gauge of our own self-worth. If they're happy with us, we're happy with us. So the tendency is to not want to do anything to confront the arbiter of our esteem, not to mention career future. If we're going to move ahead in the company, we feel we have to do it with the boss's approval.

That kind of power of approval is quite familiar to most of us from childhood, and it's not uncommon to slip into a parent-child relationship with the boss. That brings an intense need to please and an even more intense need not to disappoint. McMeekin has seen plenty of evidence of this pattern in her clients. "I find a lot of adults still treat organizations in a very parent-child kind of model," she observes. "One of the problems with our educational system and the attitudes it conveys about work is that whoever is in power somehow knows best, and if we just follow instructions, and we're a good girl or boy, we'll be okay. That isn't the truth of it at all. Corporations don't take care of people anymore."

The thought of asking for something the boss might be unhappy about can trigger feelings of guilt and shame and a reversion to the junior role again. The guilt comes from feeling as if you're letting the boss/parent down by not doing everything exactly as you're supposed to. It's saying you don't measure up. Your worth is hanging on every comment from the boss, as it once did from your parents. Since the mere thought of disappointing your employer is the same as if it happened to the caveman part of your brain that interprets wishes as acts, you feel not just guilt now but also fear. The mind takes it to the limit. There's the fear of being abandoned—fired—never getting a promotion, or being thought of as a slacker.

But you're not a child, and your manager is not your legal guardian. You owe the boss quality, conscientious work, but not blood-loyalty. You're two adults engaged in a continual process of back-and-forth. The employer pushes to see how far he or she can get you to go, and you establish the boundaries of your zone. It's a transaction for services rendered, which need to be properly valued and rewarded.

Still, there's that wait in your gait. Anita Salustro, a sales manager, knows that reluctance. "I've seen this in many places. There's a culture of fear, that if we ask to change our hours, that if we ask to work part-time, we're going to be punished. It's seen as slacking. When, in fact, if you went to your employer with a well-thought-out proposal, saying here's what I want, and here's how I intend to get there, your employer would probably embrace that."

"You shouldn't be afraid of the boss," confirms Bob Senatore, a boss himself, executive vice president of Comforce Corp. "We all suffer from that, and I suffered from that at one time." He compares it to the fear he once had about giving a public speech. After weeks of nerves in anticipation of the talk, he finally decided, "What can they do? They're not going to kill me. As long as I'm still going to live after this is over, how bad can it be? That dispelled a lot of the fear."

To give in to fear is to hold your current life hostage for a future that may never arrive. Fear is a kidnapper, snatching you from your own life on the projection of what might happen tomorrow. It's interesting to note that the people least likely to take risks are those who place a high value on future time. In other words, the more you're run by what doesn't exist, the less you can seize opportunities that do.

Don't hold on to what's not working for the vapor of tomorrow. Let go, so you can move on to the life that's been waiting for you.

The Art of Negotiating

The glorification of hard work, even when it doesn't have to be hard, as the one true goal of any breathing Amerian adult can lead to the expectation that you always have to do it the hard way, accept that pounding. Build that character. Do it yourself. Absorb the punishment. Say nothing. For those weaned on the notion that it's weak to let on you can't take it, opening a discussion on less overtime or longer vacations seems to shout wimp status. But what if you change the contraction, so it's not that you *can't* take it, but you *won't*? That shift makes all the difference, empowering you to take your rightful place at the negotiating table as someone who could work all night if you wanted to—but you don't. These aren't the words you'll want to use out loud, of course, but they indicate the place you should be coming from in your head as you bring your needs to the light of day, from a place of choice.

Negotiating for a more work-family-friendly schedule requires that you do something hard-boiled workers aren't supposed to do: ask for what you need. Unless your employer knows what you want, you can't get it. When educational-software technician Mathew Beck interviewed for his job, he did something very few people do. He brought up the subject of vacation time. It wasn't an afterthought that occurred when the following summer rolled around. "I said, 'I'd like to talk about vacation,'" recalls Beck. "They said, 'But I thought that was already agreed—two weeks. That's what everybody gets.' I said, 'Well, no. I need three weeks. I'm planning a trip.' They said 'Okay.' You have to put it on the table."

It doesn't have to be a toe-to-toe brawl. The key is finding a way to let the boss know that vacations and time for life and family are critically important to you, while demonstrating that you can meet the company's needs at the same time. Your pitch is that you are going to be even more efficient and productive, because the time to recharge will rejuvenate you.

Some experts recommend a go-slow approach. Business consultant Gil Gordon suggests seeding your plans before you get to the breaking point. "Deal with it in a series of nibbles. If your boss is calling you all day Saturday and Sunday, your first foray could be to say, 'I'd like to carve out Sunday morning as the no-call zone for the next couple of weeks. That's the time I'd like to know I'm carved out, and then you see how it that works. Then you go on to the next nibble."

Clarity Quest's Pam Ammondson, who works with the severely overworked, advises going in without threats and demands. "It's more, 'How I can make the team move ahead and be more productive if I set some boundaries for myself?'"

For those who would like to get the whole story out, a sit-down at a relaxed time and place may be the best approach. You'll need to do your homework, analyzing the boss's needs and bringing along solutions as well as problems, including backup plans if you don't get your first choice. Conduct the pitch in a way that demonstrates that you've done some thinking about the issue and its impact on the company and your manager. Here is some of the advance work you should do before your discussion:

- **Know your opposite number.** Write up a summary of your boss. Who and what does he or she respond to? What are the qualities they look for in their employees? If sheer productivity is the most important value of the boss, then that's the theme of your proposal. If your manager appreciates honesty and candor, then you can feel more free to level with them about your situation.

- **Get a weather report.** What pressures is the boss under from the next level up? Or from the market? Take these needs into account and acknowledge them in your discussion.

- **What's the manager's style?** How does he or she communicate best? Some may want a meeting, while others prefer something in writing that they can chew on.

- **Timing is everything.** What time of the day is the boss most receptive? Never make your pitch in the middle of a crisis. Find a calm day when your supervisor is in a good mood.

- **Look for precedents.** See if anyone else at the office has done what you're thinking. Precedents work. If you can't find one at your company, then look outside to another firm that may be doing what you propose successfully. One company to cite is SAS Institute in Cary, North Carolina, a company that offers everyone three weeks vacation the first year on the job and a thirty-five-hour week. This style has helped give SAS, at $1 billion in sales and 10,000 employees, one of the lowest turnover rates in the software business, and double-digit sales growth for more than a decade. Cite the experience of the Strategic Coach, a consulting company whose entrepreneurial clients have increased their earnings by 15 to 30 percent through longer vacations and valuing the role of free time in creating productive employees and owners. You might want to get some Strategic Coach materials into the hands of your boss (www.strategiccoach.com) and see what happens.

Now we come to the substance and theater of negotiation. Keep in mind what you hate about people trying to sell you things, like the car dealer. Dispense with glibness and fast talking. Be sincere and as relaxed as you can be, because you've done your homework. You know you deserve to be here. They've hired you for your expertise, and you've contributed. You need the time to be able to do your job better and take care of your personal responsibilities. Standing up for yourself is an admired quality. Try not to think of it as a showdown but as the game that it is. Make the moves as if they were on a Scrabble board and know you will still be alive when it's over.

Like any game, the negotiation process has its rules that you'll need to follow. Here are some guidelines on how to make your play:

- **Put yourself in the boss's shoes.** Try to understand the other viewpoint and let them know that you do by acknowledging it—"I see your point," "What I hear you saying is . . ."

- **Don't blame people, blame the problem.** Avoid any implication that your problem is the boss's or anybody else's fault. Stay focused on the issue of more productive hours or vacation time.

- **Don't get locked into a position.** Setting up one righteous position invites the other party to take up one of their own. The parties dig in, and then have too much face at stake to reach a solution. The Harvard Negotiation Project, which developed the style of "principled negotiation," recommends that you "reconcile interests, not positions. Behind opposed positions lie shared and compatible interests."

- **Avoid emotional reactions.** Don't let your emotions trip you up. Never react emotionally to an outburst from the other side. Continue making your points in a firm but professional way.

- **Find common ground.** Listen carefully to what the other side is saying to find areas of commonality that could help create a mutual solution.

- **Provide a graphic illustration of the problem.** The boss is usually removed from the impact that policies might be having on individual lives. It helps your case to detail in a strong way the result that overwork and insufficient vacation has had on your life and that of your family. If you don't have time to see your kids, say so. If you are seriously stressed and have been in and out of doctor's offices, tell it like it is. Let the boss know how it feels to never have a letup in work demands.

- **Don't whine.** "There's a difference between negotiating and whining," says McMeekin. "The whining approach is disastrous. In a company where everyone is overworked, you'll just be written off." Again, no blaming, no victims, just a problem with a solution.

- **Try the fairness test.** This is a tricky one, because it gives workaholic bosses a chance to trot out one of their favorite platitudes: "Life isn't fair." Try to avoid the word "fair" with tyrannical types and suggest that the current situation isn't right. Cite family values and other appeals that can show how out-of-whack the business values are with those we espouse as citizens and parents.

- **Have multiple options.** Don't go in with one answer that can easily be shot down. Put together several possible solutions to your time problem. Maybe you work late on Tuesday and Thursday nights, but the rest of the week you leave at 6 P.M. You could take your extra vacation time without pay. Try trading overtime hours for comp time. Be creative.

- **Invite participation in the solution.** Take one of your solutions that would seem to have the best chance based on the input you get in the discussion, and ask the boss, "What if we tried this?"

- **Be persistent.** "Most people aren't persistent enough when negotiating," points out negotiator Herb Cohen. "They present something to the other side, and if the other side doesn't buy it right away, they shrug and move on. You must be tenacious." If this session doesn't work, keep at it.

Since you're going up against one of the most entrenched ideals in the American psyche, there is a high probability of resistance. But a No is never a No to a persistent negotiator. It's an invitation to another approach. Maybe the idea needs to be unveiled over time.

Fanatic workaholic bosses are not going to be very sympathetic to your proposal. Their worldview is so skewed by the adrenaline haze they're floating in, that they literally take it personally when anyone doesn't celebrate killing themselves as much as they do—which is a threat to the whole upside-down universe they have concocted. Ditto for weak bosses, who are afraid to do anything out of the ordinary for fear of their higher-ups. If you are stuck with either of these cases, your best bet is to try your luck with human resources or, if your company has a safety committee or work counsel, to give that route a go. If all else fails, it may be time to move on to a saner workplace, or there's one other plan you could try: a trial case.

The Incentive Plan

If you can't get immediate approval for your plan, the best next step is to try to get some portion of it going on a trial basis. Bosses need to be weaned off the face-time obsession. Make the case that you are so convinced that the longer vacation or adjusted work hours will not affect performance that you will prove it. And, in fact, not only will it have no negative impact, it will have a positive one. Lay down a challenge: Your productivity will increase! It usually does when you take time out. And if it doesn't, you'll shut up.

As we have seen, when you're an exhausted heap of rubble, it takes you much longer to get things done than when you're fresh—particularly brain work, which is what most of us are doing these days. That memo or E-mail can take an hour or two to write when you're reeling from sleeplessness and overwork. Sales calls you make when you're fatigued aren't nearly as effective as when you're truly fired up and rejuvenated. You can bank on it. Your productivity will increase. So you need to get a chance to prove it. One salesman who sent an E-mail to Work to Live revealed how he got his boss to give him more time off with just such a trial case: "My company gives one week of paid vacation the first three years! After that you get two weeks! It is insane! I asked for extra time off without pay and went to China for two weeks. I came back and my productivity skyrocketed (I'm in sales)! My regional manager is trying to use this as an example so everyone can get more time off. It's about bloody time!"

This incentive game can get quite interesting. Take the case of Andrew Molnar, who was looking to exit the rat race at Prudential Insurance in Newark, New Jersey. He and his wife found exactly the opportunity they were looking for: a spiritual retreat that needed new management. They made a pitch to the owner of the site, located in the woods of eastern Ohio, that they would get the business out of the red, make it profitable, but there was something they had to have if they met all their sales goals. "We said we're going to be excellent visionaries for you," recalls Molnar, "and we understand from your end that you need to have these results, so if we do these results, this is what we expect: nine weeks vacation." They met their targets; they got their nine weeks, which has been an annual affair now for six years.

Bet the boss that, like these workers did, you will deliver the productivity if you get extra vacation time or two or three nights a week when you leave the office at 6 P.M. It's tough for even drill sergeant bosses to say No to potential gains in efficiency and earnings. The test case handles the boss's fear that any drop-off in face-time is going to cost him or her. It offers the prospect of increased value, as you get value, which makes it a win-win deal for everyone.

Making the Vacation Sale

One of the deep, dark secrets of the benefits world is that not everyone's perks are created equal. As in the rest of life, the squeakiest wheel gets the oil, while the rest rust. Some of the most well-oiled folks are in upper management, where four-week vacations are the norm, part of the incentive packages used to grease entry for sought-after execs. This, by the way, is prime exhibit A to illustrate the stupidity and inconsistency of the argument against longer U.S. vacations. The top brass are already getting them. What's the big deal about spreading that around?

The more valued you are to the company, of course, the more leverage you have in pushing for more holiday time. These days everybody has value, because the costs to replace you are extemely high, ranging from $15,000 up to $100,000 for the average salaried employee, and more. Unless you have a tyrant or a workaholic for a boss, everyone has a chance, if not to get more time off with pay, then to pick up another week without pay. I did this routinely at a music company I worked for. As a foreign travel buff, I needed time to spend in other parts of the world once I got there—more time than the two-week policy offered. My boss knew I was a road hound, which he found amusing and secretly envied, so he agreed to give me more time without pay, and I was able to take three-plus-week vacations from Southeast Asia to Eastern Europe.

The negotiating experience of Del Cornalio, a software engineer, shows just how far it's possible to go to score time above and beyond the office policy. Cornalio explained to a firm that wanted to hire him that vacations were an important item for him, and what he wanted was more than the two weeks they offered. "I told my boss I'd like to be able to take four weeks at a time, and two more weeks unpaid," Cornalio recalls. "I said I'd work it into the schedule and be a good trooper. He said, 'Sure, we'll work with that.'" As an illustration of how vacations can have a major impact on productivity—though not the kind we're led to believe—by the end of the year, Cornalio had the highest performance rating in the company, working a month less than his coworkers.

A posting on the website for *Workforce* magazine, a publication for human-resource professionals, shows how the negotiating game works. One HR staffer wrote, "When we hire our managers, there is a standard amount of vacation that they are entitled to. If the manager happens to negotiate really hard for more vacation (and we really want the manager), we may give the manager one or even two weeks more vacation than the standard set amount."

You are in your best negotiating position before you are hired, but once the company has indicated interest. Meredith Unger, a human-resources specialist based in San Francisco, has won extra vacation time for herself just this way. She suggests you wait "until the very end, when they really like you. I let them know that I need to either have more vacation or I need to know I can take unpaid time. I would say, 'I'm learning Italian this year, so I'll need a couple of weeks in Italy next year to study for that. And I'm going to need to take a couple weeks off in February or March. Is this okay with you?' I never say I'm going to need the time in the first four months, because they need me most then."

Here are a few keys to making a successful vacation case:

1. **Demonstrate your value.** Key employees are hard to replace. If you're a quality performer, you increase your odds of getting the time you need.

3. **Make a point of mentioning any long vacation you may have had at your last job.** Let them know you can't go backwards to a shorter holiday.

3. **Explain the importance of the extra time for you.** Touch on the need for work-life balance, time with family, and the special passions you need the time to pursue. Be specific about those interests, and let the boss feel your enthusiasm, which can be contagious.

4. **Present the evidence for more vacation time.** Cite some of the health studies in this book. A real break from the stress parade will save the company health and retention costs, enhance posi-

tive mood, and bring you back refreshed and energized to do your job even better.

5. **Push for paid leave first, but if you don't get it, go for unpaid leave.** That's hard for an employer to turn down, and it shows them how important the time is to you.

6. **Buy more time.** Some 10 percent of companies offer buying and selling of vacation time, according to Hewitt Associates. This is a very interesting trend—if you can resist the temptation of cash in hand from selling, and buy more time. You buy and sell at 100 percent of the value of your regular wages for the time period traded. The time you buy is deducted from your wages over a specified period. There's a lot of potential here. You can buy an extra week, sometimes two weeks (!!) of holiday time this way. See if your company would be open to this concept. Contact Hewitt Associates (www.hewitt.com) for information on how the program could work.

7. **Try a comp deal.** If all else fails, try trading overtime hours you probably do routinely for comp-time off. There was even an attempt in Congress a couple years ago to pass comp-time legislation. To make it work, though, you have to take the time. In companies that have this policy, not everyone takes the comp time they're entitled to, reminiscent of untaken vacations.

Bargaining For Balance

When the job hours are out of control, so is your life—but also the lives of those around you. It's not uncommon these days for the homes and apartments of high-hours workers to be little more than flophouses for sleep and showers. Besides the health consequences, the toll on personal lives is enormous. You can't have a relationship with someone who isn't around. High-hours workers, such as lawyers, have a much higher divorce rate than the general public, says Joan Williams, a professor at

American University who has studied the overwork issue's effects on women and families.

You also can't map out, can't even think of mapping out, what you want to do on this planet if you barely have time to brush your teeth. As we talked about in the prior chapter, you have to have some kind of Life Assurance, a plan to see that you live your life to the fullest, or it's not going to happen. Work will fill up any vacuum. To make way for your new Personal Life List, you have to be able to shrink or shift the hours at the office.

Creating a proposal for fewer hours is a bigger challenge than negotiating for a longer vacation. It goes to the heart of the work culture at your company, and to your own internal battle with work-ethic guilt and fear. But it can be done. Before you craft any plan for the boss, you have to put one together for yourself, spelling out what it is you really want. How are you going to measure success in the day-to-day for yourself? How do you want to spend the extra time you want to free up? What portion would go to relationship and family responsibilities and how much time to personal pursuits? By the time you're finished with this process, you'll have a strong conviction within yourself about your need to reign in the hours.

Now it's time to move on to the boss. Come prepared with a written proposal that sketches out the problem and offers a couple of solutions. The place to start is with an update of how much you're doing and accomplishing. Chances are good your manager has no clue how much you are really doing on the job. Make him or her feel the tonnage. Don't whine. Be urgent but nonblaming and non-victim about it. Next find out which of that stack of priorities is truly a priority and how things might be reshuffled so that you can take care of your personal responsibilities. Provide an energetic description of the chaos in your personal affairs as a result of unchecked job hours. Bring your relationships into it, bring your family into it, bring doctor's accounts, or any medical corroboration of stress-related illness. Make it personal, because it is. What are the golden words? Here's advice from two bosses, on how they would approach themselves.

BOB SENATORE, EXECUTIVE VICE PRESIDENT
OF COMFORCE CORP.

"I would go to the boss and say, 'This is what you've asked me to do, and this is what I've achieved. What I'd like to do is be able to do this and more, but to do it in a way that it fits into my lifestyle a little bit better. That might mean I want to work from home from time to time.' Provided the productivity is there, he should not want to lose me. If the productivity is not there, or he or she is a 1950s-mentality manager, which says that everybody has to be sitting at his desk all day, it's going to be harder. When goals are being set, and they're being achieved, there's no reason for presence or your just having to be there."

DAN STORPER, PRESIDENT AND CEO OF PUTUMAYO MUSIC

"The way to do it is to sit down, find a quiet moment, look the boss in the eye and say, 'I've really been busting my buns for the last few months. I've been really working hard, putting in extra hours. I want to still do the job and be effective, but I don't know if you expect me to continue with these hours or not. But I want to be effective, and I want to try to find a way to do it in a more reasonable amount of time, and hopefully you won't think less of me if I leave here at 6:00, instead of 7:30. I'm going to try to manage my time better.' Give the solution as well as the problem. Say 'I'm going to do my best to be here on time and give it my all, but I don't think you would want me to burn out, and I also want to be able to do the job well.'"

Be creative in your proposed adjustments of time, and once again, push for a test run to prove your case. More companies are beginning to experiment with flex time and virtual offices. Suggest a flex arrangement that would allow you to work from home a couple of days a week, cutting out commutes that would free up some time. It's certainly cheaper for the company for you and many of your colleagues to work from home. Cincinnati cleaning company, Jancoa Inc., switched to a four-day week for its administrative employees, who work longer during the week and get Mondays or Fridays off. The employees love the extra day off.

No matter how much dread you may have about bringing up the subject of work hours, nothing can ever change unless you force those words to the surface. The stress will continue to build, your health will continue to be assaulted, and you'll continue to be a stranger to your own your personal life. Imagine being able to have the space to escape the pressure cooker on a regular basis, to breathe in deeply, to get home from work before the sun sets, to feel your feet in the sand of a Bahamian beach or a rippling Teton meadow. Ask, and you may exhale.

12

Pull the Plug

Set Clear Boundaries Between Work and Home

• • •

"Breakin' up is hard to do. Now I know, I know that it's true."
—Neil Sedaka

Some of you may remember the trauma of being separated from your loved ones for the first time—the abject terror, the sense of abandonment, the sheer panic of wondering how you were going to survive on your vacation without your laptop and cell phone. It's an event so disturbing that more than a few otherwise valiant adults have not been able to face this challenge, capable of triggering such existential questions as "Am I alone on this earth?"; "Is someone outflanking me back at the office?"; or "If a vacation happens without an E-mail trail to show I was really there, did I really have the vacation?"

A study of work practices at large firms, conducted at Boston College by Mindy Fried, found that 32 percent of employees worked while they were on "vacation," while 58 percent of managers did. My own unscientific estimate is that 100 percent of those holiday workers did not have a real vacation, because they were still tethered to the office. They are suffering from a syndrome known to affect children starting school for the first time and assorted canines left alone by their masters: Separation Anxiety. Defined as a "developmentally inappropriate and excessive anxiety concerning separation from home or from those to whom the individual is attached," Separation Anxiety seems to describe quite accurately the mental anguish behind the hair-raising practice of going on vacation unwired, as well as the general fear across society today of being out-of-contact.

Technology has brought the world to our fingertips, but it's also brought convulsive hyperchange. People are afraid to be unplugged for five minutes, or they could miss, like, an E-mail! Or what's worse, fall behind the juggernaut. What we've done is confuse the messenger, the technology, with the message, the information that is piped through it. It's not the connection you need to stick to like a barnacle; it's a strategy that lets you select what's useful out of the content these delivery systems provide.

Connecting without understanding what we should be connecting to, ironically enough, feeds a growing disconnection. By obliterating the boundaries between work and home, the wired world brings the work home at night, on the weekend—and yes, on vacation—which squeezes out the free time necessary to build real social connections and have direct experiences in the non-cyber world. It creates the illusion that we are connecting with flesh and blood, instead of silicon and fiber-optic lines. "There's a paradox when people are so connected, they're disconnected," notes psychotherapist and coach Ellen Ostrow. "You're writing an E-mail, and you're on your cell phone, and your kid is tugging at your pants, and you don't even know your kid is tugging at your pants, because you're connecting electronically." Maybe that's why the more connected we are, the more we seem to need to be connected, the cell and E-mail chimes becoming a frantic fix for those too busy for intimate contact, reassuring that they are known to someone out there somewhere—even if it's just business or spam calling.

The speed and seduction of E-tools has forced a massive abdication of personal boundaries. Technology has teamed up with the rest of the overwork gang—downsizing, job insecurity, and global competition—to reinforce an Office Commandment that dramatically reduces your living time: *Thou shalt not be out of contact with the office.* This commandment has pushed the overwork tide over the top of human capacity, as the electronic creations run their masters.

This chapter will show you how to set limits on work intrusions into your personal life. You'll learn how to put a lid on the home invasion, whether it's driven by overt demands of the boss or by your own overcommitment to the job. You can pull the plug and break the addictive spell of telecom hardware and obsessive habits that bring the job home and on vacation. You'll find out how to create finishing rituals to close up shop at a reasonable hour and ways to short-circuit the loop of work anxiety that follows you home. We'll also explore the techniques of strategic worrying and mindfulness and how to create a Pressure Drop, a buffer between the workday and your home life.

Your home can be your castle again, when you clearly mark the boundaries of your property. It's time to roll out the unwelcome mat. No trespassing: electronic or otherwise.

Marking Your Territory

The line between work and home was already fading fast before the E-world explosion. We had gotten used to the encroachment of long hours into discretionary time, so the further erosion of personal life caused by technology seemed at first to carrry the weight of inevitability. But, as we know now, this was no organic next step. It was a tidal wave, swamping whatever hazy boundary was left between personal life and career. "It's like the workday never ends," says Rozanne, a public-relations executive at a firm in Washington, D.C. "You never have any time away from the constant cell calls and E-mails. Then you take it home with you and do more E-mails at home. It all creates an extraordinary imbalance in your life."

It seems like it never ends, because it doesn't—unless you put up the stop sign. The technology of instant access will just keep on doing the job that it was created to do, speeding information and crunching numbers twenty-four hours a day. We've been pushovers so far, enamored by what these devices can do and by their ego-stroking properties. Now the field of play is so completely muddled, we don't know where the foul lines are anymore.

Gil Gordon, author of *Turn It Off,* explains the revolution that has truly come home to roost. Technology "disconnected the activity we call office work from the place called the office. Just as it has unbounded the space, it's unbounded the time. It now makes many of the office tools and activities available 168 hours a week. Sure, people worked long hours in the past, but if you wanted to work on a weekend, it meant getting up and getting dressed and physically going into the office. Now you can replicate your desktop onto your laptop and do that at home or anywhere."

As we have seen, work, like water, will fill every nook and cranny it can find. In a land where identity is on the line to productivity, that means slavish devotion to the tools of that production. It brings to mind one of my favorite "Twilight Zone" episodes. A spaceship lands and aliens emerge, offering to assist the earthlings with their superior technology. They seem to be as devoted assistants as the title of one of their books seems to declare, "To Serve Man." As the first shiploads of humans get ready to take off for alienland, a code cracker manages to decipher the rest of the book. It turns out to be not a declaration of interstellar subservience; it's a cookbook. Now it's us who are on the menu of tools built to serve us.

There's no escape for Dana Sunby, the Frito-Lay distributor we met earlier. "We're on voice mail when we're on vacation," he admits. "You could sit there and check it twenty-four hours a day. You had better, because the messages will pile up. They expect you to check it three times a day normally." But in a measure of the growing restiveness of workers fed up with the invasion of their personal life, Sunby made the kind of decision that, unlike the false heroics of overwork bravado, is the stuff of real courage—he didn't check his messages on his last vacation! He had had enough. Sunby laid down a marker—and didn't lose his job.

His move points the way out of the trap: pulling the plug on office contact when it steps over the line of legitimate business need. Just because the access is there doesn't mean you have to respond to it wherever you are, or that there's anything worth accessing. Unless you love distraction. Like all the other commandments, the connection rule thrives on default behavior—inertia and nonassertion of boundaries. To prevent unlimited access from invading your personal time, you need to make it known that there's a perimeter beyond which work can't go.

This commandment can only survive to the extent you support it with your own compulsion or allow your employer to get away with keeping you on a leash. As Gil Gordon points out, "The boss who calls a person at 8 P.M. on a Sunday night or E-mails them on vacation, and gets a response, and doesn't get any push-back, figures, 'I was kind of uneasy about calling him at the ski lodge, but he gave me the answer and didn't give me any grief, so it can't be all that bad.' We unintentionally reinforce the behavior that may be driving us crazy." We've gotten so used to saying Yes at everything that's thrown our way that we've forgotten that we can say something else: No—this is out of bounds.

Holding Up the Sun

There's a motif in the Brazilian film classic, *Black Orpheus,* that crops up in various folk cultures, the idea that the sun rises because of the efforts of humankind, via offerings and ritual. For a couple of kids in Rio's slums, the sun comes up because Orpheu, the main character, sings it into the sky with a song each morning. There are some of us today who have this formidable power, holding the heavens in place by our diligent virtual vigil. We can't break E-contact or take a vacation, or the entire universe would come crashing down. It's a big responsibility, and it doesn't allow for much downtime. The perceived need to be there to keep the department or firm going can leave you tethered to the company around the clock. The guard duty is completely unnecessary, but the ego, forever trying to pump up its importance, will quite literally stop at nothing.

This is a major cause of personal life takeover by the all-consuming forces of preoccupation. It's easy to get caught up in the drama of self-reinforcing productivity to the point where you can't tear yourself away from it. "I found I could spend hours reading material, going to meetings, talking to people, and solving problems," says Tom Row, a retired scientist. "I would check my E-mail from six until eight in the morning, eat my lunch at my desk, then do E-mail from five until seven [at night]. The system will allow you to work as long as you want to." As Row found out, long enough after years of this pace to trigger a heart attack.

What happens is that, as the hours pile up, you get more and more isolated from the rest of the universe until you and your irreplaceable duties appear to be the universe. You feel quite heroic about it, as you are taught you should feel when you polish off mass quantities of tasks. The pseudo-esteem comes to depend on all the action to validate your role as the center of the universe, locking you into constant connection to the office. If you were to take an unplugged vacation, and the company—and sunrises—were to go on without you, it could mean you weren't as important as you thought you were, or, what's worse, that the way you're living, or not living, as it were, may be a galaxy off-base. That would call into question your whole modus operandi, which would not be pleasant. Perfectionists, workaholics, and busyness freaks are particularly prone to this pattern, but, luckily, it's one that can be fixed.

The answer, according to psychologist Ellen Ostrow, is to see that disaster won't strike if you loosen the extremist ideal of perfection behind the need for constant contact, a strategy she guides her overworked clients through. "I have people try to go for 98 percent of what they normally do," she says. "Then, once they habituate to that, they practice going to 95 percent. So you basically teach people that nothing catastrophic is going to happen."

A client of career-coach Gail McMeekin's was so panicked about being away from her office that she had stored up three-and-a-half months of vacation time. McMeekin forced her to take a week off. "For her, it was a terror that everything was going to fall apart when she left," recalls McMeekin. "It was really important for her to see that it didn't, and how much her life is out of balance."

This fear that the sky is going to fall in if you step back plays a huge role in the inability of Americans to relax and discover the rest of life. We've been so indoctrinated to believe that work is everything that the simple idea of not being at our posts touches off guilt-triggered visions of cosmic calamity. It's as if the chassis of your car would fall off without you at the wheel. Those who put up boundaries between the job and home or take vacations find one consistent revelation: There is no apocalypse while you're gone.

Trying to stay connected all the time is a futile attempt to control what can't be controlled—future events or the decisions of others. Despite all the work you may do, you are no more able to direct what's going to happen next week or month or secure your position with marathon bouts of hours than you can fly a 747 while sitting in coach. You are not the pilot. You're a passenger. May as well take in some scenery along the way.

The Home Invasion

Maybe what we need in order to understand the dimensions of the attack under way on personal space is more accurate terminology. Let's view these intrusions as electronic breaking and entering, as violations of your address usually are—as "home invasions." Unlimited access is stealing your privacy as surely as a thief would make off with your stereo.

Workaholism expert Diane Fassell argues that unlimited access has given the company the keys to your front door. "The American corporation has essentially violated the boundary between my personal family homelife and worklife by being able to poke into my life anytime they want through E-mail, voice mail, and pagers," she asserts. "It doesn't help that the individual worker takes all this work home and willingly does it. But the company has a responsibility. To what extent can management constantly be communicating with people with the expectation that they're going to get responses at all hours of the day and night and on weekends?"

Quite a bit, say *Dot Calm* authors Richard Swegan and Debra Dinnocenzo, who have been hearing plenty from workers harassed by out of control access. "We've gotten lots of comments about the dangers of cell phones," notes Debra. "If you think back, ten years ago you didn't get people calling you at home about work-related issues unless they were personal friends or it was an extreme emergency. We have a lot of data from people who say they get calls pretty much around the clock, if they don't control it on the business end."

The good news is that some are taking control over the incoming E-flak. It's possible to do, because the rules are all up for grabs. As with any new technology, it takes a while for appropriate behavior to be formulated in response to it. When the telephone first entered American homes, there was no agreed upon way of answering the startling device, or when to answer it—after ten rings, or should you even bother when it's rudely interrupting something you're doing. The novelty of the personal telecom hardware had us mesmerized for a while. But evidence shows that the welcome has worn thin. A survey by the Radcliffe Public Policy Center at Harvard found that 83 percent of Americans want "distinct boundaries" between work and nonwork time.

Karen Walker, a former executive with a Silicon Valley firm, used to feel she had to take home a couple of hours of work per night to get her work done. Laid off after twenty-five years of service to her company, she now is adamant that, "when it's quitting time, I have to leave work at work. I want to be able to do that, and I don't want to feel guilty about doing that."

That feeling was amplified by the events of September 11, 2001, which made it clear that a home is not a way station on the commute to the office but a sacred space apart from the fray, a place where the most important people and moments of our lives require more than our occasional presence. It's a realization that makes the case for E-boundaries an increasingly strong one. Some companies are starting to realize that keeping workers tied to the mast twenty-four hours a day is counterproductive to retaining good people, or at least functional ones. An advertising firm in Boston discovered it was driving its employees crazy with beepers that were going off on weeknights and throughout the weekend. Management was forced to sit down and figure out a less torturous way of conducting business. They discovered that, with all the overtime that was being racked up by the beeped-in brigade, they could hire someone to work the weekend shift. As easy as that, the rest of the staff had their private lives back.

Managing the barrage gets you out of reactive mode. You determine the priorities, instead of anyone with your cell number or E-mail address. The current practice is anarchy—everyone sending messages at all hours simply because they can. It exhausts staff and destroys focus with false urgency.

Where do you start to draw the line? Approach colleagues, supervisors, or human resources about setting ground rules for the new tools. The first step is to try to determine why the after-hours contact is happening. What's driving it? Not enough staff? Poor management? Workaholic habit? Clients who have been told you're on their case 24-7? What adjustments could be made to address the underlying problem? What can you turn off to make the work flow more manageable and less subject to interruption? When can you turn it off? What times should be off-limits to work contact except in cases of extreme emergency? Here are a few of the main issues to nail down:

1. What information gets priority?

2. What can be ignored?

3. Define what you consider "urgent."

4. Establish that the workday ends at the office gate. No cell calls, E-mail, or voice mail checking at night allowed.

5. What workflow and management issues contribute to late nights?

6. Have a guilt-free end to the workday.

7. Shut off cell phones and pagers after work.

8. Decide how late in the afternoon quick-turnaround projects can be initiated. They have a tendency to go home with you.

9. Make weekends no-contact days.

10. Ban work on vacation. That includes no message checking.

If you don't have any luck in getting the company to set some boundaries, set some for yourself. For example, do whatever you can to not carry a cell phone or pager, or check them only at times that you have blocked out for your maximum efficiency. Unless you are a surgeon or member of an emergency crew and have to be on call, discipline yourself to turn off all portable devices when you're at home, play or on family time. You can never be truly at leisure, present to the experience of it, if you're fielding business calls.

I'm Leaving Now

There are other ways the job follows you home, crashing your living room like an unwanted dinner guest. From the adrenaline in your bloodstream, to the worries swarming your brain, to the papers in your briefcase, the workday is not over. Unless you can develop strategies to break the pattern, you wind up having the job dictate your personal time, too. Obsessive work thoughts make you unavailable to the people and experiences around you. You're hearing your wife, husband, or friend with one ear, seeing with one eye. Your body is there, but your mind is still slaving away.

There will always be job noise that crops up at home, too, but you can dramatically turn down the volume with strategies that sharpen the boundaries between work and home and help you decompress. The first step is "believing that it's okay to leave work at the office," notes psychotherapist Steve Sultanoff. "There are behavioral ways to do that. Literally leaving your briefcase at the office. Or, if you are bringing something home, you time-bind it. Give yourself a time after which you won't work."

Many time-management experts recommend grounding the briefcase at work. Edwin Blair, author of *Getting Things Done,* suggests that the only thing that should go into your briefcase is your lunch. CEO Barbara Hemphill agrees. "If I take my briefcase home with my work, then I'm not really with my family. I'm not enjoying my family, because I'm feeling that I should be working on stuff in my briefcase. But I'm not working on my briefcase, so it's like a lose-lose."

The point of the briefcase strategy is to find ways to let your mind shift out of work gear and into civilian life. You need to be able to tell yourself, out loud at first, I'm shutting off the job switch now. Turn the office lights off, turn your coffee mug upside down. Find rituals that can help you confirm the end of one day and the beginning of another one. You have to learn to compartmentalize, leaving work to its alloted time slot, and then kissing it off for the night or the weekend.

We have avoided flipping off these switches at the end of the day because of the illusion that work is the most important thing in the solar system. This has led to an open invitation for obsessive work thoughts to bombard our brains. It's time to declare that invitation null and void, and station a bouncer at the door. You're not letting everything through anymore. You're going to run your own mind, instead of it running you. It's not a matter of eliminating all anxieties. That's unrealistic. But what you can do is engage in a little mind management, picking the time and place for job concerns. Strategies you can use to get control of the mental game include:

STRATEGIC WORRYING

Left to themselves, worries can tee off on you all day and all of the night. This is not good anxiety management. Worrying is essentially the mind's survival checklist. It wants to know you're paying attention to this or that concern. When you do, you don't worry as much. Leaving worries free rein to flit in and out without you being able to spend time on them just makes the anxiety worse. The idea here is to set aside a specific time each day to deal with worries. Spend a half hour each morning before work or just after work to go through your concerns. Weigh them, come up with action steps for some, and dismiss those you have a handle on. Some will move on to the next day. Ask yourself, What's behind the fear? What's the worst that could happen if it comes true? What are my possible options? When you've dealt with the same worries day in, day out, they start to lose their distracting powers. Strategic worrying corrals job fixations into zones that free you up to truly be off work when your body is.

MINDFULNESS

It's quite stunning how little control most of us exert over our own minds. It's as if we have no free will. Is there anybody in charge around here? Any little doubt or memory can send us careening off on a bender of insecurity, anger, or loneliness. Because we let the thought take over. All must make way for the random burp of the almighty stream of consciousness. But just because it's in your head doesn't mean you have to be cowed by it. The mind is constantly filing and sorting information, turning things over, kicking the tires of this automatic thought and that one, picking through yesterday's trash, giving ridiculous anxieties and glints of insight equal weight. Mindfulness is a process of recognizing it all as the background chatter it is and being selective about which of it you're going to entertain. And letting the rest of the thoughts fly out the same way they popped in. Most of the time we don't have any screening process, and it all just sloshes in. When you're mindful, you can catch automatic thoughts in the act, and stop yourself before you go down the sidetrack on pointless detours. You pick the thought up, look at it, and dismiss it if it's random junk. Psychologist Stephen Hayes of Hope College asserts that you don't have to take automatic thoughts seriously, because they are mere words, and only experience is real. Experience is the only truth, he says. So, since the noise is just language, you can send it packing. Mindfulness is an ancient practice that comes out of the Buddhist meditation tradition, but it's a purely practical way of lowering the off-hours anxiety, catching yourself before you go down a pointless random-thought sidetrack, by noting the thought—yes, I observe your presence, okay, fine, so what?—and letting it move on if you don't have any need for it.

The Pressure Drop

To ease re-entry back into civilian life each night, you need to decompress from the day's pressure cooker slowly. Like divers, who can't swim to the surface too rapidly from high-pressure depths or they'll get decompression sickness, we need time to adjust to changing pressures when leaving the depths of the job. Ascent must take place slowly to allow for the pressure drop, or you could explode like the nitrogen in the body of a diver with the bends.

To leave the day's stress behind, you need a decompression strategy of your own, a space where you can come up for air gradually and adjust to the different atmosphere. You've been in one mode all day—aggressive, competitive, objective-oriented—one that is the opposite of what's required for relaxation or enjoyment at home or play. You don't want to come home and start ordering your spouse around, or race through a book, or blow out your knees at the gym from a squat that carries the weight of all your job burdens. *"Pole, Pole,"* as the Kilimanjaro guides would tell you. Slowly, slowly. Create your very own Personal Pressure Drop, a zone for you to, well, zone.

Psychotherapist Mark Gorkin suggests "creating healthy transitional spaces between work and home. With couples, I'm trying to get them to give their spouse fifteen minutes before they have to start jumping into the family role." When the mind has been focused intensely in one area all day, it takes a while for it to make the cognitive shift to another role entirely. It's like trying to bring a fifty-car train to an immediate halt. The brakes have to be applied in a measured way. The best way to do that is to find buffer routines that take you out of your head for a while and switch over power to the body or help you make a clear emotional shift.

Physical activity is the perfect wind-down from the pressures of the day on several counts. Movement keeps the rational—and often irrational—left brain of the workday busy, freeing up the creative, emotional right brain to step in and help restore psychic balance. Aerobic exercise, twenty to thirty minutes of continuous activity—running, biking, swimming, walking, weight training—also provides a chemical buffer zone for you, countering the adrenaline response to stress by releasing endorphines, the body's natural tranquilizers. The one-two punch of reassigning the work-obsessed left brain to motion duty and breaking up the stress cycle through aerobic activity gives your body and mind the break they need to move into another zone. I'm always amazed at how completely a run or a lifting session can wipe the mind clean of toxic worries and fixations. A good workout for me is equivalent to waking up in the morning with a clean slate upstairs. Total restoration. Exercise forces all the troublemakers in your mind to the bench, since worries seem to be allergic to physical movement.

Despite all the education most of us have, we're still largely governed by something we can barely understand: our moods. This is what we're usually left with at the end of the working day, the raw emotion of feeling—frustration, exhaustion, unhappiness, anger, numbness. So separating yourself from the workday means finding ways to shift not only what's in your head but what's in your spirit. For this part of the disengagement process, you can turn to any number of legal mood shifters, from music, to socializing with friends, to getting out in nature, to learning a new instrument, to volunteer work. Changing attitudes is the specialty of leisure activities, which is what makes an active recreational component so important to life balance. You can't let the mood hangover of the workday turn your nights into droopy vegging. Push through that reflex to cling to fatigue and sofa cushions and do something fun—go bowling, ride a bike, hear a lecture, try a wine tasting, buy a samba album (the antidote to any foul mood) and let it rip full blast. The energy you don't think you have is usually just the mirage of mood, and will come roaring back once the activity has sent the mood packing. The longer you allow yourself to be dominated by a circular work mood, the more you allow the job to rule your personal hours. Don't let it. Change your mood, and you change your mind, leaving job fixations at the office and your home once again your castle.

13

Shove It

Quit a Job That's Killing You

• • •

"Present dangers are less than future imaginings."
—William Shakespeare

The one trait of successful people that you never hear about (because it's a national taboo) is that they are experts at cutting their losses. Success requires risk, and risks don't always pay off. Behind most success, you'll find setbacks. It took Rowland Macy seven attempts before he found success with his retail store. Even Donald Trump suffered major setbacks, with big financial losses in 1990. Success, like life, is a game of trial and error, and the ones who fare best are able to treat the error part as it's done in science—where you find out what works by finding out what doesn't. They have the ability to distance themselves from the event personally, which allows them to commit one of the biggest sins from sea to shining sea: They quit a dead-end course.

Persistence is one of our greatest virtues, but it's also one of our biggest vices when fear of being a "quitter" is used to keep you doing something you hate. No job is worth risking your health, your family, and the obliteration of living time. Yet many people continue to subject themselves to jobs that are making them sick and breaking their spirit—for the security, of course, but also because they have been trained to believe that quitting is more shameful than armed robbery.

Decisions motivated by fear of other people's disapproval cannot move you forward. They block risk, not to mention IQ, and you wind up killing yourself to do what others want you to do because of a commandment you're not supposed to break: *Thou shalt never quit your job.*

Sometimes the only way out of an unbearable work environment is to exit stage left or right for healthier pastures. No one wants to get to this point, and you always have to weigh the factors carefully, but if it's a choice between an abusive job and keeling over, losing your family or integrity, or having no space to live, a change of scenery may be the best course of action. In this chapter we'll explore some of the things that make it so difficult to leave even the worst of jobs, such as the need for security, the overspending habit, and the investment in time and energy that we've sunk into a given company or profession. What is job satisfaction anyway, and how will you know when you've found it? We'll hear about people who've made the break and carved out lives they want to lead, shifting professions or just plain downshifting to a place with room to breathe.

No matter how miserable a job is and how ill it's making you, the fact is you are there because you choose to be there. That you may choose to not be there is simply another decision you are free to make. Despite the supposed rule against quitting, more and more are doing it. According to *U.S. News and World Report,* some seventeen million Americans quit their jobs in 1999. So you're not alone. And these workers will be getting raises in the 10 percent to 20 percent range, compared to 4 percent if they stayed where they were. Leaving a job that you can barely drag yourself to is not the end of the world, but it may be the beginning.

To Stay or Not to Stay

The court of public opinion is the toughest judicial venue in the land. The rulings it hands down to us are so convincing, no enforcement is even needed. We police ourselves. And do an extremely good job of it. It's unknown how the decisions are transmitted to all of us self-deputies, but within our internal code there are rules that we just know to be true. Such as: I should stay at my job for (pick a year) one year, three years, five years, even if I despise it. The goal is to show commitment to your company and, thereby, look good on your resumé. It's not a bad idea to stay with an employer, except when it causes you to do something stupid, like overwork until you're in the back of an ambulance.

Susan, the editor who wound up flat on her back on her office floor at World Bank, is a sobering example of how arbitrary notions of what you "should" do, based on your interpretation of what other people say about job loyalty, can get you in serious trouble. It was clear within a few months at the job that she was hung out to dry by her superiors. Staffers left and were never replaced, leaving her with eighty-hour weeks that were quickly caving in her body. But she felt she had to stick with her job several years to show the appropriate job time span on her resumé for her next move up. By the time Susan finally quit three years later, she could barely sit or stand, her back had been so ravaged by the stress and nonstop schedule. Had she left earlier, she could have saved herself a spine and thousands of dollars in medical bills. The irony is that the job was so horrific, she doesn't even care what's on her resumé anymore and wants to do something in a totally different profession.

Career counselor McMeekin sees plenty of people who continue to subject themselves to unhealthy working environments, because of laws they invented from their perception of the court of public opinion. "People come in and say, 'I can't leave my job, because I have to stay there five years, even though I hate it and they're being horrible.' And I say, 'Where did that axiom come from?' 'Well, you have to stay there five years.' People have these ideas about loyalty that are not being reciprocated by their employers."

When you feel you "should" stay at a job much longer than you want to, that word is the unmistakable sound of guilt. All the work-related things you feel "you really should" do, don't come from you; they come from others, and from the guilt you'll feel if you don't do what you think they want you to.

Nowhere is it written that you must work for a company for a certain arbitrary period of time—unless you're under contract. You are as free to opt out as your employer is to relieve you of your duties, which these days is quite free, indeed. Layoffs have become as routine a feature of the American economy as pruning back the rosebushes. If you are in an unbearable working situation, you can't afford to let the "shoulds" give you any bright ideas. None of them will be yours, for one. Behind them all is the tell-tale hand of others, demanding that you bend to their will. Despite the drumbeat of overwork messages, you are not obligated to make yourself a project for the medical school textbooks.

There's no "should" in job satisfaction. You do it because you want to. The industrial psychologist Frederick Herzberg, known for his ground-breaking work in the study of job motivation, identified six factors in job satisfaction:

- **Recognition**

- **Achievement**

- **Possibility of growth**

- **Advancement**

- **Responsibility**

- **The work itself**

These are the motivators that influence positive attitudes about the job, and you'll notice none of them are orders or guilt-inspired commands. They fire us up because they appeal to the need within everyone for self-actualization, to be all you are. That's the goal your psyche is striving for, growth of the unique individual that you have to be. But you can never fulfill that need when you're going through the motions doing what others or you think you "should" do at a job you want to leave.

The other part of the job-satisfaction equation is values. Unlike the aspirational needs that everyone has, each of us brings our own set of values to the workplace, a lifeview that reflects our belief system— which includes how we feel about everything from integrity, to kindness, honesty, morality, the environment, family, happiness, community, sprituality, money, and politics. The increasing frenzy to cut staffs and costs, drive up hours and share prices, and focus on short-term gains to the exclusion of everything else has created a conflict in values for many workers, who find themselves cogs in wheels they don't believe in. This has the same effect as a lack of motivators, slamming the door on our ability to act as who we need to be to realize our ultimate nature. So there's a lot behind that generalized feeling you have of being stuck and that it's time to move on. You're built for progress. Those boots were made for walking.

What Security?

I think we can all agree now that job security is dead. It wouldn't be the first casualty in the certainty sweepstakes. As many prognosticators as we have out there, no one really has a clue as to what's going to happen next or how we can achieve ultimate security. Because we can't. That doesn't stop us from trying, though. Propelled by the survival imperative, we spend most of our lives shoring up defenses against who knows what and desperately seeking all that makes us feel safe. Many a goal in life has gone down the drainpipe of security, particularly job security— now a contradiction in terms. The pink slip could come at any moment, your company could be bought, or rapid changes in your industry could make your position obsolete in a nanosecond.

With all the volatility today, real security may lie in accepting an idea shared by street-corner and Eastern philosophers—that there is no security, at least of the financial or immortal kind. The security lies in knowing that you don't need all the anxiety of trying to be secure anymore. You're not, which can be a very freeing notion. Think of all you wouldn't put up with if you weren't trying to secure a future that can't be completely guaranteed.

There's nothing wrong with planning and being prepared. But as nice as it is to feel secure, it's never a good enough reason for compromising your physical or emotional well-being or postponing the experience of living. We are taught to go for the security, i.e., the money, but it can't deliver. We're trained to buy security with piles of possessions, but that doesn't work, either. They can't provide internal security, the only one that counts—life satisfaction, the sense of making a contribution, the thrill of the new, all of which require leaving the secured perimeter. Having a moat around your castle doesn't promote the security of openness and well-being that come from happiness; it creates a defensive posture, the need to protect and amass. The Taoist philosopher Lao Tzu observed this futility: "When gold and jade fill your rooms, no one will be able to guard them for you."

A more realistic approach may be to act like there isn't any security. This way you keep your eye on many options and don't get reamed by a toxic job or slavish devotion to a resumé. Career coach McMeekin agrees that the upheaval all around requires a new approach to employment planning. "You need to anticipate that you may not be at the company you're at for very long," she advises. "It doesn't mean you don't work really hard and try to maximize the time. But you really need to be looking for better opportunities and not put all your eggs in one basket. We need to look at every job as really kind of a consulting gig, and evaluate very carefully up front who these people are, what they have to offer and do we really want to be there."

That's a crucial shift, from servant to contractor, and it can empower you to embrace the reality of the multiple gig world, instead of clinging to a destructive job until it creates irreparable damage. It's a cliché but true: The only thing we can really be secure about is change, now more than ever. Going with that inevitable motion, instead of resisting it, lets you swim with the tide of impermanence, instead of against it. Accepting this reality offers more of a sense of security—in its acceptance of the unexpected—than futilely trying to buck it by holding on.

What Keeps You Stuck

We tend to get stuck in jobs we should have left years ago, because we are nothing if not champion creatures of habit, which soon becomes a rut. Sometimes your head has already left the company, but your body just keeps showing up every day, as if under the spell of a diabolical personnel director. Why is this? Why can't you just make the move you know you have to make? The answer is the devil we know is always preferable to what we don't know. What's out there could be worse. But it also could be the job that could give you back your life. How much risk would that be worth?

Our risk-taking ability, though, is hampered by certain mental barriers and lifestyle habits. Let's take a look at several of the chief culprits that keep us stuck:

RESUMÉ RIGORMORTIS

It's quite astounding the power that this piece of paper has over lives. Millions of people are controlled, written, and directed by the resumé, not the person who appears on it. Like Susan, the woman who wound up on her back at her cubicle, they sacrifice their health to it. They give up jobs they may want to do because they wouldn't look good on the resumé. They dismiss thoughts of traveling around the world for a few months after college or between jobs because it would be seen as flaky on the almighty document of human worth. When you let your story be dictated by how things will look on this fragment of who you are, someone else is the author. To break out of the box, you need to think not how job and life moves will look to others, but how they will address your needs and desires. Don't reduce your potential to the size of a resumé. The paper should have to fit your life, not the other way around. Being run by your resumé is like the shoes running the human. If you're extremely unhappy doing what you're doing, try something completely different. Take a direction your resumé would hate, which means you'll probably like it.

PRISONER OF THE PAST

Sometimes what keeps you stuck is a profession you don't want to be in anymore. It's hard to admit that the course you're on isn't working, because you've put long years of dreams, education, sweat, blood, and investment into it—in cash and time. These sunk costs can be a huge barrier to taking another path. All that time and effort—how can you walk away from it? If you've given it the best shot you've got, and it hasn't turned out the way you wanted it to, it's pointless to stick with a choice you made years ago as a very different person to avoid having to admit it's not working. You already know it's not. There's nothing strange about a career change. We're supposed to have five of them apiece over our lifetimes from here on out. You're a lot smarter now than you were when you made your first career choice. You have a much better idea of what you want, because you know clearly what you don't want. Cut your losses like the pros do, and you may find yourself invigorated by a new direction.

WORK AND SPEND

The annual spending of the average American increased by 30 percent to possibly as much as 70 percent in the two decades between 1975 and 1995, according to economist and author Juliet Schor in *The Overspent American.* Meanwhile, the savings rate of the average American household plunged to half the rate it was in the mid-1980s. Schor makes a persuasive case that we are spending more than we ever have—and more than some ever have, period—due to changing social ideals and relentless marketing. Schor believes that our raging spending habit is a major contributor to the overwork trend, forcing us to work high-hours jobs to support the consuming. As the pioneer who first called attention to runaway work in *The Overworked American,* she knows of what she speaks. Overconsumption not only can keep you working longer to pay the bills, it can also limit your ability to change jobs. Record-high consumer debt may be keeping some of you stuck in a field or position you'd like to exit, because the money's good. You'll never find the balanced career you're looking for if you let out-of-control spending cut off your escape routes. Money worries box you into the material comfort zone, which is what keeps you at that job when you're already gone mentally. You'll need to discipline your spending ways to give yourself the flexibility to move, hang loose between jobs for a while, or shift down the earning totem pole, if that's where the balance is.

The reason I'm here writing this and you're reading it is because we humans are especially talented at change. We may not like it, but we know how to get used to it, which is why there are no Neanderthals launching high-tech companies or doing brain surgery. So you've got what it takes in your genes to change, adapt, and move on to greener pastures. Resumé blockage, sunk costs, or work-and-spend are only as effective in barring your path as you allow them to be. The key to the lock is in your hands. There's a lyrical line of Joseph Campbell's that has served me well over the years and maybe it will help you in your decision: "When everything is lost, and all seems darkness, then comes the new day and all that is needed." There is another day, another way, that you can't see until you allow the unknown to show it to you.

Quitting Time

If you've tried everything to make your job more inclusive of the rest of your life and are butting up against a dinosaur overwork culture that just doesn't get it, it may be time to weigh a departure. Dr. Wes Patterson says it's all about fulfillment. "When it ceases to be fulfilling, you have the physical symptoms, and that's when you have to step back and take a look at your life. The reason to change is when it's not coinciding with your goals and your desires and needs. Otherwise, you burn out."

Texas computer tech Julie Masser made a decision to quit a company that was slamming her with seventy-hour weeks and road trips that would never end. It came from the tragic clarity and perspective brought on by the sudden death of her husband. She was only thirty-one when he died of a brain aneurism. "It was a very frightening thing to leave the security of a job," she remembers. "But when I lost my husband, I really didn't give a shit if I had anything. I didn't care if I had clothes. You could have taken everything I owned, and it didn't matter. I spent a lot of time thinking. Do you really want to have to look in the phone book to see what city you're in? I was changing cities every day.

I recognized that I didn't have to play that game and have a healthy life. And money isn't the end of the world. Money doesn't mean you're a strong person, a moral person, a decent person, a good friend, a good parent." She quit an abusive job and now has a boss who "respects the right of an employee to have a personal life and time off."

The emotional exhaustion of burnout robs you of the ability to think clearly and the energy to turn discontent into action. So it's best to consider carefully the costs and benefits of moving on well in advance, asking the pertinent questions: Is there any possibility of improvement in work-life policies at this job? Or is this work culture intractably workaholic and dysfunctional? What constitutes job satisfaction for me? How could I incorporate my life goals and values with my professional occupation? What type of work could provide me with not only income, but a sense of mastery and fulfillment as well? What's my plan? Am I covered if something goes wrong? Do I have a plan B, C, and D?

Leaving a job is always a wrenching process, even if you can't stand the place. It's like moving to a new house. A lot of stuff has to come out of the closet. It's painful, but when it's over, you've been able to offload some of the junk that was cluttering up your life. One of those items ready for the Salvation Army is the corporate culture that you tried in vain to make work and that can leave you doubting yourself on the way out the door. "Sometimes you get so caught up in the system and the values of the system, that you feel like you've failed, even though on some level you feel like you didn't want to win in this ball game," explains Lawyerslifecoach.com's Ostrow.

You have to return to your goals again, and to what constitutes success and life satisfaction. Those things are your compass, not a work culture blatantly incompatible with them. Use this compass to detach yourself emotionally from the company, something you need to be able to do to find a new job, maintains McMeekin. "Most job searches never truly begin until you've let go of the past. You have to embrace change and your future."

HOW TO MAKE YOUR MOVE

There are a number of strategies to downshift and carve out a lifestyle reflective of who you are. They range from entrepreneurial and subcontractor roles that allow you the independence to set your own schedule, to career shifts that provide a sense of meaning, to targeting companies that have a reputation for employee balance, to a switch from private industry to government, where vacations are decent and the days end before the roosters wake up.

The Entrepreneurial Route. Andrew Molnar had been a harried manager at Prudential headquarters in Newark, New Jersey, stressed and torn by the conflict between his own values and the "position, power, money" mentality that drove trucks over everyone in their wake. One day a crisis erupted in the department he was managing. A key tech person was out for a week, and Molnar had to put out the fire. After three twenty-four-hour days, he went home exhausted and sick, and said, "This is defintely not for me." He and his wife started to map out an escape route. How they did it is a perfect lesson in the potential that lies within, once we embrace change, instead of holding on to what we don't want.

"Using our management experience, we got all the characteristics down of what we wanted," recalls Molnar. "We sat down and said, 'Well, what kind of thing would this look like,' instead of doing it the other way around—'What is out there,' and trying to fit our skills into that. So when we put together a list of things we'd like to do, the number one thing was running a spiritual-retreat center. We put out a powerful prayer, and three months later we got an offer to be at this place, where we're co-directors."

Molnar and his wife run Camp Frederick, a retreat center in the woods of eastern Ohio. They took an operation in the red and turned it into a thriving business, one that blends their values with their livelihood. Today they get a mere nine-week vacation every year, and they just built a house on the rustic grounds. They have exactly what they wanted, because they stopped, determined what they were looking for, and cast security to the wind. Put together your own Top 10 List of what you'd like to do. The opportunity, like Camp Fred, might be sitting out there waiting for you.

Government Benefits. If you've been burned by the workaholic ways of private industry, you might find a more sane pace in state or local government. That was Tom Garrison's solution to the boot camp world of McLain Co., a national food distributor in Texas. "They drove you hard and burned you out quick," says Garrison. He had a fifty-four-hour week, with one week's vacation. "It was nuts." He quit and took a job with the state of Texas, where his days end at a predictable hour and where he gets twice the vacation time.

Meaningful Work. The soul can't live on billable hours alone. That was the realization for Maureen, a Washington, D.C., regulatory attorney, who decided to walk away from the power and prestige of a top law firm to do something that had more meaning—and more time. She was going to be at her office until 11 P.M. the day we spoke. "Am I a slave to the billable hour?" she asked herself. "Is this what I was put on this earth to do? I'm trying to reorient my career more to what I got into this in the first place for, to do some good in the world."

Going Independent. Remember Del Cornalio, the software engineer who negotiated a six-week vacation with his boss? Well, it wasn't enough, not for someone with all the interests that Cornalio has. He wound up going solo. As a consultant in Northern California who adapts software to function in other languages, he has been able to open up a few more *months* of free time on the schedule. "I probably do one or two contracts a year—six or seven months of working," he says. "The rest I take off deliberately. For every contract I take, I probably turn down a dozen. Maybe it's not wildly lucrative. I'm not as rich as I could be if I was working my brains out. But I'm a lot happier. I press my own olive oil and grow my own olives. I've written two cookbooks, and I spend a lot of time volunteering." What would it be like to have as much time for your life as Cornalio? Think of what you could do, of all the things there are out there to see and learn and discover and experience. Then figure out a skill that you have or could go to school to acquire that would allow you to live a life you design. Goodbye, cubicle!

Target the Best. If you're not ready for a full downshift yet, try targeting your job search to companies that show up regularly in job-satisfaction and quality-of-life surveys. Check out the annual listing put out by the Great Place to Work Institute (www.greatplacetowork.com, 415-503-1234), which appears in *Fortune.* A better survey may be the one done by *Business and Health* magazine (www.businessandhealth.com), which rates the healthiest companies in America. You can find the firms out there that have model wellness and work-life programs.

The lessons of downshifters across the land make it clear that it pays to quit—when what you're quitting is a work culture hazardous to your health and values that's as blind as a mole in a hole to the life-denying tunnel world it speeds back and forth in. Look up, and you'll see it. A crack, an opening you can take to the surface of the earth, where there is sky and mountains and grass to walk on in your bare feet.

14

The Time of Your Life

Travel and Leisure as Good as It Gets

• • •

"The more a person is able to direct his life consciously, the more he can use time for constructive benefits. The more conformist and unfree he is, the more time is the master. He serves time."

—Psychologist Rollo May

As I tiptoed through reeds higher than my head on a bushwalk in Zimbabwe's Chizarira Wilderness, I noticed something I'd never heard before: the loudness of stillness. It was so quiet I could hear anything that interrupted it. Birdsong by the bird. Rustling branches by the tree. Every reed I brushed, every twig I stepped on exploded like a sonic boom, leading to the loudest sound of all, my own nervous breathing. I was trying to keep it down, because I didn't want to disturb the three male elephants I was tracking with a local guide and four other travelers, not to mention whatever else was grunting and whooping out in that thicket.

I was paying special attention to the wind, since our objective was to stay downwind from the pachyderms, whose acute sense of smell would tip them off to our presence. They could be aggressive, as I suppose we all are when we get drop-ins. Every few minutes the guide would lift a wet index finger to the sky for a hint of the latest developments. We walked a little while, stopped, cocked our ears, and raised index fingers, then started creeping again in a lane not made by guys in orange flak jackets. A corps of tusker engineers had just trampled this corridor into shape, leaving behind basketball-size reminders of their work for me to trip over. It was a thrilling game of hide-and-seek, which had me feeling like an extremely tall 10-year-old, which is to say, that despite being an adult, I was having fun.

We scrambled up an embankment and darted behind a termite mound. On the other side, only fifteen feet away, the three tuskers ripped away at a spindly tree, oblivious to our presence, their great trunks tearing off branches and tucking them into their mouths. Peering around the side of the mud stack, I was riveted by this image of classic Africa. It wasn't coming from a TV screen. The picture was real. And so was my elation at being able to witness this authentic slice of living history. It was as if I was peeling back the curtain to something "closer to the beginning," as novelist Graham Greene once put it.

My participation had made it happen. Being on foot, instead of in a vehicle, changed the whole dynamic of the experience. As the turf changed, so did my perspective—from that of a detached observer to a biped mammal feeling vulnerable and awed. The usual wandering mind had shifted to total focus in the moment. I wasn't thinking about E-mails I had to send or videos I had to return. I didn't have to crouch better than anyone else or judge the bushwalk against any other event to enjoy it. No tusker had to balance a baboon on the end of its trunk for me to get my money's worth. All was splendid exactly as it was in its unstaged state.

When you're having the time of your life, nothing is missing from the picture. That tends to happen often when you're immersed in the participant experience, absorbed in things that get you out of the deep space of brain-lock and into hands-on living. You're transported out of autopilot and order-taking to full engagement, which is transformative. You come back different than when you left, charged with a sense of possibility about all there is to see and do out there beyond the speck of your own day-to-day. It's not necessary to chase large animals with big ears to get this feeling. You can find it any time you leave the spectating bleachers and plunge into participant leisure experiences. There are hundreds of them out there, and we'll take a look at some of the options in this chapter.

Along the way we'll dispel some myths about leisure, which is not at all about counting the threads in your shirtsleeve. Quality leisure is an active process of engagement and discovery. It requires your involvement and direction, and that takes a proactive approach to time off—a leisure ethic. Since few of us are given many clues about what to do in our free time, we'll examine some of the skills required for this elusive realm and get to know the whereabouts of the Discovery Zone. We'll also learn the keys to the main ingredient of great vacations, direct experience, where you are no longer living in fear of the future or regret about the past, merely getting through the day. You're immersed in the rapture of being fully alive. Let's get to it.

You're the Director

Habit has a way of obliterating memory. We've been breaking rocks so long now that many of us are too exhausted to imagine anything else. We have forgotten how to relax, if we ever learned. If you don't know anything else, you tend to keep doing what you do know—work. I'm convinced this obliviousness is the leading reason why we have $19 billion in unused vacation time annually. We just don't know what's on the other side of the grindstone. It's high time, then, that we made the acquaintance, or reacquaintance, with leisure, an item quite unlike its reputation.

First of all, leisure is not suspended animation until you get to the next planet. It's not doing nothing. In fact, it's the opposite. It's an active state of engagement in pursuits of your own choosing that bring enjoyment, growth, and meaning to your life. Leisure's bad rap comes from the old Puritan superstition and from the spectating nature of most off-hours today, zoning in front of TVs or cash registers. As David Myers points out in *The Pursuit of Happiness,* "Well-being resides not in mindless passivity but in mindful challenge." Aristotle couldn't have agreed more. He noted in *Ethics* that "It is commonly believed that happiness depends on leisure." For the ancient Greeks, leisure was a time of action, to experiment, discover, and tap individual potential.

It still is. Leisure is nothing less than your expression of how you spend your freedom. It's your declaration of independence from the necessities of life. As the ultimate arena of free choice, leisure should be as all-American as monster trucks. It's more ruggedly individualistic than work any day. Unlike the job, where you are at the command of others, you are completely in charge of your leisure. You're the entertainment director.

You may have a half dozen bosses running the work end of your life, but you are the boss when it comes to your time off. Maybe that's why Herman Melville once declared that "the dignity is in leisure, not labor." If you use your leisure authority, you gain even more initiative. Leisure participation has been shown to contribute to a sense of self-determination. "An active leisure lifestyle is marked by an enhanced sense of freedom and control over one's behaviors," notes sociologist Seppo Iso-Ahola. Since it's your choice, leisure can provide benefits the best job can't, which is why it has been found to be a crucial component in well-being. Researchers have documented that frequent leisure participation is a leading indicator of life satisfaction—the more you're involved in leisure activities, the higher the satisfaction level.

But first you have to know what to do in your spare time besides fidget. In traditional cultures, people learned a variety of creative skills to use in their free time—carving, dancing, weaving, storytelling, making pottery. Half the population of Bali today can play a traditional instrument or perform a ceremonial dance. Our leisure talents lean more to gourmet popcorn popping. So maybe it's time we did a little brushing up on free-time skills. What are the keys? It starts with awareness, a conscious redirection of time, "an ethical context that says, 'I value my time,' or 'I'm going to do something I really enjoy,' or 'I'm going to be with people,'" says David Compton, professor of recreation and leisure at the University of Utah. "You need to understand why it's important for you to disengage from work and engage in activities that bring pleasure and happiness, not for hedonistic or materialistic benefits, but for genuine satisfaction."

In other words, you need to have a leisure ethic, an identity outside the job that comes from doing things you are passionate about, and the willingness to indulge those interests for your own intrinsic satisfaction. Having a leisure ID is critical to your work-life balance. The interests, enjoyments, and relationships that create that identity are the "living" you're making for yourself.

How do you get a leisure ID? You have to be a self-starter, because none of the work drones around you is going to do it for you. No one can. Only you know what rings your personal bell. The skills you need for it are similar to those in the entrepreneurial arena—a desire for competence or mastery, the ability to be intrinsically motivated, and what the psychologists call "activation," the ability to convert that motivation into reality. That's all just a fancy way of saying that it takes some curiosity and the inclination to follow it wherever it leads, even into areas you might be a rank amateur in. Trying new things is an essential ingredient in the leisure experience, a key to the discovery and stimulation that will keep you coming back for more. Experiment. Dabble. And you're on your way to an ID that's all you for once.

HOW TO STIMULATE YOUR LEISURE TOOL KIT:

- **Take the lead.** Don't wait for leisure opportunities to come to you. Start conversations and make invitations to get things going.

- **Explore.** Be nosy. Wonder your way into new activities and passions.

- **Go solo.** Fear of doing things alone is a huge block to developing your leisure ID. Remember, it's your satisfaction that is at stake here, nobody else's. In the course of doing things solo in areas of interest, you'll meet many fellow travelers.

- **Talk about nothing.** If your calls these days are all about business or objectives, there aren't going to be many leisure opportunities coming up. Talk about nothing—i.e., the life outside the office—and something will.

- **Get diverted.** Allow yourself to get lost in pleasurable diversions from work life. The adventure is in the detours.

- **Activate your social network.** The leisure terrain lies fallow unless you work it. Get back in touch and schedule regular outings.

- **Join the club.** Find a club or organization that represents an interest of yours and get involved. Participation leads to activation of leisure potential.

Unpack Your Bags

Once you've cleared time for a vacation, you'll need to start unpacking. That's right. With a year of work and home tensions weighing you down, before you can get out of town you have to get the town out of you. Put together an unpacking list of the stuff that has no business going with you—work worries, the boss, colleagues, career progress, laptops, pagers, cell phones. Just drop all that deadweight completely. Stash it somewhere—there's probably room in the garage—until you get back. Make sure no one and nothing from your work life is stowing away on the trip with you when you're paying all the bills.

That goes just as much for work behavior as it does for obsessive thinking about work. It's reflex to bring the hard-charging, results-oriented approach of the office on vacation with you. But don't let the drill sergeant tag along. It defeats the whole point of the vacation, which is about the journey, not speeding to your return flight as soon as possible. Using the production yardstick and hurry-worry to pace your holiday is like wanting to know where a jazz concert will go before it starts. It's all in the playing.

One large chunk of the excess baggage that needs to be offloaded is guilt. You've worked hard for this trip and deserve it. Ditto with other limiting routines such as closed-mindedness and judgmental behavior. Be open to new experiences and strand the critic, of yourself as well as others, at home. Do pack plenty of curiosity and patience.

The control freak isn't going anywhere, either. That killjoy stays home. To get the most out of your vacation, you're going to have to give up the wheel and excess steering of events. Figure out what you want to do, but in a way that lets you roll with it and improvise. Allow yourself the freedom to enjoy whatever happens.

That will be easier when you unpack another albatross, the to-do list. Leave behind the pressure to accomplish an agenda, or the trip isn't going to be successful. That's the work mode you're trying to ditch. Leave room for improvisation and whims. That's part of being free. If you don't want to do anything one morning, stay in bed and enjoy that rare pleasure. It's your time, and you can do anything you want with it. Getting the most out of your holiday doesn't come from cramming every minute of the day with activities. You want to find a good balance of participant elements and carefree hours that you can use as you like. The goal should be fulfilling time, not filling time. Let things unfold as they will, and you will, too. Notching off agenda items leaves you inevitably miserable at the end of the trip that you didn't do all you wanted to. Nobody's counting!

Another item you can do without is consigning yourself to the hermetic tourist cocoons that isolate you from the experience of the new and unknown, which is the main route to re-creation. I know this is weird, but you have to actually do the traveling yourself to really go somewhere. That's the rule. Remember, you're the entertainment director. Step out from the comfort zone into a participant approach, and the real breakout from the box begins. You no longer have your I-know hat on, screening things out because they're different from your routine or too risky. You're out of the headlock.

And finally, before you take off, you have to dump the adult bias against play. Play is recognized as a critical component of health and growth in kids, but we have the idea that it's beneath us solemn grown-ups because it's nonproductive and, therefore, frivolous. But we can no more deny the shouts of "Red Rover" in our biochemistry than we can unzip our skins and walk away from ourselves. The enjoyment equipment is all built in—mouths to laugh with, legs to run with, arms to throw with, hands to clap with.

Thou should play. Not only because you can, but because you have to. It's a major antidote to stress and the leading cause of that anxiety—taking yourself too seriously. And here's the kicker: Because it gives you what you really want, intrinsic satisfaction, play is more productive on the esteem and well-being fronts than a stadium full of flow charts. It gives you the permission to enjoy yourself without the pressure to succeed or the fear of failure. You are free from expectations, which allows you to try new things, spurring the learning process. While you might feel stuck in your job, play can keep you growing, expanding your emotional range, developing new skills, and offering outlets for self-expression. So don't be childish and ignore a vital part of who you are. As Picasso said in his later years, "It took me a long time to become young."

Here are some guidelines to help you get your vacation off the ground and leave the party crashers at home:

1. **Don't wait till it's too late.** Start thinking about what you want to do on your holiday at least six months ahead of time.

2. **Don't abbreviate.** Push for all the time you can get. Three-day weekends are fine interludes, but they're not vacations. Go for two weeks and more, if you can get it. You need time to fully recharge and rejuvenate.

3. **Target passions.** Build your vacation around the things that you like to do for intrinsic pleasure or that you've always wanted to learn.

4. **Find the participant element.** The job keeps you in observation mode; now it's time to get involved. Participation changes everything, and is key to the transformational possibilities of vacations. Try a bike trip through the California wine country, learn some new recipes at a cooking school in Tuscany, or hike the backcountry of Colorado.

5. **Lose the watch.** Home front impatience and hurry-worry can destroy your holiday. Don't bring the rush hour on vacation, which

is like taking a bullet train to your mailbox. You're already there. Ratchet back the pace a few dozen miles per hour, and just relax. Take the watch off and bury it in one of your socks.

6. **Push the Play button.** Drop the work ID and put on your kid hat. You are now officially at recess.

7. **Drop agendas.** It doesn't matter whether you see two museums or one or none in a given day. The point is being there for the ride to whatever happens.

8. **Get lost.** Lose yourself in the experience, and you'll find something that was missing, the joy of spontaneity.

9. **Take a leap.** Get out of your box and do something completely different. Take some risks, try new food or activities. Growth is the most valuable souvenir you can bring home.

10. **Be a fool.** To get the most from your experience, you have to plunge in, whether you know what you're doing or not. It's okay to be completely inept at something new. Vulnerability is the road to discovery and authenticity. The less you let your I-know mind run things, the better time you'll have. People like you better when you're not in control.

11. **Don't get canned.** Avoid canned vacations that leave you out of the equation. If they're doing it all for you, you are still in a box, sealed off from the life awaiting you.

12. **Try a new personality.** The vacation setting allows you to be however you want to be in a world where no one knows you. Trade shy for outgoing and negative for positive.

13. **Take the inside track.** Make sure you have time for the stuff you never do at home, inside activities—reflection, contemplation, and general spacing. That's where you'll find new routes and attitudes—and a re-created mental outlook.

14. Cut the E-leash. For your holiday to really be a holiday, there can't be any reminders of work in the vicinity. No E-mail or phone messages are allowed. Pagers will be impounded. This is your time, not the company's.

Get Out of Your Head

Most of us spend our days locked in cerebral combat, analyzing, reanalyzing, weighing, worrying, speculating. We're so wrapped up in thought that we're just going through the motions of life from the neck down. But participant travel can get you out of your head and into something your whole body can feel: direct experience. When you enter this full-contact world, the buffers between you and full immersion in life fall away, and you're back to your old self again. It's the way you used to do things as a kid—plunging in, learning through doing, absorbing without judging.

Direct experience is so concentrated it screens everything else out, including the constant din of the nattering mind. The background noise of doubts, demands, and fears is silenced, leaving you in the rare position of complete receptivity and openness. You enter the realm of what Maslow called "peak experience," and what Mihaly Czikzentmihalyi dubbed "flow," a state when you are fully involved in an activity to the point that you lose awareness of everything else but what you're doing. You are so focused that even self-consciousness doesn't dare get in your way. There's a complete integration with the experience and the moment, where, for once, you are fully inside your own time, undistracted by the constant comparatives of this moment with another one, by self-critical yammering, or the drumbeat of future dreads. Like a surfer peeling across the face of an endless curl, you have become the ride. Czikzentmihalyi calls it "flow," because that's the feeling, that all is sailing effortlessly along to your cues. I've experienced it many times in travel, and it is one of the most sublime sensations on earth. As random strangers, luck, and serendipities pop into my path without any conscious direction from me, it's a sense of being plugged into the planetary opposite of Murphy's Law: Anything that can go right, does. It's my very own harmonic convergence. I feel like a ball floating down a mountain stream that Alan Watts once described. I "cannot be blocked, stopped, or embarassed in any situation." I am "simply continuous."

I'm not surprised that these flow experiences are as good as it gets for *Homo sapiens,* according to Czikzentmihalyi. These are the times when people report they are at their happiest and life is at its most satisfying, when they are lost in the moment of complete involvement. The reason, explains Czikzentmihalyi, is that these "optimal experiences add up to a sense of mastery—or perhaps better, a sense of participation in determining the content of life—that comes as close to what is usually meant by happiness as anything else we can conceivably imagine."

Determining life content is not an item in big supply back in cubicle country. As a result, we can develop limiting beliefs around the pigeonholes we're restricted to, defining ourselves by our sales for the day, how well we did in the meeting, or whether we've got enough pull to get that primo parking spot. The direct experience of travel makes you realize that you are more, much more, than those limiting gauges, that they, in fact, don't define you at all. Fired by the power of possibility, you know there's more beyond the office and its limited version of you.

How do you make the magic happen? Just as you have to step out from the work bunker to find life, you have to get out of the tourist bubble, out of the role of audience member stuck with the entertainment served up. You have to plunge in and allow yourself to be swept up. Follow the road less traveled, more authentic, less commodified, and these simple directions to the Discovery Zone of direct experience:

THE DISCOVERY ZONE

- Go one more step beyond your comfort zone. Then another.

- Talk to one more stranger. And then another.

- Immerse yourself into one more activity you've never done before. And then another.

- Linger one more minute. And then another.

Adventures To Go

Unlike traditional travel, where observation is the goal, adventurous travel is your ticket to participation. You travel closer to the land and the people, which lets you interact with both instead of being sealed off by the tourist cocoon. Immerse yourself into the world around you, and the world within you, calcified by excess career focus, also comes to life.

Your destination is the journey of personal exploration. It's a mode that is appealing to more and more people lost in the concrete jungle. Adventure travel now makes up about 40 percent of the entire travel dollar. The action usually takes place in outdoor or natural settings, but adventure really can take place wherever you are, because it's a state of mind, a willingness to explore unfamiliar territory—to you (it doesn't matter how many people have been there before you). It's about the vast landscape of incognita territory within each of us, revealed through the magic of the journey.

You can head out on an adventure on your own, with a Lonely Planet guidebook and a spirit of independent wanderlust, or you can buy adventure off the shelf from one of thousands of companies offering trips, from backcountry hikes in the Rockies to sailing trips along the Turkish coast. Or you can mix and match, traveling independently but hooking up with a guide for a portion of the trip.

Most adventurous travelers do it the independent way. I've always traveled this way, because it guarantees maximum freedom, which is what I love about travel. The schedule's open enough to change your route when you get a hot tip from a fellow traveler or you can hang out longer if you like. Software engineer Del Cornalio and his wife decided to do just that on a trip through the Mediterranean. They rented a house for a month in the town of Kloxylos on the Greek isle of Náxos, which gave them a full loaf or two of cultural adventures. Cornalio's landlord turned out to be the village baker, who Cornalio helped out, baking bread in an old, olive wood-fire oven. "It was magical," recalls Cornalio. "We kept our days unstructured and let the travel spirit evolve, and amazing things happened every day."

Getting inside other worlds gives you a new latitude. You see things you can't know unless you're there. Boulder, Colorado, marketing consultant John Ricks got his outlook altered on a packaged adventure trip to East Africa. Climbing Mount Kilimanjaro gave him a bogglingly new perspective, on the world from 19,000 feet, and on his ability as a 50-year-old to do things he didn't know he could do. But meeting local Africans left him with an even more lasting impression. "They were so friendly," he recalls. "Their per-capita income is about $200 a year, but they're the happiest people I've ever been around. What you realize is you don't need all the stuff that you have. We've got too much."

The participant adventure fired up Ricks so much that he and his wife were ready to go again as soon as they got back, which is standard procedure for people who've just had their heads spun around like a top by the sensory explosion of direct experience. The next year they trekked through the Peruvian Andes, and now they're planning a climb of Europe's tallest peak, Mount Elbrus, in the Georgian Republic. Once you go, you want to keep going, to live the exciting possibilities you know are out there.

You can come out and play now.

TAKEOFF TIPS

There are thousands of adventures that you can dream up or buy already designed—from mountain treks, to rainforest trips, to whitewater raft outings. Here's what you need to do to get yourself out the door on one of them:

1. **Get moving.** You need to quickly move from the idea that you'd like to do something to concrete action. Home in on some areas of interest and start researching.

2. **Target the geography.** Prepare a Top 5 List of geographical areas you'd like to explore, from your own state to far-flung destinations.

3. **Choose a genre.** What genre of adventure are you interested in? Choose from nature, sports, wildlife, cultural, wilderness, arche-

ological, biking adventures, or a host of other categories that might fill the bill.

4. **Select an activity.** What type of participant experience are you looking for? Sailing? Hiking? Whitewater rafting? Or maybe just independent exploring? Keep a Top 5 List here, too, and winnow it down to a winner.

5. **Choose your travel style.** Are you an independent traveler? There are many rewards for going this route—authenticity, price, the fun of planning and navigating on your own, finding unexpected places, spontaneous adventures, and meeting a host of other independent travelers along the way. If you're too busy to plan your own trip, or where you want to go is too remote to do on your own, or you just want built-in company, you might want to buy your adventure from a tour operator.

6. **Don't let money be a barrier.** It's cheaper to travel than you think. I stayed last year at a very nice pensione in Lisbon, Portugal, for $30 a night. You can have a bungalow on the beach on a Thai island for $10 a night. Book your flight early. Use a consolidator to cut as much as 50 percent off your airfare. Take a longer trip. You pay through the nose on three- and four-day trips. You can save money booking trips with European or Australian tour operators, which are cheaper than American companies because they offer fewer amenities. You can find these companies on the Web.

7. **Don't let fear of traveling solo get in your way.** If there's no one to go with, go yourself! Veteran travelers know that you're not solo very often when you're on the Fellow Traveler Circuit. You'll bump into folks all over the place, some of whom will become lifelong friends. It's easy. You need each other to figure out where the hell you are and where you're going. There are tens of thousands of solo women travelers exploring every nook and cranny on the globe. I ran into a 20-year-old Canadian girl at

Victoria Falls in Zimbabwe who had traveled all over Africa by herself, and hadn't had a single problem. Get out there, and you'll never want to stop.

8. **You can let other people figure it out.** If you don't have time, and you've got the budget, there are thousands of adventures to go available through trip outfitters. Try companies such as GeoExpeditions (*www.geoexpeditions.com;* 415-922-0448), which specializes in Himalayan hikes and exotic Asian destinations. Or try: Journeys International in Ann Arbor, Michigan (*www.journeys-intl.com;* 800-255-8735); Southwind Adventures, for South American escapes (*www.southwindadventures.com;* 800-377-9463); or Down Under Answers for Australia and New Zealand adventures (800-788-6685).

9. **You don't have to be an athlete to have adventure.** If you can do a few laps around the average mall, you can handle most of the adventures out there. There are some fitness and skill levels needed for certain climbing and rafting trips, but those will be detailed in tour operator catalogs.

10. **Families can have adventures, too.** The family that plays together stays together. With a little planning, the whole crew can partake in an adventure. The national parks are a great base camp for affordable adventurous activities. There is also a growing number of companies offering programs tailored to families. Check out Rascals in Paradise, in San Francisco; Are We There Yet in Corte Madera, California; and Away.com.

11. **Ignore the fear mongers.** Don't let the acts of the deranged and the sensation-peddlers keep you from leaving your house or getting on planes. They've gotten exactly what they wanted when that happens. Don't let them take your life away. One of the better things travel does is to let you see first-hand that the world isn't clamoring to slice you up. The trust is out there, one more step beyond fear.

Inner Journeys

To function in the workplace you have to be not just good at producing things, but good at not producing some things, too—mainly, revelations about who you really are. You're kind of a secret agent. You've got your assigned identity—double-O job title; a special power costume, and an exotic language, office-speak, which allows you to talk with colleagues for years without really saying anything about yourself. It's a minuet of personas, the business masks we all wear.

Spend too much time in deep cover, and you lose touch with the character behind the role. The result is suffocation inside and confusion outside about who you really are, about what your priorities are underneath that mountain of organizational duty. It stems from the fact that we don't like being secret agents. We're bad actors. We all have a deep-seated urge to be known for who we are, the individual, not the collective face, to live as much as we can from an authentic place. As the hours in the persona role dominate and squeeze out all else, we're cut off from the source of real identity, the interior world, which doesn't thrive in a setting where bloodlessness is the admired ideal. That makes it critically important to carve out time outside the office to feed the soul.

A vacation is the one time a year when you can step back from the fray and get the bigger picture. It can locate the identity behind the mask that's been buried deep in layers of career sediment. You're back to doing things you like to do, which reminds you of other long dormant interests and emotions, and you're moving back to your center again. By slowing you down and focusing all of your attention on what's in front of you now, a good journey can open your eyes to things obscured by the filters of the workday and your own self-awareness. Planted completely in the moment, you begin to see through to the truer nature of things, what the Japanese poet Basho called the "hidden glimmering" behind it all. You're able to get to an essence that lies just behind the everyday surface of perception. This is why it's so easy to get past appearances with people you meet while traveling. You quickly move beyond difference to commonality, since the judges are on vacation, too.

The change of venue lets you see things with new eyes. In Morocco I hired a guide and rode a camel into the Sahara Desert. The night sky in the Sahara was worth the trip alone, a ceiling of horizon-to-horizon sequins. I stood on the sand outside my tent, spellbound by the usually hidden glimmerings of infinite twinklings and a Milky Way I'd never seen before, one that looked like a white-water river, it was so sharp and frothy. Shooting stars streaked like firecrackers. At that moment the galaxy became for me, not something distant and other-worldly, but rather nearby, like the neighborhood, and I could feel my star-stuff connection to the whole spectacle in the way Carl Sagan used to describe it, which sent me spinning through my own inner galaxy. Those are the kinds of scenes that are out there when we're really looking, when the glare of preoccupation isn't drowning them out.

Experiences like these prompt inner journeys while you're taking the outer one. The spirit is restored by wonder when you can feel the size of the world and your relation to it. In the open moments of travel and especially amid natural wonders, you can feel the interconnective magic, which rouses you to something larger than yourself and your circular anxieties and desires. Natural inspirations whisk you out of the judgmental left brain, returning you to the reflective and creative right brain, where you can taste that elusive quality of belonging—to more than a workstation in this world.

Dr. David Cumes, a physician and wilderness leader in Santa Barbara, California, calls this sense of wonder "wilderness rapture." He argues that it "is our birthright. We should be feeling this rapture all the time. It's just that we're all so screwed up from all the pressure." Author of *Inner Passages/Outer Journeys,* Cumes learned this lesson back in his medical school days in South Africa, when he'd go on breaks into the outback with the Bushmen of the Kalahari Desert. The Bushmen got him "tuned into the idea that wilderness is probably the most powerful thing we can do for ourselves," by getting us out of the rational left brain and into the feeling of the right.

Cumes and a growing number of like-minded people offer a variety of spiritual adventures for those inclined. The outings include Native American experiences, such as sweat lodges; pilgrimages to the world's great sacred sites, such as Tibet's Mount Kailas, the center of the earth for Hindus and Buddhists; spiritual retreats at Zen monasteries in Japan; and trips to meet tribal shamans in the Amazon. Of course, you can always have your own inner journeys on your own, anywhere you can lose the fixation on destination long enough to find the hidden glimmerings in what's right before you.

Life University

One of the reasons we get as stale as yesterday's half-eaten donut in our work rut is the lack of intellectual stimulation. The mind needs to move beyond the scintillating realm of in-boxes and integrated software solutions just as the body does. You have to use it, or you lose it. Neuroscientists have discovered that dendrites, the conduits through which information flows to brain cells, need to be stimulated by information flow, or they shrink and disappear. To keep your dendrites in shape, you need to keep the lessons coming.

Learning adventures do that, getting you on the road while offering hands-on experiences in archeology, biology, history, languages, botany, zoology, paleontology, and a whole lot more. You can study dolphins on location in the Bahamas, do a chimpanzee census in Tanzania, or go on an archeological dig in Hawaii. It's all for the advancement of science and your dendrites. The trips are real scientific outings led by professors and researchers. You roll up your sleeves to help the academics uncover the mysteries of the universe, and they help you understand your world. They're not luxury outings. You'll stay in modest to rustic accommodations, and you'll have to survive without a minibar. But you'll be on the frontlines of science and discovery, and may even be the one to find what everyone was looking for.

You do have to pay your way, and it's not inexpensive. But the money goes to a good cause, helping fund important research. The best-known supplier of research adventures is Earthwatch. Get your hands on their latest catalog at *www.earthwatch.org* (Tel: 617-926-8532), and you can drift off for hours imagining the possibilities, from documenting musical traditions in Ireland to a wooly mammoth dig in South Dakota. Another longtime organizer of field-research trips is the University of California Research Expedition Program (*www.urep.ucdavis.edu;* tel: 530-757-3529). UREP's trips put you on the ground in a research locale for a couple of weeks on average, which allows you to interact with local people and get to know your destination from the ground up.

If you're interested in adventures that make a contribution, another route is to take a volunteer vacation. These programs allow you to pitch in to help a local community or environment less fortunate than yours, and provide the most rewarding souvenir of all—knowing you made a difference. Think of these trips as the Peace Corps for two weeks, instead of two years. You'll help villagers in West Africa or farmers in the Caribbean. Check out the possibilities with Global Volunteers (*www.globalvolunteers.org*), Amizade Ltd. (*www.amizad.org*), or Volunteer America (*www.volunteeramerica.net/vacations.htm*).

Have you ever wished you could learn another language, but one class a week just can't get you off the mark? Try a full-immersion language adventure. You'll get intensive study in the language of your choice in a place where everyone speaks it. You can practice what you learn every day at the market, coffee houses, and restaurants. Some programs offer accommodations with a host family, letting you work on your skills as you make friends in the neighborhood. You can study Spanish in Costa Rica, Spain, or Chile; or Dutch, Italian, Danish, Chinese, Japanese, Russian, and many more languages in the host lands.

Through a Chicago company, Language Link (*www.langlink.com;* 800-552-2051), you can study Spanish in Quito, Ecuador, for a week, seven hours a day, for $245. The cost to stay with a local family is only $154—and that includes meals and laundry. Or you could study Spanish in the Ecuadorian Amazon, at a jungle school on Anaconda Island, where your classmates will include the local beaked contingent of parrots and macaws, plus monkeys, turtles, and ocelots.

When you can extract yourself from the default leisure of spectating and become the director of your own personal life, there's a world of adventures out there. No longer at the mercy of others for your personal activities, you are free to make time truly your own. The years suddenly widen and expand, and you feel like you're doing just what you're supposed to be doing here, because you are—following the script of your Hierarchy of Needs. Once you plunge into the world of direct experience, there's no doubt about it. These are the times of your life. And you know then where a lot of idling has been going on. Back in the job-is-life box.

15

Where Vacations Rule

How Europeans Get Six Weeks Off

• • •

"I work for a global company, and have done so for the last six years. It makes my blood boil to know that European workers for my company receive three times the vacation time I do, and it makes me feel like a big, fat sucker. We are getting screwed, big time."

—from an E-mail sent to Work to Live

Time flies in the netherworld of cubicle country, where one year of droning hard drives blends into the next. Looking up from his workstation one day, Milwaukee adman John Ricks noticed it was the end of December. Another year had bit the dust, and he hadn't used all his vacation time. He had 16 days left that would now be squandered because he couldn't carry them over to the next year. Like so many Americans, his focus had been so completely on the job that a vacation was an afterthought. The result? One unremarkable year had just blended into another.

It was a little embarassing, inasmuch as his job was promoting tourism for the state of Wisconsin, which he trumpeted with the line, "Don't Let Your Life Shrink to the Size of Your Job." "That's just what I had done," admits Ricks. "At the time I had no leisure identity other than being the ad guy on a travel account. It dawned on me how nuts that was." He had a vacation epiphany and vowed to never miss a holiday again. He's made good on his vow, taking off ever since on four-week trips all over the world.

Across the Atlantic in Mannheim, Germany, Juergen Lattenkamp and his wife, Sanni, have no such problem with unused vacation time or, for that matter, distinguishing one year from the next. "Well, '92 was Bali and Malaysia," recalls the friendly German, who I met on a trip to Belize. "And in '93 we traveled around Thailand. Then '94 was Greece. We went to California in '95 and also Tunisia. Then we met you in '96 in Belize. After that, France in '97. Costa Rica was amazing in '98. An absolutely super trip. In '99 we visited Cuba and in 2000 the Yucatan."

A medical assistant who runs MRI and imaging equipment for a radiology practice, Lattenkamp, in the style of his countrymates, gets plenty of living in right in the middle of his working years. Where he comes from, the two are not mutually exclusive. His adult years aren't a blank, because he has the time to make life memorable. He and his wife don't have that black hole between the ages of 25 and 65, where the all-consuming tentacles of the job squeeze out everything unrelated to earning the daily bread.

Of course, it's easier to make time for life when you've got six weeks off, like Lattenkamp and his fellow Germans. That's six weeks without guilt, without wisecracks, without fear of retaliation for being away too long—six weeks to thoroughly relax and explore without an anxious mind. It's a concept that seems inconceivable to overworked Americans. But it's all based on down-to-earth policies that make good common sense, and, yes, even business sense—if we can be open enough to take a look. We're going to do just that, finding out in the pages ahead what the Europeans know that we don't, how many nations on the Continent manage to be as productive as we are while their citizens work a couple months less than we do, and how they got there and we didn't. It's time for the facts of balanced life: You can work hard, have a high standard of living, and still have the time for a vacation—or two, or three, every year.

VACATIONS AROUND THE WORD

COUNTRY	DAYS BY LAW	AVERAGE
Australia	20	25 days
Austria	25	30 days
Belgium	20	five to six weeks
Brazil	24–30	
Canada	10	
China	15	15 days
Denmark	25	30 days
Finland	24	25 days
France	25	five to six weeks
Germany	24	30 days
Greece	20	23 days
Ireland	20	
Italy	20	30 days
Japan	10	17.5 days
Netherlands	20	25 days
Norway	21	five to six weeks
Portugal	22	
Spain	25	30 days
Sweden	25	five to seven weeks
Switzerland	20	five to six weeks
United Kingdom	20	25 days
U.S.	0	10.2 days*

Sources: European Industrial Relations Observatory, World Tourism Organization, Balance EWLA; *Los Angles Times* *Bureau of Labor Statistics, paid leave after three years on job

The Rise and Stall of Real Vacations

For most of human history, leisure was not something you had to explain or debate, it being as natural as breathing. The Athenians celebrated two months' worth of festivals every year. The Romans outdid the Greeks, with 175 holidays annually. Even folks in the Middle Ages had more leisure time than we do today, letting their robes down on countless religious holy days. The Hopi Indians were able to take off half the year, while the Kung Bushmen still manage to squeeze in 230 personal days beyond hunting and gathering duty.

Leisure has been the main aim of all societies this side of the former Soviet bloc—and us. As the home of authentic life beyond the struggle for dinner, leisure is where we live, play, love, and explore the boundless possibilities, where culture is born, where we tell the tales and sing the songs of our imaginings. How many museums of work are there outside North Korea or Cuba? Judging by the walls and galleries of the world's exhibit halls, civilization does not seem to be based on how many hours its citizens work but on how they express themselves at rest.

We had our best chance at some of it in the early twentieth century. The advocate was that forgotten superhero of the workingman, President William Howard Taft, who believed that American workers deserved a break, and a decent-sized one, too. "The American people have found out that there is such a thing as exhausting the capital of one's health and constitution," Taft declared in a speech in 1910. As chronicled by Cindy Aron in *Working At Play,* Taft proposed that "two or three months' vacation after the hard and nervous strain to which one is subjected during the autumn and spring are necessary in order to enable one to continue his work the next year with the energy and effectiveness which it ought to have."

Taft's brainstorm went exactly nowhere, probably because he was about a century ahead of his time and on the wrong continent. Paid vacations became available to the majority of American workers only in the 1930s. Strangely enough, it wasn't unions that were responsible for the emerging annual holiday; it was employers, who came to believe that vacations could increase profits with more rested and productive workers. In those days American and European workers had equivalent vacation time, a week to two weeks annually. But the American vacation remained solely at the whim of employers, while in Europe, unions and then lawmakers made annual paid leave a right of employment and citizenship, making it the law of the land. Vacation time in most European countries rose from two to three weeks in the 1950s to four to six weeks in the early 1980s.

U.S. unions went for the money, explains Swedish professor Orvar Lofgren, author of *On Holiday,* while "the unions in Europe went for longer vacations. The state in many European countries was very much concerned that vacations were good for you, that everyone should have holidays, that there should be legislation about vacation time. I don't think the state played the same role in the U.S."

Not hardly. But there is a precedent for a legislative approach to vacation time in the U.S. In 1936 the Department of Labor formed a group called the Committee on Vacations with Pay to look into the haphazard state of vacations in the U.S., where a little more than half of all workers had one to two weeks off, and the rest had none. According to Aron, the committee issued a report slamming the lack of a national policy, pointing out that thirty other countries had laws on annual vacations with pay. It recommended that the Secretary of Labor draft a bill on paid leave. But nothing emerged from the desk of labor secretary Frances Perkins, who played a key role in getting the minimum wage, but missed a big one here.

That was the great fork in the road, where the U.S. went one way—back to work with a couple more bucks—and the Europeans went the other, bagging a couple more weeks. Today the holiday systems across Europe retain a foundation of statutory protection that has legitimized the holiday experience, which our lack of a law leaves illegitimate. Each country has its own mandatory minimum amount of paid leave, ranging from a minimum of twenty days to twenty-five days. You can see from the chart on page 273 that the most generous holiday laws are found in Holland, Denmark, Sweden, Finland, Spain, and France. Since so much of the continent is unionized, most workers get more time through collective agreements, which add another week or two or more to the legal minimum. That makes the average Danish holiday six weeks, with many getting seven and eight weeks, while the British, Italians, and Dutch take five and six weeks by agreement.

Europeans still like to take one of their several holidays each year in the traditional summer rites they're famous for, the Italians and French vanishing in August, and the Dutch in July, but holidays are spread around more now. Despite the myth that Europe closes in July and August, business goes on. "Europe doesn't really shut down," points out Walter Perkins, an American executive who worked in Holland. "A lot of people do go away, but not everyone goes away at the same time." The Finns offer more vacation days to people who take their holidays outside the April to September peak period. Spanish work shifts are now organized so that not everyone takes their holidays at the same time. Germans stagger school terms, providing for a varied holiday season in each German state.

Another custom in many European countries is to take off the final two weeks of the year during the Christmas holidays. This informal vacation is the rule in Sweden, which, added to the five weeks Swedes get by law, brings them to seven weeks, not counting squeeze days and extra weeks won at the bargaining table. Now there's a great idea. Why can't we get into the swim of more time off by taking off for the Christmas holidays? How much really gets done in your office after December 15? Not a heckuva lot, I would suspect. Yet we take up space anyway, going through the charade out of habit.

Employees in most European countries are eligible for their minimum paid leave after a year on the job. Up until then, though, they can claim a pro-rata chunk of the mandated time. This is a neat solution to a problem many have in volatile job sectors of the U.S.—how to get some time off before waiting a full year for benefits to begin. If you've worked six months in Denmark, for example, you would get fifty percent of five weeks, or 2.5 weeks.

Because European holiday time is federally mandated, that solves the portability dilemma that keeps workers grubbing for time in the U.S. For example, Cleveland software specialist Ken Kunkel had to drop down from four weeks to two at the age of fifty, since he just got a new job. He was outraged. "Absolutely pissed," he roars. "I worked in Canada for a while and you get three weeks after one year." When you change jobs in European countries, your holiday time goes with you, because it's guaranteed by law. "This is your legal right, and it is not affected by the time you have worked for your employer," says Denmark's

Kim Benzon Knudsen. Any additional time beyond the law that accrues with an employer does not transfer.

Some countries take holiday policies one astounding step further, offering a vacation bonus. You don't have the excuse of being too broke for a decent holiday in Holland, Denmark, Spain, and Finland, which all have plans to help workers finance their vacations. Denmark has its Holiday Fund, which sets aside a percentage of earnings through the year for each employee. Holland has its holiday tax, tagging 8 percent of the paycheck for a payoff come holiday time. Collective agreements give Finnish workers a 50 percent vacation bonus on top of their regular pay.

When you talk to European experts about these benefits, there's no sense that these are wild-eyed or hallucinatory policies. They're simply a given, staples of a consensus that cuts across thirteen different cultures. "Holidays are very useful for us, to rest and repair ourselves, to enhance personal and family life, to diminish the importance of work conflicts and get distance from them," explains Spanish economist Anna Escobedo of the CIREM Foundation in Barcelona. "We believe we would get very stressed/depressed/crazy if we could not have our beloved vacations."

The People Sport

All the negative associations with vacations in North America—guilt, anxiety, boredom, nonproductivity, laziness—are reversed in Europe, where folks feel guilty, anxious, bored, nonproductive, and lazy if they don't take a holiday. That someone could perceive a holiday to be worthless time-wasting is unfathomable on the Continent. "You'd be considered stupid, if you didn't take a holiday," declares Zurich-native Sybille Hartman. "Leisure is like a people sport in Europe. It's very important that you take this time. It's something that you're proud of. People travel all over the world—New Zealand, the Caribbean. The topic of conversation at work is often about holidays."

This is the cultural part of the equation, why Euro managers and bosses love their month-plus breaks as much as their employees do. Elliot Robertson, an American who worked and indulged in long vacations in Germany for eight years, says Germans live for their holidays. "It's the highlight of their year. It blew my mind some of the places just regular warehouse guys would go on their vacations. Islands in the Pacific you've never heard of. It's just a completely different mentality. Most people would take a summer and a winter vacation. In the U.S., you've got to shove so much into a vacation, it's hardly a vacation at all. Having six weeks keeps you more refreshed the whole year. You know a break is coming. It's not like, 'Well, I've used my five or ten days, and I have to suck it up for the next eleven months.'"

Medical assistant Lattenkamp gets in more trips than that. He has his year broken up so well he always has an escape just around the corner. He takes his "big holiday," three weeks, at the end of the year when the weather in Germany is cold and gray. He likes to "go to the sun" during that trip, to warmer climes such as Bali and Costa Rica. Every Easter he meets a batch of friends for a week in a place like Tuscany or Greece, where they pool resources for a hideaway spot, cook their own meals and hang out. Every September he and a group of fourteen friends visit a different European capital for a five-day adventure. Last year was London, next up is Prague. But that's not all. He also converts overtime hours into long weekends by arranging it with his colleagues, who do the same. This gives him six or seven Fridays off each year, enough for three-day outings. Beyond that, there are ten national holidays, which Germans also like to attach to weekends, offering more long weekend possibilities. Swedes call these "squeeze" days, the Spanish "bridges." Europeans use their supply of them reverentially—which is as it should be, since most were originally religious dates. The "holy day," of course, is the origin of "holiday."

All around Europe people are maneuvering for a squeeze day here, plotting a trip to some exotic port there, taking an active role in experiencing life on their terms. It's about grabbing as many real-life experiences as you can from a world that will keep you in a workaday box if you don't. The holiday serves as a breakout, and as such, the very thing one-track work nuts in the States think it isn't: an achievement. You take control for once. You put one over on the survival game. The engaged holiday, something you design, plot, and experience, puts you at the helm of accomplishment for its own sake, which provides a level of fulfillment the job and its back pattings can't.

Dr. Desiree Ladwig, director of one of the top work-life organizations in Europe, Balance EWLA, in Hamburg, Germany, explains the activist take on vacations. "It's a question of personal strategy, whether you want to be your own manager, or whether you're managed by all the things surrounding you. It's a skill to be able to manage your free time. If you have no strategy for your free time, you keep working."

"Work hard, play hard" is the attitude that has made long vacations possible for Europeans. You can do both. There is no contradiction. Lattenkamp, for instance, loves his radiology job and often puts in a forty-five to fifty-hour week. As a German, he comes equipped with a ferocious work ethic of his own, as do the Dutch and Swiss, not known as slackers. Having a strong work ethic doesn't have to preclude time off and enjoyment. American exec Perkins saw that when he was posted in The Hague. The finance VP developed a deep respect for the Dutch commitment to a balanced life. "They obsess about their jobs as much as Americans," he adds. "But they also have the realization that to keep everything in balance, to have the good life, you need to have time off, and time to pursue hobbies, time to pursue athletics, and just time to pursue nothing, time to go off to southern Spain or your cabin in the woods somewhere and relax. That's just as important to them as getting up and going to work in the morning and doing a good job."

The vacation gap between North Americans and Europeans is about priorities, not dedication to the job. Family, social interaction, and travel are as important in the scheme of things as career for Europeans, so they make the time. That doesn't make them any less able or inclined to perform when they get back to the office. In fact, Europeans feel the time off makes them better workers when they return. Maria das Dores Guerreiro, a professor and work-life expert in Lisbon, Portugal, puts it this way: "We have the philosophy that we must rest sometime to become more productive in our jobs."

That logic doesn't convince rabid workaholics in the U.S, for whom long vacations mean only one thing: Europeans are lazy. Briton Karen Fornash, who is married to an American in Fort Lauderdale, has had it with that IQ-challenged view. "We have to break the myth here that, if you're not working full blast all the time, you must have a low work ethic." She's had countless conversations about why Americans, including her husband until he got off his work butt finally and traveled with her, felt this way. "I think Americans define quality of life by what we have—cars, house, stuff. And Europeans define quality of life by time spent doing what they want to do. It's not that they don't want stuff. But it's not how to measure happiness."

The split comes down to tense. Many Americans see well-being as something that will occur in the future, with a given level of achievement or success. The European approach is to partake now, that by making time for holidays and two-hour dinners you improve the quality of your life by actually living it.

Better Vacations Through Teamwork

It's no secret. The keys to month-long holidays and more balance between work and life aren't locked away in some Swiss deposit box. The practices that could fix your Vacation Deficit Disorder are all out there in full public view, ratified and vetted by tens of millions of people and a host of thriving First World economies. There is no need to reinvent the wheel. European nations can accommodate long holidays from their workers because they do two things we don't: They plan for the time off, and they cross-train fellow employees to pick up the slack.

Because American companies don't really want you to be gone, they do nothing to prepare for your time away from the office. They don't cross-train and have no contingencies in place for work flow when you take your vacation. So how could you even think about taking two whole weeks when your job becomes a black hole while you're gone? Europeans I've talked to are amazed that our hallowed management system has no clue about planning for benefits it supposedly offers. Holiday time in Denmark, for instance, "is an integral part of the work planning," states Kim Benzon Knudsen, a Danish labor expert. "Five to six weeks holiday here is 10 percent of the year, and management must provide that the workforce of the company has the ability to cover people while they're gone to that extent." Holidays are factored into budgeting, production, and every facet of the operation.

One of the first orders of business every new year at Lattenkamp's radiology company is to plan out the year's holiday schedules. "We sit around a big table and have a convention," notes Lattenkamp with a laugh. "Everyone says when they would like to go for their big holidays, and we work it out together." Though his company is small, twelve people, the work flow is organized so that everything runs smoothly when people are on holiday, which is a lot in Germany, the holiday champs of Europe, where eight weeks of vacation are not uncommon for union members. Employees negotiate holiday dates in conjunction with co-workers and employer needs, making sure the company is covered while they're on their getaways. Since the absences are planned, gaps can be headed off by completing time-sensitive work ahead of departures. The most common solution is for co-workers to lend a hand through cross-training.

At Lattenkamp's small office he and his co-workers make their own breaks by spreading the expertise around. "My boss says, 'I need to keep the camera [MRI] going and the office functioning—how you do it is your problem,'" states Lattenkamp. "I give my job to different persons. Twenty percent there, 30 percent there, 50 percent there. I've been doing that for ten years, and it's going good."

What he's talking about isn't having a colleague move a pile from the left side of the desk to the right side. The cross-training that makes long holidays possible involves real sharing of skills and knowledge with colleagues, the ability to trust one another, which is discouraged by the fear and loathing created in American command and control organizations. "You have to give up a little responsibility," urges Lattenkamp. "If you can do that, you will have more free time and a lighter working style."

Tennessee Technology buyer Elliot Robertson supervised a department of five when he worked in Germany. "You couldn't shut the department down because someone went on vacation," he recalls. "So we would all cross-train. We all knew pretty much the mechanics of each others' jobs. Every department did their own cross-training."

There was nothing strange about the process for Robertson. He had learned all about the wonders of cross-training on his last assignment, which was actually with an American outfit, the U.S. Army. (Could cross-training be the reason why U.S. military personnel get four weeks of vacation the first year on the job?) "The army mentality is that at any minute you could become a casualty and someone has to pick up where you left off, so the whole idea is to have at least the basic skills," explains Robertson. "Everyone knows how to read a map, how to run a radio, how to receive orders, write orders. I see it the same way in business. Someone could get sick for a long period of time or die crossing the street tomorrow. If they're in a position where they had almost exclusive knowledge of a certain subject, you're going to be hurting."

This happens all the time in U.S. companies. People have accidents, they get seriously ill, and they're out of action. In the interim, others pinch-hit, urgent stuff is reassigned, and the work somehow gets done. If we can do it then, it's a lot easier to do it when it's a planned absence, as vacations are supposed to be. Cross-training would keep efficiency humming during employee vacations. It increases the knowledge base and camaraderie in a no-cost way, and provides an insurance policy that companies will still run smoothly if key personnel fall prey to illness or accidents. For employees it could result in guilt-free vacations and the end of the nonvacation vacation, where the lack of company backup forces you to stay in contact with the office on your holiday.

The lessons of Europe—and the U.S. military—are that when skills and knowledge are shared and teamwork emphasized, expanded free time results. Could cross-training methods work in American companies? The revelation is *they already are working*—as are four- to six-week vacations—in U.S. firms operating throughout Europe. Companies from Xerox to Ford must by law provide employees with the holiday benefits of the host country. Since U.S. businesses have been working and profiting handsomely for decades under local European holiday plans, we can safely conclude that American companies can both cross-train and offer four-week vacations without the sky falling in.

Hundreds of American companies doing business in Europe and tens of thousands of European businesses—with a track record of profits and multiple vacations annually for decades—say longer vacations are doable. "American companies are seen as very professional," notes Denmark's Benzon Knudsen. "They should be capable to plan the implementation of better vacation policies. Whether that is something they wish to do, that I don't know."

The Good Life *and* Productivity

The public perception is that the U.S. is swamping Europe with our productivity machine, and that we can't stop for a second or we'll be, god forbid, like them, unproductive and practically on CARE packages. But despite all the extra hours we work, the U.S. is not wildly more productive than our European competitors. By the mid-1990s, in fact, Europe had caught up to U.S. productivity rates, with Belgium, France, Holland, and Germany leading the way, according to the International Labor Organization (ILO). Yet some flatly refuse to believe the facts. I remember one guy on a call-in radio show, who, after I explained how the Europeans had caught up, responded with, "We don't want to do anything like those lazy Europeans! They're socialists!" The opponents of minimum paid leave remind me of the O. J. Simpson jury, dismissing the DNA evidence for long-held emotional judgments.

U.S. productivity numbers are often padded by using output-per-person, instead of per hour, numbers, which are inflated by the massive number of hours Americans work. For instance, in 2001 Norway was 12.2 percent more productive than the U.S., according to researchers at the University of Groningen's Growth and Development Center, in Holland, who analyzed figures in the U.S. and Europe in conjunction with the U.S. Conference Board. But since the Norwegians worked 28.9 percent fewer hours than Americans, their total gross domestic product per person winds up 16.7 percent less than the U.S. workers. So the Norwegians are more productive, but because they choose to work fewer hours, their total output is lower. On an hourly basis, Belgium, France, and Holland were also more productive than the U.S. in 2001, but the U.S. came out number one in the GDP-per-head contest because of the huge gap in hours worked, eight to twelve weeks more than the Europeans in total hours per year according to the ILO. Our perceived productivity supremacy is increasingly the result of "working longer, not more efficiently," concluded a report by the Economic Policy Institute.

The increasing parity of many European economies with the U.S. undercuts a couple of arguments used to oppose longer vacations, that European-style holiday time damages their economies, and that our productivity would nosedive if we had their scandalous vacation time. Well, U.S. efficiency skidded for fourteen years from 1981 to 1995, while European economies with generous holidays beat the U.S. in labor productivity growth over the same period, according to the U.S. Federal Reserve Board.

Walter Perkins saw "no loss of productivity whatsoever" as a result of the six-week vacations at Frederick R. Harris in Holland. I got the same reaction from Dr. Minna Salmi, a workplace expert in Helsinki, Finland. "The productivity rate in Finland is high, so we can conclude that long holidays do not damage productivity," she said.

Europeans face the same global economic challenges that we do, even overtime pressures. "Families have to fight for their time, but not for holidays," says Dr. Desiree Ladwig. The difference is they *do* fight, choosing to control hours instead of letting them run amuck. They have stoplights: maximum forty-eight-hour workweeks, minimum daily rest periods of eleven hours, and shorter workweeks reached in collective bargaining agreements—37.4 hours a week by agreement in Germany, 37.5 in Norway, 37 in Denmark—or by legislation, such as the thirty-five–hour week in France. As hours have decreased, productivity has increased, points out German economist Gerhard Bosch in *Working Time*. "Reduction of working time . . . has provided much of the impetus behind productivity growth and economic growth." When BMW switched to a thirty-seven–hour week at its Munich plant, it also added a new shift system that improved efficiency.

The European experience shows that there is another way. But can we buy it, if we didn't invent it? Tom Freston, CEO of MTV Networks, has "been in meetings with people from other companies where they make fun of the European one month off," he says. "Like how do they think they're really going to make it in the race, if they're going to do that? Or the siesta—that has to go. There's the certainty that we have the right way. There needs to be more awareness. The more traveled people get, the more outside interests they get, they might realize there's more to life."

Elliot Robertson, who used to get six weeks off in Germany, knows there is. "There's just so much better out there, if people could make their lives more than work," argues Robertson, who has written letters to his congressman and senators urging a more family-friendly workplace. "If people would go out and take real vacations and get to know their family and enjoy other things, they would see that work isn't the only thing in life."

And that each year doesn't have to blend unremarkably into the next.

16

Principles for a Sane Workplace

How to Take Back Our Time

• • •

"He who considers too much will perform little."

—Friedrich Schiller

Before Columbus discovered America, the prevailing wisdom was that there was nothing west of Portugal except a very large waterfall into cosmic oblivion. The naysayers were so convinced they were right that they had their own soundbite, *Ne Plus Ultra,* or "No More Beyond." After the dogged Italian found the New World and lived to tell the tale, the story suddenly changed. The most rabid doubters had to eat crow, and did so happily to cash in on the riches that, of course, were out there. *Plus Ultra,* or "More Beyond," became the new anthem, leading intrepid explorers to the four corners of the globe.

Entrenched positions can do a complete about-face with the facts. Today the engineers of the overwork culture—corporate downsizers, Wall Street greed barons, outmoded command-and-control managers, cocksure workaholics—are as certain as Flat Earthers were then that there is nothing out there beyond the known world of 24-7 work but total calamity. But just as the skeptics and fear-mongers of the fifteenth century were turned around by reality, we can do the same with the opponents of free time. Because the evidence is out there: the success of American firms offering real vacations and flex schedules; the high productivity rate of European countries with five-week vacation laws; the studies showing the counter-productivity of chronic overtime; double-digit increases in health insurance; the 93 percent of Americans who feel time off is necessary for productivity. We just need to build that evidence into a social consensus through the example we set by following the Counter-Commandments. We need to demonstrate through our deeds, including support of legislative efforts to get new workplace protections, that we want our time back. And we want it now. Because there's more beyond endless fifty- and sixty-hour weeks. More beyond having to prove worth and commitment by sacrificing your health and even your life in pointless displays of bravado. More beyond forfeiting families, to be "ideal" workers. More beyond a black hole for a personal life until retirement. More beyond the invasion of work into homes and vacations. More beyond, way more beyond, the absurdity of having to feel guilty about enjoying ourselves because work is the only item of value in the universe.

We can change the life-killing overwork culture if we can abandon alienation and competitive lockstep and come together, the way we used to. The fact is, we have a long tradition that values life apart from the job and has been willing to fight for it. For one hundred years, from the 1840s to the 1940s, American workers fought for their time—and got it. Public outcry led President Martin Van Buren to reduce the working day from twelve to ten hours in 1840. Workers through their labor unions waged a concerted fight throughout the nineteenth century and into the early twentieth to bring hours down. With a war cry of "Eight Hours for Work, Eight Hours for Rest, and Eight Hours for What We Will," labor was able to trim hours for many workers to nine per day and to a half day on Saturday by the turn of the century. Strikes by garment workers from 1924 to 1927 won the five-day, forty-hour week for the clothing industry, and the idea caught on with the public. So much so that a shorter workweek was part of *both* Democratic and Republican platforms in 1932. Astounding, isn't it? We almost had a *thirty-hour week* when the Thirty-Hour Bill passed in 1933. The law was diluted soon afterwards by the National Recovery Act, which set hours at an average of forty per week. After a long legislative battle, the Fair

Labor Standards Act enshrined the forty-hour standard, which began in 1940. A century of people caring about time to live had cut the American workweek in half.

We can do it again. Join with Work to Live and take back your time and your tradition of standing up for a healthy workplace. In this chapter you'll learn how we can do it by taming an anarchic workplace that's equivalent to a city without stoplights. It's time for some traffic enforcement, including reform of the FLSA, to create a minimum-paid-leave law and curbs on excessive overtime, and an overhaul of the counter-productive, head-banging workstyle we don't have to pursue to the intensive-care ward. Learn how Work to Live's Principles for a Sane Workplace can restore order to the asylum, focusing on the content of what we do at the office, instead of the duration.

At one time the prevailing wisdom was that smoking was harmless and that driving drunk was nobody's business. The combination of facts and the conviction of anti-smoking and anti-drunk driving advocates turned public opinion around, which turned voters around, which turned politicians around, saving thousands of lives. We can do the same with the deadly overwork habit. Starting right now.

The End of Vacation Starvation: Minimum Paid Leave

I'd like to think business could expand vacation schedules out of its own enlightened self-interest, but we can't wait for the year 5000 to get here. With more and more vacations on paper only, with unions representing a mere 9 percent of workers in private industry, with job insecurity so rampant that people are afraid to take all of their vacation or any vacation, and with no other recourse to stop the slide, it's clear that the only solution is for the people, through their elected representatives, to exercise their democratic prerogative in favor of public health, safety, and common sense, and put minimum paid leave legally on the books.

It's time to join the rest of civilization, working Americans of the 19th and early 20th century, and the framers of the Constitution in recognizing that there's a fundamental right—our inalienable right as Jefferson put it, to the pursuit of happiness—to have time for life. It's time to realize that we, the people, who brave a fifty- and fifty-one-week work tunnel every year with barely a letup, who create the nation's wealth and standard of living, who pay the taxes that fund national defense, whose belief in hard work is so unstinting that we will drive our bodies and families to the edge for the job, ought to be able to share in the economic dividends we create enough to have our vacations protected by law.

Why have a dreaded federal regulation on the matter? Isn't that about as evil as it gets? The end of the world as we know it? Why a law? Because we are a nation that believes in the rule of law, and yet we don't have any protecting working citizens against vacations that are stalled, shrunk, and pressured into nonexistence, not to mention that are barely long enough to qualify as real vacations in the first place. We need a minimum-paid-leave law for the same reason that we have a minimum wage, for the same reason business has come under regulation in the past, to protect those who can't protect themselves. Franklin Roosevelt believed that regulation of industry was necessary from time to time because of what he called the recklessness of unfettered capitalism. The result was the minimum wage and social security, protections fought tooth and nail by business, but that are accepted universally today as essential features of American citizenship and human dignity. It's the same with vacation protection. And we need a minimum-paid-leave law for the same reason that Congress passed tough new accounting and executive compensation regulations in 2002—because a completely unregulated market is an unlimited disaster for people. As we have seen in the parade of arrested execs doing the "perp-walk" shuffle across our television screens, business knows the color of only one traffic light: green. It can't put up its own stoplights. Pioneering economist Sydney Chapman, whose research established that there is an optimal length of working time in the day, determined that industry could only adhere to that limit if it acted in enlightened accord, which, given the competitive nature of business, was never going to happen.

When millions of hard-working Americans are afraid to take their vacations for fear they will be replaced or bypassed for promotions if they do so, we have to have the protective recourse of a law. When the volatile economy forces workers in their forties and fifties to start their paid leave banks over again at one or two weeks when they join a new company, as if they were at their very first job, it's not too much to insist from the political leaders that we empower that they make every effort to right this ridiculous state of affairs. Having to constantly prove ourselves worthy of vacation time until the day we retire is an insult to the efforts beyond the call of duty that working Americans put in every day to keep this country's economy growing.

The case for vacation protection is best made by the people who desperately need it, as employees around the country made clear in hundreds of E-mails to Work to Live like these:

- "I work for a small company of about twenty people. The boss here hardly takes any time off and hates it when someone else does. He is always making the comment, 'I have been here twenty-five years and have never taken a full week of vacation.'"

- "I earned five weeks of vacation for twenty-three years of service with my former company and then was downsized. My new company said that their policy would not allow them to give me any vacation for the first year and then only two weeks after that. They liked my twenty-three years of experience in engineering, but they could not compensate with vacation. I had to start all over again. Congress could change all this."

- "I will have to work twenty-five years to get four weeks off!! Absolutely absurd. Managers who have lost sight of balance in their own lives demand ridiculous hours and often degrade those who try to get time for themselves. Time for reviving oneself produces more, not less, productive workers. Let's get civilized like all the other industrialized countries!"

- "I have worked for the same company for seven years and only receive ten days vacation and five sick days. Two weeks vacation versus fifty weeks of work time is just not enough. I feel after all those years of dedicated service, could it be that difficult to increase my vacation time to fifteen days? I am a single parent. My son is 9 years old, and I am very involved in his school and sports activities. Having three weeks vacation would enable me to spend more time with him and be involved in his activities."

Work to Live has proposed that Congress amend the outmoded FLSA, the country's main labor law, with language stipulating a mandatory minimum paid leave of three weeks for anyone who has worked at a job for a year, increasing to four weeks after three years. Among other features, the law would:

- protect you against any retaliation for taking all the vacation coming to you, and end the fear of replacement, demotion, or promotion fallout as a result of taking a vacation.

- protect you against employers stalling or chilling vacations with chronic cancellations.

- prevent your vacation from shrinking when you change jobs. You will always get three weeks after you spend a year at a job.

- provide after three months with a company and up through the first year a pro-rata share of vacation. For example, at six months you would get 1.5 weeks off.

You would still need to get your employer's approval for the best time in the workflow to take the leave, but that process would become much more organized after there is a paid-leave law on the books. It would force holidays out of the afterthought column and into the planning of operations. Everything would be much more coordinated, so the impact on business would be less interruptive than it is now in its current anarchic state. Cross-training, as in Europe, will become the norm, with co-workers picking up the slack for those on vacation. In other words, taking a vacation will be as normal a part of working life as taking a meeting.

Employers already offering three-week vacations, from small businesses like the H Group, an investment services company in Oregon with a handful of employees, to giants like the SAS Institute, have found that adding another week of time off results in huge gains in productivity and retention—at almost no cost. "For many jobs, a vacation is one of the cheapest benefits an employer can offer," explains Rick Service, editor of *Business and Health* magazine. "It's built into the system. It's not like they're going to hire a temp, and carry your salary and the temp cost. It's a scheduled absence. The expensive stuff is the unscheduled absence. It's a benefit you can be generous about without breaking the bank."

For Cincinnati cleaning firm Jancoa Inc.,"the three-week vacation has been the most successful retention program that we've had," enthuses co-owner Mary Miller. She and her husband Tony resisted adding an extra week of vacation for six years, until Dan Sullivan of Strategic Coach was able to persuade them to take the plunge. Their turnover problem dropped from 360 percent to 60 percent within two months. Productivity shot up, as did sales and profits. The whole program, 468 vacations last year, cost a total of seven cents. "We quickly realized that, with the money we were putting out for recruiting, retention, and background checks for new employees, it really cost us nothing," notes Miller. Their administrative staff is now on four-day weeks, as are the Millers themselves. They also take a week off every *month* and a three-week vacation in the summer.

Work to Live's proposal to make these benefits a national law got a supportive reception in Washington, D.C. Penn State economist and overtime-expert Lonnie Golden and I pressed the case for minimum-paid leave, and I left the Hill feeling that we've got an excellent shot of getting a paid-leave law—if we make enough noise and rally voters. One congressional aide asked me if I knew how many business interests were going to be lined up against Work to Live. It was a long list. I asked, naively, "Who's on the citizens' side?" A few moments of silence was followed by the mention of a couple of unions. And certainly unions such as the Service Employees International Union (SEIU) have been doing a good job attacking forced overtime. But it was very clear that given the tonnage of business lobbies, citizens are up against it in the house of their very own government. That means we're going to have to do some governing by the people and for the people, and get involved the way the advocates of Mothers Against Drunk Driving did. The time is right. With the fiascoes coming out of corporate America, there is a belief that workers need protection from a culture of greed operating without limits. The stoplights going up for accounting and executive loans have to extend to paid leave and excessive overtime.

And there's one other thing that makes this a propitious moment—the current president has shown a marked preference for the month-long vacation. If George W. Bush can take four weeks off, as he did in 2001, it ought to be possible for the rest of us to get real vacations.

Social consensus can change the entire equation. Join with Work to Live at *www.worktolive.info,* call or E-mail your congressional representatives (written correspondence can take three months to clear security these days), and tell your friends to do the same. Participation, remember, is the key to the life you need—and a democracy by the people. You can find the contact numbers on the Web. The best place to start is with an excellent guide to contacting your representatives that takes you through the do's and don'ts: *www.eff.org/congress.html#e-mail.* There's a great congressional directory at C-Span's Web site page, *www.c-span. org/questions/house.asp#h6* (click on "Congressional Directory," under Resources on the left nav bar). You can also get congressional phone and E-mail numbers at *www.visi.com/juan/congress/* (for both local districts and D.C.); and links to House and Senate info as well as to Web sites for each member of Congress at *http://usgovinfo.about.com/cs/emailwashington/.* Contact info for the Senate is listed at *www.senate.gov/contacting/index.cfm.*

Anyone concerned about minimum paid leave should be sure to express their support for it to the chairman of the Committee on Health, Education, Labor and Pensions, who would be the pivot point for legislation in the Senate. If the Democrats retain their current control of the Senate, that's Senator Ted Kennedy (317 Russell Senate Office Building, Washington, D.C. 20510; 202-224-4543). If there is a Republican majority, you can find out who the chairman of the committee is at the senate.gov site by clicking on "Committees" on the top nav bar. You should also contact the chair of the House of Representatives' Health, Education, Labor and Pensions committee, which would handle legislation in the House, as well as every member of that committee. The same thing goes for all the members of the Senate committee. You should be able to get the information on committee members from the C-Span site, or senate.gov. If you don't have access to the Internet, your local library should have what you need, as well as the phone numbers of the main switchboard for both the Senate and House. Remember, the opponents of paid leave have all the resources, so it's critical that we show what we've got—the votes—and follow through on this.

Let them all know that you support paid leave legislation, and other life- and family-friendly policies, such as these, proposed to Congress as part of an overhaul of the FLSA:

- a mandated contract provision for every employee that spells out up front how many hours that person will be expected to work.

- an amendment to the Fair Labor Standards Act that would put a cap on overtime, as some states have done.

- tax incentives for employers who initiate flex-time and other more modular work schedules for all employees, particularly for working parents.

- a third category of worker under the FLSA under which workers who are currently exempt get some sort of compensation for overtime, such as comp time.

- comp-time credits for overtime worked with straight time pay for select groups of nonexempt employees.

- tighter legal enforcement of existing regulatory rules on the misclassification of employees as exempt, and employees as "contractors;" and for overtime work unpaid.

- strengthened language on the managerial test for salary exemption, specifying the amount of time that must be devoted to managerial duties.

- an adjustment of the salary test in the FLSA for inflation. A 1999 report by the General Accounting Office found it exempted only one percent of employees.

Will business scream to the rafters about these changes? You bet. Just like it did with the minimum wage and social security. But if you can scream louder and demonstrate that a massive number of votes are on the line as it with this issue, the political winds can shift faster than a hummingbird on a honeysuckle. Just as a giant conifer can sprout from a solid granite cliff because, a seed found a crack in which to grow, we can turn it all around with a foothold.

Six Principles for a Sane Workplace

How do we disconnect the self-destruct buttons of the overworked place? The answer is very simple. We have to shift the emphasis from our crazed, hyperventilating, all-hours work*style,* to the substance of what we're doing. Harder, faster, longer, and more painful doesn't mean more succesful outcome, more quality, more volume, or certainly more innovation. It means runaway medical costs for business, more illness and disease for employees, reduced productivity, and more mistakes all around, as so many studies show. The belief that we have to be grinding our teeth and popping veins to really be working is a tragic failure. Straining is a guarantee of bad performance in any realm of endeavor, a sign that effort is not being channeled effectively.

So let's dump the masochism that comes from fear and insecurity and replace it with a new work culture based on confidence and trust, on principles that can lead to increased productivity for business and healthy, balanced lives for workers and their families. Those start by embracing a foundation of ideals more in line with who we say we are as a people, citizens, and parents: by valuing 1) **workers as much as the work; 2) how well you do your job, not how long; 3) time off as much as productivity—because it creates it; and 4) how well we can adjust job hours to fit the real world of private, family,**

and civic responsibilities. These notions are at the heart of Work to Live's 6 Principles for a Sane Workplace, which would bid *Sayonara* to the wacko engines of workaholism and face-time.

SANE WORKPLACE PRINCIPLE #1
Quality time off creates quality time on.

Time off is a prerequisite for optimum performance. Everything starts here. Because time off restores and refreshes, it produces more in less time. Rest and recreation generate productivity, innovation, and creativity. As hard as it is for some managers to believe, beaten-down burnout cases just can't do the job of a rested, energized employee. The torture-rack route to success has been fueled by the idea that free time has no value. As long as we buy this whopper, we'll continue to be marooned in overwork. The way out is to junk the habit of always looking beyond where we are to the next task or achievement, and, instead, focus on the moment we are living and working in. If we do that, we'll be able to see the supreme dumbness of the no-life workstyle. Free time can never be valued when worth is contingent on what happens tomorrow, nor can excessive work habits be moderated when you're racing to the next objective. You also have to refuse to justify time off. It's a human necessity as crucial to the act of living as water.

Free time is so valuable in its ability to regenerate fried brain cells and failing bodies that it upgrades all your time, producing dividends across your life—from revitalized job performance to personal health; creativity; greater life satisfaction and well-being; to improved family time. With these enormous payoffs, continuing to fear time off and feel guilty about it is counter-productive, which is to say, anti-American. So let's be patriotic, and break the cycle of self-destruction.

SANE WORKPLACE PRINCIPLE #2
It's not how long but how well the job is done.

The central fallacy that runs the overworked place is that quantity of hours, sheer time that you are glued to your chair, is the supreme gauge of productivity—whoever goes through the most Preparation H gets the promotion! As we know by now, all the evidence proves that excessive hours don't contribute to productivity; they take away from it. The story we've bought up till now is that someone who takes ten hours to finish a report is doing a better job than someone who gets it done in six. The incentive of this reverse logic is to be inefficient.

The Sane Workplace gives the heave-ho to face-time, a yardstick that has nothing to do with performance. Management has to start rewarding employees based on the content of the work, not the volume of painkillers in the bloodstream. As economist Juliet Schor argues, "We need a new managerial culture. We have to get away from that direct-supervision mentality. The research shows that when people and teams are given more autonomy to organize themselves, they're able to work more efficiently."

Face-time is a factory-era gauge of productivity that's obsolete in the information age. Long hours don't tell managers anything about quality these days, which is a function of brains, rested ones. They're also an abysmal gauge of commitment, leaving advancement to anyone willing to sacrifice health and family and take up space like a squatter. It's results that count in the Sane Workplace, not stakeouts.

SANE WORKPLACE PRINCIPLE #3
When you don't treat employees as liabilities, your assets multiply.

The prevailing command and control attitude of valuing only the work, the output, not the person doing it, was best illustrated to me by an anecdote Rodney Hilpirt told me. Hilpirt, a business consultant and management professor at the University of Dallas said it's always the same when he's called in to executive offices to try to troubleshoot personnel problems. He asks for the organizational chart, and he's handed one with the hourly employees at the bottom. Hilpirt tells the execs to invert it. "They say, 'Are you insane?' I tell them, 'Those are your most important people, and you've got them at the bottom of the food chain. They ought to be on the top of the chain, because without them you don't have a job.' They tend to start listening then."

People have been drastically devalued in the downsizing madness, seen as "head counts" to be slashed or added at the whim of mergers or stock buff-ups. The staffs at many companies are viewed, not as assets, but as liabilities, which is, in fact, where they appear on the balance sheet. It's a fatally flawed psychology that leads directly to inefficiency, absenteeism, burnout, retention problems, and skyrocketing medical bills. In a Sane Workplace, management understands the connection between a valued staff and customers who feel valued, and see employees as an investment. As financial-services boss Ron Kelemen tells it, "I can't think of any other investment where I could put in "$30,000 to $50,000, get a tax deduction for it, and start getting a return on it within a couple of months."

When you treat people as an investment, you don't burn them out and make them sick, which saves big money. The cost of company medical plans was up 11 percent in 2001 and 15 percent in 2002, according to *Time*. But the healthiest companies in the nation, as awarded by the Wellness Councils of America and profiled in *Business and Health,* are actually making money by keeping people healthy. Lincoln Plating, a company in Lincoln, Nebraska, reports an $800,000 return on its investment of $85,000 in employee health. Omaha, Nebraska-based Union Pacific Railroad has saved $1.2 million with its wellness program, which has been effective enough to actually cut the company's health-care costs.

No executive would think of overloading the company's new multi-million dollar information system until it crashed. Investments are treated to last; employees seen as stock fodder aren't. When employees are trusted and enfranchised to find better ways of working, everyone wins.

SANE WORKPLACE PRINCIPLE #4
Hours for the real world bring real results to work, home, and community.

We have to start making work schedules accommodate the obligations of real lives. Parents with full-time careers "can't have any sort of family life," says Penn State economist Robert Drago, a work-family expert. The solution lies in more flexible hours through alternative schedules such as telecommuting. We already have the tools to move in this direction. Technology makes it possible for us to do more in less time and work from any number of locations besides under somebody's nose. Managers have to give up control over employee time, because in the knowledge economy, it's no longer relevant. You can't watch what's going on in someone's skull. In return, sane managers get higher productivity, retention, morale, efficiency, and cost savings.

We need to expand flex schedules. A Boston College study by Mindy Fried that surveyed companies such as Honeywell and Motorola measured the three main flex options: daily flexibility, where you control your hours on a daily basis; flexibility over start and stop times only, the most common flex style; and telecommuting. It found that flex schedules can lower the intensity of the time squeeze, because workers feel they can accommodate their lives more. But they don't solve the issue of long hours. Flex time has to be combined with the key to the Sane Workplace: a return to boundaries. We've got to reset the norm back to 40 hours.

A Work in America Institute study in 2000 showed that employee-oriented, work-life practices resulted in huge savings for a variety of companies, from Hewlett Packard to Ernst and Young. Those practices at Ernst and Young proved that a work culture rooted in work-life balance pays for itself—and then some. The efficiency ideas and flex-time changes adopted from employee suggestions resulted in a savings of $14 million to $17 million.

SANE WORKPLACE PRINCIPLE #5
Part-time is a big part of the time-bind solution.

Most Americans would prefer a workweek a little over thirty hours. Despite the assumption that everyone around you wants to work around the clock, most of us would secretly like to cut back. That's hard to do when the only options available, as American University's Joan Williams has pointed out, are full-time, overtime till you drop—being the "ideal worker"—or else "wipeout," part-time and off the success track. Which is why we have so many people chasing around and around on the overtime hampster wheel. Anything less than full-time work has such a stigma, particularly for men, that it's akin to career suicide. We need a way out of the cage: a third way, part-time parity.

Part-time parity offers proportional pay, benefits, training, and advancement, with fewer hours. That choice doesn't exist right now, since part-time is equivalent to malingering and brings with it a high price tag in social stigma and a thinner wallet. As Drago explains it, "If you cut back on your hours, you lose income more than proportionately. You lose health insurance, you lose pensions. People are forced into the overtime situation because that's their only option if they want to make a family wage."

A Sane Workplace offers an upgraded part-time *track,* offering a viable career option to the family-gutting, ideal-worker scenario. With quality part-time work, you could still be seen as a bona fide working American. Men could trim hours without feeling emasculated. "It goes to masculine gender performance," explains Williams. "The man, because of his sense of manliness and to maintain a sense of home, has to work more and more. That ends up marginalizing his life. So the key is quality part-time work to which stigma is not attached. If you had a situation where a man could say, I'm going to work thirty-five hours a week, and I will not fall off the map professionally, huge numbers of men would do that."

Let's offload black-and-white thinking. Overtime or slacker. Full-time or no commitment. We can break through this vicious cycle with the commodity we are famous for: innovation. If our families are more than props to trot out at company Christmas parties, if our lives are worth more than the prescriptions sitting in our desk drawers, if community is something more than a couple words a year to a phantom neighbor, we need to provide a third way.

SANE WORKPLACE PRINCIPLE #6
Share the work, share the life.

The missing ingredient in the burnout culture of fear and loathing is trust. Managers don't trust employees and treat them like children. Employees don't trust bosses who are pink-slipping them and burning them out. Co-workers don't trust each other because of epidemic job insecurity and nonstop competition that makes us see everyone around us as the enemy. The only way out of the terminal exhaustion of suspicion and doubt we're caught up in is to realize that we're not separate but together in this mad scramble to find a life. We have to move to a cooperative model based around quality. The Europeans are already well on their way there. Belgian work-life expert Professor Steven Poelmans feels strongly that, "The time has come to enjoy and give depth to the content in everything you do, and Europeans have an edge over Americans here, because we have an attitude of putting more quality in our lives."

Why should we let the Euros be number one in quality of life? We don't have to, if we can cut back on the reactive, I-can-take-it posture and share the load. We can start with cross-training. Find fellow employees you can trade skills with, so that they know enough about what you do to fill in for you when you're on vacation. And you can do the same for them. Can our deeply ingrained competitive instincts allow others to know our business? The only other choice is fear, and that gets us where we are now, in a race to extinguish our lives. We got into this mess together, and the only way we can get out of it is together, sharing the pain—and the gain.

Seize the Day

The Europeans have had the help of labor parties, strong unions, and a committed social consensus that taking care of families and people should be a national priority to spur on paid-leave laws, reduced hours, and work-family protections. Unions in the U.S. have been able to put some limits on excessive overtime, such as in the nursing and telecom fields, but only one in ten workers in private industry is unionized, and there is still forced overtime for union workers. So collective bargaining, while important where it exists, isn't going to get the vast majority of Americans longer vacations or shorter hours anytime soon.

The road ahead for us will have to be led by us, with support from unions and community organizations, through national legislation. We need to press the case for change in the workplace with a grassroots movement that makes the social toll of overwork a national focus, along the lines of the campaign waged by Mothers Against Drunk Driving. The reason that all of us don't work six days a week, twelve hours a day—yet—as we did in the 1840s, is because of the battles our ancestors fought and won. No reason we can't do it again, since the case for limits is more compelling today than it was in the 1930s. With middle-income families now working four months more than they did in 1979, according to economists Barry Bluestone and Stephen Rose; almost one in two marriages ending in divorce; 40 percent of children of divorce ending up in poverty; one out of two workers reporting symptoms of burnout; 75 percent to 90 percent of all visits to physicians due to stress-related causes; 60 percent to 80 percent of work accidents due to stress; 18,000 people assaulted at work every year and 764 killed, according to NIOSH; worker's comp costs at $60 billion a year and climbing 20 percent in 2002, according to *Forbes;* and the wasteland we all see around us in drained, fatigued colleagues and friends you never see because everyone's always working, there is no shortage of health and safety reasons to draw the line. We have laws limiting the number of hours pilots, flight attendants, and truckers can be on duty for a reason—fatigue kills.

The events of September 11, 2001, showed us all the steep cost of working to the exclusion of all else, making it as clear as it ever has been, that the point of all our ceaseless striving is not a future gold mine but today's—home, family, and that incredibly fragile organism called Life.

I was struck by how the eulogies and articles about those who died in the tragedy focused, not on what they did *for* a living, but *on* their living. Profiles of victims in the *New York Times*'s "Portraits of Grief" series highlighted their passions, interests, and personalities. Mentions of job were incidental. Antonio Rocha, a Cantor Fitzgerald broker, was remembered as a "big kid," who loved going to Disney World with his children and traveled around the country to follow Formula One racing. Digital strategist Waleed Iskander was described as "an inveterate adventurer," who had traveled to Africa and South America and was "known for his zest for life and his devotion to Pink Floyd." Trader Stephen Joseph was remembered as a pied piper who loved to party at Mardi Gras and had a booming laugh.

The lesson here is powerful, and it's this: We all sweat blood to leave our mark, the professional accomplishments that we think are necessary to make our lives significant or worthwhile. But they already are—in the ways that make you who you are, not what you think you have to be. The job doesn't make you; your nature does. What we'll be remembered for is our humanity, enthusiasm, and individuality—the stuff that makes us one of a kind—not how many weekends we worked or the number of awards hung on the office wall. The *Times*'s profiles of passions interrupted say eloquently in four column inches what couldn't be said by a year's worth of talking heads: life is in the living.

Aspiration without participation along the way is abdication of the privilege of being here. Woodrow Wilson said that only once in a generation do we rise above material things. Now is that time. We need to summon up the courage to push aside the fear and taboos, the knee-jerk ideology about federal regulations. The market doesn't care whether your marriage or family falls apart because you're slammed with sixty-hour weeks. It doesn't care how many latchkey kids we have. And it doesn't care whether we destroy our golden goose, the folks who give it all they've got fifty to fifty-one weeks a year, who ask only for a modicum of time to step back, to care for their families and themselves, to breathe in some life. Only people care.

That means you. That means all of us. And in this debate we will have a chance to put forward a new vision of success, one that's not about job titles, or ability to "take it" for marathon hours, or absurd denial of life through skipped vacations, or compulsive buying of stuff we don't need to fill up the holes in our lives. It will be a success that celebrates the experience of living, not its avoidance; one that reflects our ideals and values, not Madison Avenue's; one that values time by the act of being in it; one focused on the WORTH ETHIC, which, as we have learned, is the key to the quality of your life. People motivated only by materialistic values report less life satisfaction, less happiness, worse relations with others, and less involvement in community. Things are ephemeral. Things don't run the interior equation that, in turn, runs well-being and fulfillment; you do through intrinsic experiences that provide growth, joy, and meaning. You are your destination. You, right now, as you are.

So let's start prioritizing what really counts. Family. Friends. Love and happiness like Al Green sang it. Freedom. Wisdom. Participation. Purpose. Play. Process. Soul. Learning. Connection. Values. Discovery. Balance. Risk. Authenticity. Fun. Wonder. Compassion. Art. Music. Travel. Spontaneity. Trust. Community. Two-hour meals. Ten-year-old daughters. The shapes of clouds. Castles in the sand. A shoulder for your head. An island in the sun. Samba in your stride!

In the sunset of your days, you're not going to look back and wished you worked more. But you can't wait until it's too late for that insight. It's a thought you need to take with you every day to avoid a life of regrets and assure one that's fully experienced. Because in the end what will matter will be that toast on the Italian coast, a child's first bike ride, a secret waterfall in Kauai, the warmth in a lover's eyes—the time when you had time, a commodity more precious than all the diamonds at DeBeers. So let's treasure it while it's still here, by vowing to not spend it on any old busyness, by tossing the fear and guilt of the Office Commandments, the doubt and insecurity bred by master marketers, the pointless panic of the Race, the Ass Backwards mentality that makes us feel that an absentee life is an accomplishment. Let's value a job well done, not overdone. And let's join together to create time for life in the tradition of those nineteenth-century working Americans who rallied behind the cry of "eight hours for work, eight hours for sleep, and eight hours for what we will." They knew then what we know now, that the greatest task in life is making sure you have time to live it.

So no more postponing. Clear the calendar, grab your Personal Life List, load up the camera, and start snapping. Give yourself a life to remember, so you can say someday—like today—I was there.

Work to live!

Bibliography

Adler, Alfred, *The Individual Psychology of Alfred Adler.* Harper Torchbooks, 1964.

Ammondson, Pamela. *Clarity Quest.* Fireside / Simon & Schuster, 1999.

Ardrey, Robert, L. *The Territorial Imperative.* Atheneum, 1966.

Aron, Cindy S. *Working at Play.* Oxford University Press, 1999.

Bergler, Edmund. *The Battle of the Conscience.* Washington Institute of Medicine, 1948.

Bluestone, Barry, and Stephen Rose. "The Enigma of Working Time Trends." *Working Time: International Trends, Theories and Policy Perspectives.* Routledge, 2000.

Bosch, Gerhard. "Working Time Reductions, Employment Consequences and Lessons from Europe: Defusing a Quasi-Religious Controversy." *Working Time: International Trends, Theories and Policy Perspectives.* Routledge, 2000.

Branden, Nathaniel. *The Psychology of Self-Esteem.* Nash Publishing Corp., 1968.

Branden, Nathaniel. *The Six Pillars of Self-Esteem.* Bantam Books, 1994.

Brooks, Nancy Rivera. "Most Workers Who Call in Sick Really Aren't, Study Finds." *Los Angeles Times,* September 23, 1999.

Business Roundtable. "Scheduled Overtime Effect on Construction Projects." November, 1980.

Cette, Gilbert. "Reform and Reduction of Working Hours." Embassy of France, Web site, 2002.

Chapman, Sydney J. "Hours of Labour." *The Economic Journal,* 1975.

Chenoweth, David. "Sitting Around, Burning Money." *Business & Health,* February 2001.

Compton, David M., and Seppo E. Iso-Ahola. *Leisure and Mental Health.* Family Development Resources, Inc., 1994.

Conner, J. Robert. "Napping on the Job: Good!" Health.medscape.com.

Creighton, Judy. "Workplace Stress Leads to Snacking—Much of It Indiscriminate." The Canadian Press, Canoe.com.

Cryer, Bruce A. "Neutralizing Workplace Stress: The Physiology of Human Performance and Organizational Effectiveness." Paper presented at Psychological Disabilities in the Workplace, The Centre for Professional Learning, Toronto, Canada, June 12, 1996.

Czikzentmihalyi, Mihaly. *Flow.* Harper & Row, 1990.

Davis, Stan, and Christopher Meyer. *Blue.* Perseus Books, 2000.

Deardorff, Julie. "NFL Player's Death Highlights Heat Risk." *Chicago Tribune,* Aug. 2, 2001.

Decarlo, Donald, and Deborah H. Gruenfeld. *Stress in the American Workplace.* LRP Publications, 1989.

Department of Labor. "U.S. Department of Labor Nursing Home 2000 Compliance Survey Fact Sheet."

Department of Labor. "U.S. Department of Labor Poultry Processing 2000 Compliance Survey Fact Sheet."

Diener, Ed, Eunkook Suh and Shigehiro Oishi. "Recent Findings on Subjective Well-Being." University of Illinois, 1997.

Diener, Ed, and Richard Lucas. "Subjective Emotional Well-Being." *Handbook of Emotions.* Guilford, 2000.

Diener, Ed, and Robert Biswas-Diener. "New Directions in Subjective Well-Being Research: The Cutting Edge." University of Illinois, 2000.

Drago, Robert. "Trends in Working Time in the U.S.: A Policy Perspective." Paper for the IRRA National Work/Family Policy Forum and the Sloan Work/Family Policy Network.

Dyer, Wayne W. *Pulling Your Own Strings.* Funk & Wagnalls, 1978.

"Employment and Social Affairs." *New Ways: European Family and Work Network,* Volume 3, 1998.

Eden, Dov. "Vacations and Other Respites: Studying Stress On and Off the Job." *International Review of Industrial and Organizational Psychology,* 16, 2001.

Eden, Dov. "Job Stress and Respite Relief: Overcoming High-Tech Tethers." *Research in Occupational Stress and Well-Being.* JAI Press, 2001.

Etzion, Dalia, and Mina Westman. "Vacation and the Crossover of Strain Between Spouses—Stopping the Vicious Cycle." 1999.

Fassell, Diane. *Working Ourselves to Death: The High Cost of Workaholism and the Rewards of Recovery.* Harper, 1990.

Fernas, Rob, and Dan Arritt. "A Field of Glory, and Pain." *Los Angeles Times,* February 2, 2002.

Fierst, Glenn A. "The Case for Updating the Fair Labor Standards Act." *Employee Rights Quarterly,* Vol. 1, No. 2, 2000.

Figart, Deborah M., and Lonnie Golden. "Understanding Working Time Trends." *Working Time: International Trends, Theories and Policy Perspectives.* Routledge, 2000.

Fisher, Roger. *Getting to Yes.* Houghton Mifflin, 1981.

Freeman, Lucy and Herbert S. Stream. *Guilt: Letting Go.* Wiley, 1986.

Galinsky, Ellen, Stacy S. Kim, James T. Bond. "Feeling Overworked: When Work Becomes Too Much." Families and Work Institute, 2001.

Galinsky, Ellen, James T. Bond, Jennifer Swanberg. "The 1997 National Study of the Changing Workforce." Families and Work Institute, 1997.

Gallwey, Timothy W. *The Inner Game of Work.* Random House, 2000.

Gardner, Marilyn. "New Mothers Return to Work Sooner Than Ever." *Christian Science Monitor.* May 23, 2001.

Gemignani, Janet. "Breaking Away." *Business & Health,* July, 1998.

Gemignani, Janet. "Can Your Health Plan Handle Depression?" *Business & Health,* June 2001.

Geurts, Sabine, Evangelia Demerouti, Laura den Dulk, and Anneke van Dooren-Huiskes. "Managing Work-Family Conflict in Europe."

Girion, Lisa. "Infuriated Managers Suing for Overtime—And Winning." *Los Angeles Times,* June 8, 2001.

Girion, Lisa. "More Overtime Lawsuits Expected." *Los Angeles Times,* July 12, 2001.

Girion, Lisa. "Massive Award in Overtime Lawsuit." *Los Angeles Times,* July 11, 2001.

Girion, Lisa. "Office Pressure Cookers Stewing Up 'Desk Rage.'" *Los Angeles Times,* Dec. 10, 2000.

Girion, Lisa. "Employee Inner Views." *Los Angeles Times,* September 10, 2000.

Goetzel, Ron Z., and Ronald J. Ozminkowski, Lloyd I. Sederer, and Tami L. Mark. "Working with Depression, Part I: The Business Case for Quality Mental Health Services." *Business and Health,* August 1, 2002.

Golden, Lonnie. "Work Schedule Flexibility Among U.S. Workers and Policy Directions." *Working Time: International Trends, Theories and Policy Perspectives.* Routledge, 2000.

Golden, Lonnie. "Flexible Work Schedules: What Are We Trading Off to Get Them?" *Monthly Labor Review,* March, 2001.

Golden, Lonnie. "Overemployment: Theory, Types, Empirical Determinants, Policy Responses." Economic Policy Institute.

Golden, Lonnie, and Deborah Figart—editors. *Working Time: International Trends, Theory and Perspectives.* Routledge, 2000.

Golden, Lonnie, and Helene Jorgensen. "Time After Time: Mandatory Overtime in the U.S. Economy." *Briefing Paper,* Economic Policy Institute, 2002.

Goldman, Debbie. "Today's Work and Family Issue: Curbing Abusive Mandatory Overtime." Communications Workers of America.

Goodman, Danny. *Living at Light Speed.* Random House, 1994.

Gordon, Gil. *Turn It Off: How to Unplug from the Anytime-Anywhere Office Without Disconnecting Your Career.* Three Rivers Press, 2001.

Graham, Baxter W. "The Business Argument for Flexibility." *HR Magazine,* May, 1996.

Gump, Brooks B., and Karen A. Matthews. "Are Vacations Good For Your Health? The 9-Year Mortality Experience After the Multiple Risk Factor Intervention Trial." *Psychosomatic Medicine.* September–October 2000.

Harris, Mark. "The Game of Life." *Conscious Choice,* reprinted in *Utne Reader,* March–April, 2001.

Herman, Roger E., and Joyce L. Gioia. *Lean & Meaningful.* Oakhill Press, 1998.

Hobfoll, S. E., and Arie Shirom. "Stress and Burnout in the Workplace: Conservation of Resources." *Handbook of Organizational Behavior,* 1993.

Houtman, Irene, Frank Andries, Karin Bosch. "Monitoring Stress Risks, Outcomes and Prevention in the Netherlands: A State of the Art and Follow-Up."

Howe, Kathleen. "The State of the Nation Is Drowsy, Sleep Watchers Say." *Los Angeles Times,* Mar. 28, 2001.

Hunnicutt, Benjamin Kline. *Work Without End: Abandoning Shorter Hours for the Right to Work.* Temple University Press, 1988.

Hunnicutt, David. "Discover the Power of Wellness." *Business & Health,* March, 2001.

Hunnicutt, David. "America's Healthiest Companies." *Business & Health.* March, 2000.

Karasek, Robert, and T. Theorell. *Healthy Work.* Basic Books, 1990.

Jeffers, Susan. *Feel the Fear and Do It Anyway.* Ballantine Books, 1987.

Johnston, Victor S. *Why We Feel: The Science of Human Emotions.* Perseus Books, 1999.

Joyce, Amy. "Meditation Rooms Offer Employees a Refuge from Stresses of the Workplace." *Los Angeles Times,* November 22, 1998.

Jung, Karl. *The Portable Jung.* Viking Press, 1986.

Kaufman, Leslie. "Some Companies Derail the Burnout Track." *New York Times,* May 4, 1999.

Koestler, Marina. "Stop the Madness: Stress in the Workplace." *Business and Health,* August 1, 2002.

Kohn, Alfie. *No Contest.* Houghton Mifflin, 1986.

Kong, Dolores. "Vacation Deprivation." *Boston Globe,* July 8, 2001.

Kornfield, Jack. *A Path with Heart.* Bantam Books, 1993.

Kotbe, Hoda. "Sleeping on the Job." MSNBC.com, June 6, 2001.

Kundtz, David. *Stopping: How to Be Still When You Have to Keep Going.* Conari Press, 1998.

Landsbergis, Paul A., Susan J. Schurman, Barbara A. Israel, Peter L. Schnall, Margrit K. Hugentobler, Janet Cahill, and Dean Baker. "Job Stress and Heart Disease: Evidence and Strategies for Prevention." *Scientific Solutions*, Summer 1993.

Lichfield, John. "The French Miracle: A Shorter Week, More Jobs and Men Doing the Ironing." *The Independent.* June 24, 2001.

Little, Bruce. "Leisure Often Responsible for GDP Gaps." *Toronto Globe and Mail,* July 8, 2002.

Lofgren, Orvar. *On Holiday.* University of California Press, 1999.

Maslach, Christina, and Michael P. Leiter. *The Truth About Burnout.* Jossey-Bass, 1997.

May, Rollo. *Man's Search for Himself.* Delta, 1973.

Mayo, Elton. "The Hawthorne Studies." Harvard Business School.

Mendels, Pamela. "Rest More—and Work Just as Hard." Businessweek Online, June 15, 2000.

Mendels, Pamela. "Finding Time When Little Is Left." Businessweek Online, June 26, 2000.

Mendels, Pamela. "Memo to Workaholics: It's Called 'Leisure Time' for a Reason." *Business Week,* October 30, 2000.

Monmaney, Terence. "Living with a 9/11 State of Mind." *Los Angeles Times,* February 26, 2002.

Montagu, Ashley. *Man and Aggression.* Oxford University Press, 1968.

Moore-Ede, Martin C. *The Twenty-Four Hour Society.* Addison-Wesley, 1993.

Myers, David. *The Pursuit of Happiness.* Avon Books, 1993.

Myers, David, and Ed Diener. "Who Is Happy?" Hope College, Univ. of Illinois, 1995.

New York Times. "A Nation Challenged: Portraits of Grief." January 6, 2002.

Nguyen, Hang. "Leisurely Lunch Hour Is Thing of the Past." *Los Angeles Times,* February 25, 2001.

Osbon Diane. *Reflections on the Art of Living: A Joseph Campbell Companion.* Harper Perennial, 1999.

Peterson, Thane. "Take a Break, and the Rest Is Easy." Businessweek Online, August 28, 2001.

Plaschke, Bill. "It's Time to Start Turning Up the Heat on Demanding Tough-Guy Coaches." *Los Angeles Times,* August 5, 2001.

Poe, Andrea C. "When In Rome." *HR Magazine,* November, 1999.

Randolphi, Ernesto A. "Developing a Stress Management and Relaxation Center for the Worksite." *Worksite Health,* Vol. 4, No. 3, Summer 1997.

Rybczynski, Witold. *Waiting for the Weekend.* Penguin Books, 1991.

Schaef, Anne Wilson, and Diane Fassel. *The Addictive Organization.* Harper, 1998.

Schnall, Peter L., Paul Landsbergis, Katherine Warren, Thomas G. Pickering, Joseph E. Schwartz. "The Effect of Job Strain on Ambulatory Blood Pressure in Men: Does It Vary by Socioeconomic Status?" State University of New York at Stony Brook, 1999.

Schor, Juliet B. *The Overworked American.* Bantam Books, 1992.

Schor, Juliet B. *The Overspent American.* Basic Books, 1998.

Sessions, Don D. "Ten Myths at Work." *Equal Opportunity Career Journal,* July–August, 1995.

Shepard, Edward, and Thomas Clifton. "Are Longer Hours Reducing Productivity in Manufacturing?" *International Journal of Manpower,* 21 (7), 2000.

Shields, Margo. "Long Working Hours and Health." *Health Reports,* 11, 1999.

Shirom, Arie, Mina Westman, Ora Shamai, and Rafael S. Carel. "The Effects of Work Overload and Burnout on Cholesterol and Triglycerides Level: The Moderating Effects of Emotional Reactivity among Male and Female Employees." *Journal of Occupational Health Psychology,* 2, 1997.

Shirom, Arie. "The Effects of Work Stress on Health." *Handbook of Work-Related Stress on Health,* 2nd Ed., 2002.

Shirom, Arie. "Job-Related Burnout. A Review." *Handbook of Occupational Health Psychology.* American Psychological Assoc., 2002.

Smith, Lynn. "Finding Good in 'Normal'." *Los Angeles Times,* June 12, 2001.

"State of Working America 2000–2001." Economic Policy Institute.

Stamford, Bryant, "The Real Cause of Heart Disease? Macho Ostriches." *Louisville Courier-Journal,* September 30, 2001.

Tietjen, Mark A., and Robert M. Myers. "Motivation and Job Satisfaction." *Management Decision,* 36/4, 1998.

Sobel, Rachel K. "Mind in a Mirror." *U.S. News and World Report."* November 12, 2001.

Tumulty, Karen. "Health Care Has a Relapse." *Time,* March 11, 2002.

Swann, William. *Self-Traps: The Elusive Quest for Higher Self-Esteem.* WH Freeman and Company, 1996.

Tzu, Lao. *Tao Te Ching.* Bantam Books, 1990.

United States General Accounting Office. "White-Collar Exemptions in the Modern Workplace." September 1999.

Van Egeren, L. F. "The Relationship Between Job Strain and Blood Pressure at Work, at Home, and During Sleep." *Psychosomatic Medicine* 54, 1992.

Van Slambrouck, Paul. "A Culture Obsessed with Time." *Christian Science Monitor,* March 5, 1998.

Walker, Tom. "The 'Lump-of-Labor' Case Against Work-Sharing." *Working Time: International Trends, Theories and Policy Perspectives.* Routledge, 2000.

Walljasper, Jay. "Speed of Life." *Conscious Choice,* September 2000.

Watts, Alan. *This Is It.* Vintage Books, 1973.

Watts, Alan. *The Meaning of Happiness.* Harper & Row, 1968.

Watts, Alan. *The Wisdom of Insecurity.* Vintage Books, 1951.

Watts, Alan. *Nature, Man and Woman.* Vintage Books, 1991.

Watts, Alan. *The Book.* Vintage Books, 1991.

Weber, Max. *The Protestant Work Ethic and the Spirit of Capitalism.* Charles Scribner's Sons, 1976.

Westman, Mina, and Dov Eden. "Effects of Vacation on Job Stressors and Burnout." *Journal of Applied Psychology,* 83, 377–585, 1997.

Westman, Mina, Dalia Etzion, and Merav Aharon-Madar. "Vacation, Burnout, and Absenteeism." 1999.

Weston, Liz Pullam. "Planting Seeds for Simpler Life." *Los Angeles Times,* November 25, 2001.

White, Ronald D. "Work Sliding Down on List of Priorities." *Los Angeles Times,* November 4, 2001.

"Working Time Developments: Annual Update 2000." European Industrial Relations Observatory.

World Tourism Organization. *Changes in Leisure: The Impact on Tourism.* World Tourism Organization, 1999.

Index

· · ·

Page numbers in *italic* indicate figures; those in **bold** indicate tables.

311

Joe Robinson founded the Work to Live campaign, which is lobbying for a minimum of three weeks of vacation for all Americans. He has appeared in *Time, Utne Reader,* the *Los Angeles Times, Financial Times,* and *Chicago Tribune,* as well as on *The Today Show, CNN, NBC Nightly News, CBS Sunday Morning,* and National Public Radio to discuss the Work to Live campaign. He lives in Santa Monica, California.